Athletics, Gymnastics, and *Agōn* in Plato

ALSO FROM PARNASSOS PRESS

Philosopher Kings and Tragic Heroes
Edited by Heather L. Reid and Davide Tanasi
2016 ISBN 978-1942495079

Politics and Performance in Western Greece
Edited by Heather L. Reid, Davide Tanasi, and Susi Kimbell
2017 ISBN 978-1942495185

The Many Faces of Mimēsis
Edited by Heather L. Reid and Jeremy C. DeLong
2018 ISBN 978-1-942495-22-2

Plato at Syracuse
with a new translation of the *Seventh Letter* by Jonah Radding
Edited by Heather L. Reid and Mark Ralkowski
2019 ISBN 978-1-942495-28-4

Looking at Beauty: to Kalon *in Western Greece*
Edited by Heather L. Reid and Tony Leyh
2019 ISBN 978-1-942495-32-1

Conflict and Competition: Agōn *in Western Greece*
Edited by Heather L. Reid, John Serrati, and Tim Sorg
2020 ISBN 978-1-942495-35-2

Athletics, Gymnastics, and *Agōn* in Plato

edited by
Heather L. Reid
Mark Ralkowski
and Coleen P. Zoller

Parnassos Press
2020

Copyright © 2020 Fonte Aretusa LLC
Individual authors retain their copyright to their articles, which are printed here by permission. All rights reserved. This book or any portion thereof may not be reproduced or used in any manner whatsoever without the express written permission of the author and publisher except for the use of brief quotations in a book review or scholarly journal.

First Printing: 2020
ISBN: 978-1-942495-36-9 (paperback)
ISBN: 978-1-942495-38-3 (ebook)

Parnassos Press
Fonte Aretusa Organization
Sioux City, Iowa USA

www.fontearetusa.org

Cover illustration: Terracotta bell-krater, Greece, ca. 410–400 BCE. Attributed to the Kekrops Painter. Metropolitan Museum of Art, Accession Number:56.171.49. CC Public Domain Image.

Epigraphs

μέγας γάρ…ὁ ἀγών, ὦ φίλε Γλαύκων, μέγας, οὐχ ὅσος δοκεῖ, τὸ χρηστὸν ἢ κακὸν γενέσθαι

for the struggle to be good rather than bad is important, Glaucon, much more important than people think.

Plato, *Republic* 10.608b

παρακαλῶ δὲ καὶ τοὺς ἄλλους πάντας ἀνθρώπους, καθ᾽ ὅσον δύναμαι, καὶ δὴ καὶ σὲ ἀντιπαρακαλῶ ἐπὶ τοῦτον τὸν βίον καὶ τὸν ἀγῶνα τοῦτον, ὃν ἐγώ φημι ἀντὶ πάντων τῶν ἐνθάδε ἀγώνων εἶναι

And I call on all other people as well, as far as I can— and you especially I call on in response to your call—to this way of life, this contest, that I hold to be worth all the other contests in this life.

Plato, *Gorgias* 526e

Acknowledgments

The editors are grateful to all the participants of the Fifth Interdisciplinary Symposium on the Heritage of Western Greece in 2019, and to those who submitted papers specifically for this book. Harvard's Center for Hellenic Studies supported Prof. Reid during the conference and during the editing phase of the book. We would also like to thank the Exedra Mediterranean Center of Siracusa for their help and hospitality.

Table of Contents

Epigraphs v

Acknowledgments vi

Introduction 1

Heather L. Reid
Plato's Gymnastic Dialogues 15

Matthew P. Evans
Architectural and Spatial Features of
Plato's *Gymnasia* and *Palaistrai* 31

Erik Kenyon
Socrates at the Wrestling School:
Plato's *Laches, Lysis,* and *Charmides* 51

Christopher Moore
Critias in Plato's *Protagoras*: an Opponent of *Agōn*? 67

Mark Ralkowski
A Contest Between Two Lives: Plato's Existential Drama 87

Stamatia Dova
On *Philogymnastia* and its Cognates in Plato 107

Guilherme Domingues da Motta
The *Agōn* between Philosophy and Poetry 127

Marie-Élise Zovko
Agōn and *Erōs* in Plato's *Symposium* 143

Nicholas D. Smith
Socrates's Agonistic Use of Shame 157

Jure Zovko
Agōn as Constituent of the Socratic Elenchos 173

Lidia Palumbo & Heather L. Reid
Wrestling with the Eleatics in Plato's *Parmenides* 185

Daniel A. Dombrowski
Four-Term Analogies and the *Gorgias*:
Gymnastics, *Agōn*, and the Athletic Life in Plato 199

Lee M. J. Coulson
The *Agōnes* of Platonic Philosophy:
Seeking Victory without Triumph 211

Coleen P. Zoller
Plato's Rejection of the Logic of Domination 223

Index of Platonic Dialogues 239

Index of Greek Terms 241

General Index 243

Heather L. Reid, Mark Ralkowski, and Coleen P. Zoller
Introduction

Staring back from the modern academy to the world of Classical Antiquity, it is easy to forget that the ancient Academy was a gymnasium and that Plato was an athlete—a wrestler serious enough to compete at the Isthmian Games—before he became a philosopher. The athletic settings, techniques and terminology that pepper his work are routinely overlooked, lost in translation, or written off as cultural commonplaces with little or no philosophical relevance.[1] To be sure, *agōn* was characteristic of ancient Greek culture in general,[2] but there is something special about Plato's relationship with athletics, gymnastics, and *agōn* that deserves attention from anyone wishing to understand his philosophy. The purpose of this book is to explore that relationship from a variety of perspectives. The sum of these accounts is far from comprehensive, but we hope it will serve as impetus to further study and more serious consideration of the agonism inherent in Plato's philosophy.

Athletics

According to Diogenes Laertius (3.1.4), it was his coach, a wrestler named Ariston, who gave young Aristocles the nickname Plato, on account of his *"euexia"*—a gymnasium term that would

---

[1] Robert Metcalf, *Philosophy as Agōn: A Study of Plato's* Gorgias *and Related Texts* (Evanston IL: Northwestern University Press, 2018) is a recent exception. Metcalf argues that Plato's philosophy is essentially agonistic, and he cites Nietzsche (*Twilight of the Idols* §23) as an authoritative precedent for the idea.

[2] A view primarily attributed to Jacob Burckhardt, *The Greeks and Greek Civilization*, ed. Oswyn Murray, trans. Sheila Stern (New York: St. Martin's, 1999). For a complete analysis, see Tobias Joho, "Burckhardt and Nietzsche on the *Agōn*: the dark luster of ancient Greece," in *Conflict and Competition: Agōn in Western Greece*, eds. H. Reid, J. Serrati, and T. Sorg (Sioux City: Parnassos Press, 2020), 267-288. Lisa Wilkinson, *Socratic Charis: Philosophy Without the Agon* (Lanham, MD: Lexington Books, 2013) challenges the idea, arguing that *agōn* is incompatible with equality, and thus democracy. She argues that Plato's dialogues may be more profitably read as challenging agonism.

be associated by Aristotle not just with good physical condition, but also moral virtue (*aretē*). The same passage confirms Plato's participation as a wrestler (probably as a boy) in the Panhellenic games at Isthmia.³ Diogenes goes on to describe Plato meeting Socrates and beginning to study philosophy at the Academy (3.1.5), but we would be wrong to think of this place as a philosophical school. In those days it was simply a gymnasium, a parklike space reserved for nude exercise (*gymnastikē*) with little more than shaded paths, open areas for wrestling and games, a variety of religious monuments, and easy access to water for bathing.⁴ At the Academy, there is no archaeological evidence of a *palaistra*—the square peristyle building with an open court for exercise, *exedrae*, and undressing rooms, sometimes called a gymnasium— until the second half of the fourth century BCE.⁵ The Academy that Plato knew in his youth better resembled the one described in Aristophanes's *Clouds*: a leafy park where "the plane-tree whispers to the elm."⁶

Of course Aristophanes's Academy is presented as the antithesis of Socrates's "Thinkery," but it would be rash to suggest

---

³ Diogenes Laertius 3.1.4: "ἐγυμνάσατο δὲ παρὰ Ἀρίστωνι τῷ Ἀργείῳ παλαιστῇ· ἀφ᾽ οὗ καὶ Πλάτων διὰ τὴν εὐεξίαν μετωνομάσθη, πρότερον Ἀριστοκλῆς ἀπὸ τοῦ πάππου καλούμενος [ὄνομα], καθά φησιν Ἀλέξανδρος ἐν Διαδοχαῖς. ἔνιοι δὲ διὰ τὴν πλατύτητα τῆς ἑρμηνείας οὕτως ὀνομασθῆναι· ἢ ὅτι πλατὺς ἦν τὸ μέτωπον, ὥς φησι Νεάνθης. εἰσὶ δ᾽ οἳ καὶ παλαῖσαί φασιν αὐτὸν Ἰσθμοῖ, καθὰ καὶ Δικαίαρχος ἐν πρώτῳ Περὶ βίων."

⁴ On Greek gymnasia, see Jean Delorme, *Gymnasion: Etude sur les Monuments Consacres a l'Education en Grece* (Paris: Editions e. de Boccard, 1960).

⁵ That is, decades after Plato's school was inaugurated around 387 BCE. According to Delorme, *Gymnasion*, 325-329, the philosophical school at the Academy ultimately consisted of the garden, the house, the *mouseion*, and the exedra—which was probably built as a place to give lessons to the *ephebes*. For the archaeology of the Academy, see Ada Caruso, *Akademia: Archeologia di una scuola filosofica ad Atene da Platone a Proclo* (Athens-Paestum: Scuola Archaeological Italiana di Atene, 2013), esp. 96-106.

⁶ Aristophanes, *Clouds*, trans. Jeffrey Henderson (Cambridge, MA: Harvard University Press, 1998), 1005-1008. The comedy was first performed in 423 BCE, when Plato would have been a young child.

Introduction

that Plato is responsible for bringing philosophy into the gymnasium. Not only did Socrates, Antisthenes, Prodicus, and various other fifth-century intellectuals frequent gymnasia, they were all preceded by the proto-philosopher Pythagoras.[7] Diogenes Laertius reports that in 588 BCE, the Olympic boxing crown was won by a Samian youth named Pythagoras, who triumphed by fighting "scientifically" despite having to compete against the men.[8] Like so many stories about Pythagoras, this one about Olympic victory is doubted, but the philosopher's connection to athletics appears credible.[9] He was indisputably connected to Croton, a city noted for its dominance in the Olympic Games; and sources report a relationship with the city's famed wrestler Milo.[10]

---

[7] In addition to Plato, Xenophon, *Memorabilia,* 1.1.10, attests to Socrates's habitual gymnasium visits. The Socratic Antisthenes (ca. 444-ca. 365 BCE) was said by Diogenes Laertius (6.10.13) to converse (*dialegetai*) in the Cynosarges gymnasium. Evidence for Prodicus's presence in gymnasia comes from the pseudo-Platonic dialogue the *Eryxias* (399a-b), where the sophist is said to have been expelled from the Lyceum by the gymnasiarch for expressing dangerous views before a youthful audience.

[8] Diogenes Laertius (8.47): "Ἐρατοσθένης δέ φησι, καθὸ καὶ Φαβωρῖνος ἐν τῇ ὀγδόῃ Παντοδαπῆς ἱστορίας παρατίθεται, τοῦτον εἶναι τὸν πρῶτον ἐντέχνως πυκτεύσαντα ἐπὶ τῆς ὀγδόης καὶ τετταρακοστῆς Ὀλυμπιάδος, κομήτην καὶ ἁλουργίδα φοροῦντα· ἐκκριθέντα τ᾽ ἐκ τῶν παίδων καὶ χλευασθέντα αὐτίκα προσβῆναι τοὺς ἄνδρας καὶ νικῆσαι."

[9] This is the conclusion of Nigel Spivey, "Pythagoras and the Origins of Olympic Ideology," in Barbara Goff and Michael Simpson, eds. *Thinking the Olympics* (London: Bloomsbury, 2011), 21-39. Pythagoras's biographer Porphyry (15) reports that "Pythagoras trained the Samian athlete Eurymenes, who though he was of small stature, conquered at Olympia through his surpassing knowledge of Pythagoras' wisdom." The trainer story is denied by the more reliable biographer Iamblichus (25), but he nevertheless affirms that Pythagoras recruited athletes in Samos's gymnasia (21) and went to the gymnasium in Croton as soon as he arrived (37). Iamblichus also relates that Pythagoreans were subject to a battery of tests (*dokimasia*), including their physical aspect (*eidos*), gait (*poreia*) and 'mobility' (*kinēsis*) (71).

[10] Milo's connections to Pythagoras and Pythagoreanism, including his marriage to Pythagoras's daughter, Myia, are explained in detail by J-M Roubineau, *Milon de Crotone ou l'invention de sport* (Paris: Presses Universitaires de France, 2016). An English review of the book by Heather L. Reid appears in *Classical Review* 67.2 (2017): 457-9.

Many of Plato's ideas have roots in Pythagoreanism, perhaps even his decision to teach in a gymnasium—an act that followed his first trip to Western Greece, where athletics and Pythagoreanism were prominent.[11] Like Pythagoras, Plato believed that philosophy is not a skill, a profession, or even a subject of study, but rather a way of life that involves habituation or training (*ethos*), including daily exercise, and regular testing, which may take the form of athletic contest.[12]

We should not imagine that Plato himself, or any of his students, had Olympic victory as their goal. Athletics had become "professionalized" since Pythagoras's day, and both *Republic* and *Laws* criticize the intense training required as an impediment to the pursuit of *aretē*.[13] He clearly sees value in competition, however, for men, women, children, and the community itself. In *Laws*, athletic festivals are to be held every month, and everyone in the community, including women and children, is encouraged—if not required—to compete.[14] Events include footraces ranging from 200 to 20,000 meters, almost all of them in armor (832e), as well as ballgames (830e), single and team combat events (833e), as well as armed equestrian events (834c). The function is partly martial: "if it helps us to train for war we must go in for it and put up prizes for the winners, but leave it strictly alone if it does not" (832e).[15]

---

[11] That Plato met with several Pythagoreans, especially Archytas or Taretum, on his trip west is attested by a variety of ancient sources, including the *Seventh Letter*. For an overview of the topic, see Heather Reid and Mark Ralkowski, eds., *Plato at Syracuse with a new translation of the Seventh Letter by Jonah Radding* (Sioux City: Parnassos Press, 2019).

[12] That Pythagoras thought this is attested by Aristotle (Fr. 195). Plato describes philosophy as a way of life at *Repuplic* 600ab.

[13] *Republic* 404a, *Laws* 807c. Ruobineau, *Milon de Crotone*, argues credibly that the Pythagorean Milo was the first truly professional athlete.

[14] The festivals are discussed in *Laws* VIII. The text wavers on whether participation will be mandatory for everyone at all times, but clearly emphasizes that the rules will apply to men and women alike (829e). See H. Reid, "Plato on Women in Sport," *Journal of the Philosophy of Sport* 47:3 (2020): 1-18.

[15] Unless otherwise noted, all translations of Plato are from Plato, *Complete Works*, eds. John M, Cooper and D. S. Hutchinson (Indianapolis: Hackett, 1997).

Introduction

Ultimately, however, the goal of athletic contests in *Laws* is to preserve the "ways of virtue" (*agathon*) and to avoid injustice (*adikein*) from oneself and others (829ab). In his own life and in the ways of life he describes in his work, athletics has a role, but *aretē* is always the goal.

Gymnastics

Athletic training and contests in an explicitly educational context are best described as gymnastics. Athletic contests and horse races (as well as dancing and hunting) are called *gymnastikē* at *Republic* 412b, not because they weren't part of the games, but because they were aimed at cultivating *aretē*.[16] Combining philosophy and gymnastics in education was not a new idea,[17] but most people thought the latter served only the body. Plato's Socrates explicitly rejects that idea at *Republic* 410c, saying, instead, that both *gymnastikē* and *mousikē* were established "chiefly for the sake of the soul." Gymnastics, in particular, is useful for harmonizing the spirited and wisdom-loving parts of the soul (411e). In other words, it promotes *aretē*, which is understood as a kind of health and harmony in the soul, which, like bodily health, requires exercise.[18] Since Plato believed that the soul is the origin

---

[16] On the goals of gymnastic education in Plato's *Republic*, see Heather L Reid, "Sport as Moral Education in Plato's *Republic*," *Journal of the Philosophy of Sport* 34:2 (2007): 160-175; and "Plato's Gymnasium," in *Athletics and Philosophy in the Ancient World: Contests of Virtue* (London: Routledge, 2011) 56-68. Plato's focus on the soul, rather than the body, may be part of the reason that he promotes gymnastic education for women just as much as men in both *Republic* and *Laws*; for an analysis, see Heather L. Reid, "Plato on Women in Sport," *Journal of the Philosophy of sport* 47:3 (2020): 1-18.

[17] Isocrates, *Antidosis*, 182 declares that philosophy and gymnastics are "twin arts—parallel and complementary—by which their masters prepare the mind to become more intelligent and the body to become more serviceable, not separating sharply the two kinds of education, but using similar methods of instruction, exercise, and other forms of discipline."

[18] Plato uses the virtue-as-health analogy in many dialogues, for example *Republic* 444d-e.

of human movement,[19] he concluded that moving the body can actually train the soul. Socrates states explicitly that a fit body does not produce virtue in the soul, but rather that the soul's *aretē* makes the body as good as possible (*Republic* 403d). Performance in athletic contests is, accordingly, an indicator of healthy souls, and it is used in *Republic* to select who will receive higher education and become philosopher-rulers (537bc).[20]

The goal of Platonic gymnastics, as we said, is not Olympic victory, but rather to acquire what Socrates calls a "helper for philosophy" (498b); and by this he means a psychic state rather than a physical one. He seems to think that the kind of character that remains resolute in the face of temptation and adversity in sport will have what is needed to

> take the longer road and put as much effort into learning as into physical training, for otherwise, as we were just saying, he will never reach the goal of the most important subject and the most appropriate one for him to learn." (504cd)

"People's souls give up much more easily in hard study than in physical training," explains Socrates; they need a love for hard work (*philoponon*) that can be directed at learning, listening, and inquiry just as much as *gymnastikē* (535b-d). In *Republic*'s educational theory, the competitive spirit cultivated through sport is eventually applied to philosophical argument (539d). That

---

[19] A common view in ancient Greece, see Bruno Snell, *The Discovery of the Mind in Greek Philosophy and Literature* (New York: Dover, 1982), 8–22.

[20] Plato does not say that only the winners of the contests would be selected; he simply implies that the contests will test their mettle, so to speak, "more thoroughly than gold is tested by fire" (413cd). The testing of gold metaphor is repeated a bit later, "We said, if you remember, that they must show themselves to be lovers of their city when tested by pleasure and pain and that they must hold on to their resolve through labors, fears, and all other adversities. Anyone incapable of doing so was to be rejected, while anyone who came through unchanged—like gold tested in a fire—was to be made ruler and receive prizes [*athla*] both while he lived and after his death" (*Republic* 502d–503a).

Introduction

something similar was probably practiced in Plato's Academy is suggested by the dialogues themselves.

The real-life competition between Plato and his rival educators helps to explain his dialogues' agonism. Plato had a professional interest in pitting Socrates against rival sophists,[21] or, more specifically, the sophistic understanding of education.[22] For Plato, *aretē* is not something that can be bought and sold, it must be earned through training and competition. So when sophists like Protagoras claim to teach *aretē* for a fee, he sends Socrates in to strip them bare and expose the fraud.[23] The attempt to commercialize *aretē*, among gymnastic and sophistic educators alike, corrupts the process of pursuing it. It tends to value external appearance over internal excellence, or to confuse the trappings of victory with the virtue that gives victory value in the first place. Sophists like

---

[21] We use the word 'sophist' here in a stipulative way to identify Plato's philosophical rivals. In fact, the distinction between sophist and philosopher was not so clear-cut in fifth and fourth century BCE Athens. See John Patrick Lynch, *Aristotle's School* (Berkeley: University of California Press 1972), 41. In a letter from the late second or early 3rd century BCE, Philostratus (*Epistles*, 1.73) tells Julia Domna that Plato is not so different from the sophists and has, in fact, borrowed some of their tricks.

[22] For a comparison of sophistic and Socratic education, see Coleen P. Zoller, "To 'Graze Freely in the Pastures of Philosophy': The Political Motives and Pedagogical Methods of Socrates and the Sophists," *Polis* 27; 1 (2010): 80-110.

[23] *Protagoras* (313c-d): "Then can it be, Hippocrates, that the sophist is really a sort of merchant or dealer (*kapēlos*) in provisions on which a soul is nourished? For such is the view I take of him [...] And we must take care, my good friend, that the sophist, in commending his wares, does not deceive us, as both merchant and dealer (*kapēlos*) do in the case of our bodily food. For among the provisions, you know, in which these men deal, not only are they themselves ignorant what is good or bad for the body, since in selling they commend them all, but the people who buy from them are so too, unless one happens to be a trainer or a doctor. And in the same way, those who take their lessons (*mathēmata*) the round of our cities, hawking (*kapēleuontes*) them about to any odd purchaser who desires them, commend everything that they sell, and there may well be some of these too, my good sir, who are ignorant which of their wares is good or bad for the soul." W.R.M. Lamb, trans., *Plato in Twelve Volumes*, vol. 3 (Cambridge: Harvard University Press, 1967).

Isocrates, who habitually confuse *aretē* with practical (especially rhetorical) skill because it is "recognized by all" (*Antidosis* 84), run afoul not only of Platonic metaphysics, which posits universal ideals, but also ancient Olympic values, which rewarded victors with only a sacred wreath of vegetation.

Platonic gymnastics orients the *agōn* toward *aretē*, replacing the love of victory (*philonikia*) with the love of wisdom (*philosophia*). It is no coincidence that in Plato's *Apology*, Socrates chastises Meletus for carelessly and ambitiously bringing people to court, literally *eis agōna*—into the contest (24c). The competitive spirit of sophists, social climbers, and perhaps even athletes, needed to be directed toward a higher good.

Agōn

Plato routinely describes Socratic dialogue in agonistic terms. In *Euthydemus*, the argument is compared to a ball game (277b) and wrestling match (277d, 278b, 288a). In *Protagoras*, it is called a verbal contest (*agōna logōn*), and Socrates compares Protagoras to the champion runner Krison of Himera (335e). In *Theaetetus*, Socrates is compared to Antaeus, a mythological athlete who lived in a cave and forced passers-by to wrestle him (169b). At *Philebus* 41b, Socrates says: "So let us get ready like athletes to form a line of attack around his problem," and in *Cratylus*, he says "once we're in the competition, we're allowed no excuses" (421d). Socrates's opponents even suggest that he is too competitive. "You love to win, Socrates," says Callicles (*Gorgias* 515b). Observes Protagoras, "I think that you just want to win the argument, Socrates" (360e). Thrasymachus accuses the philosopher of competitiveness and love of honor (*Republic* 336c), adding "without trickery you'll never be able to overpower me in argument" (341b).

But the method of Plato's Socrates is not a zero-sum game. Socrates responds to Callicles's charge of *philonikia* by saying, "it's not for love of winning that I'm asking you. It's rather because I really do want to know" (*Gorgias* 515b). To Protagoras, he replies, "I have no other reason for asking these things than my desire to answer these questions about virtue (*aretē*)," especially what it is and whether it can be taught (361a). This contrasts with the sophists' approach, which he criticizes in *Euthydemus* for confusing the defeat of their opponents with the achievement of wisdom: "They think that if they place these persons in the position of appearing to be worth nothing, then victory in the contest for the reputation of wisdom will be indisputably and immediately theirs, and in the eyes of all" (305d). But this kind of victory amounts to settling for plausibility rather than truth, says Socrates; it confuses the reputation for wisdom with wisdom itself. One is reminded of the ancient Sicilian wrestler Leontiskos, who won matches not with wrestling skill, but by breaking his opponents' fingers.[24] The problem with victories won through trickery, whether athletic or *eristic*, is that they subvert the ultimate purpose of the contest, which is *aretē*—for both opponents. Enlightened athletes and Socratic philosophers recognize this and come to regard agonistic struggle as mutually beneficial; their *philonikia* becomes *philosophia*.

When Critias accuses Socrates of trying to refute him rather than address the "real question at issue," Socrates demurs, claiming that he is "examining the argument for my own sake primarily, but perhaps also for the sake of my friends" (*Charmides* 166d). Once Critias agrees that such clarification of concepts is part of the common good, Socrates tells him to ignore who is being refuted and instead to "give your attention to the argument itself" (*Charmides* 166e). He reminds his interlocutor Protarchus that "we are not contending here out of love of victory for my suggestion to win or yours. We ought to act together as allies in support of the truest one" (*Philebus* 14b). He tells Polus that friends must help each other up when they fall (*Gorgias* 462c), and when the sophist complains he is hard to refute, Socrates responds that he himself would be grateful to be refuted: "Please don't falter now in doing a friend a good turn," he says, "Refute me" (470cd). Socrates believes in providing an agonistic challenge even to one's beloved, as evidenced not only by his treatment of his own *eromenoi*, but also in the advice he gives to *erastes*.[25] Enlightened agonism,

---

[24] The story is told in Pausanias, *Description of Greece,* 6.4.3.
[25] See for example, *Lysis,* 210e.

inspired by the athletic model of the heroes, is for Socrates the ultimate form of friendship. As he explains to Theodorus,

> I have met with many a Heracles and Theseus in my time, mighty men of words; and they have well battered me. But for all that I don't retire from the field, so terrible a lust has come upon me for these exercises. You must not begrudge me this either, try a fall with me and we shall both be the better. (*Theaetetus* 169bc)

Essays

The essays in this volume address several aspects of *agōn* in Plato's dialogues, from their dramatic setting and characters, to their methods, metaphors, and goals. Heather L. Reid opens the discussion by arguing that Plato's dialogues not only employ athletic settings and metaphors, some of them actually function as virtual gymnasia, presenting Socrates as a coach who guides readers—as well as interlocutors—toward an innovative ideal of *aretē*. Matthew P. Evans's essay examines the interplay between Plato's philosophy and the architecture of the athletic buildings in which he sets *Lysis, Charmides, Euthydemus,* and *Theaetetus.* Evans argues that Plato encodes philosophical meaning into these spaces, thus reinforcing the power of his dialogues. Understanding the structure and function of gymnastic spaces in Plato's time can enhance our understanding of his meaning. Next, Erik Kenyon analyzes the interaction of dramatic and philosophical *agōn* in *Laches, Charmides,* and *Lysis,* revealing how all of these layers of competition aim ultimately to promote virtue. These dialogues, set in or around wrestling schools, use care for the body as a framework for thinking about care for the soul.

Christopher Moore's essay examines the character of Critias in the *Protagoras.* On the one hand, Critias serves as a negative example of one who fails to enter the philosophical *agōn* by subjecting his views to the scrutiny of others, and lacks self-knowledge because of it. On the other hand, as an opponent of Socrates, he contributes constructively to the debate by nudging it toward a higher moral plane. Moore surmises that the historical

Introduction

Critias may have performed a similar role. Mark Ralkowski also examines a character, this time Alcibiades, in whom he sees the embodiment of an *agōn* between two ways of life in fifth c. BCE Athens. The battle is between the life of philosophy and that of politics, and the fact that Socrates lost Alcibiades to the latter is more an indictment of Athenian politics than of Socratic method.

Next, Stamatia Dova takes a philological approach to Plato's interest in *gymnastikē,* analyzing his use of *philogymnastia* and its cognates in several dialogues. In contrast to the assumption that Plato is an unabashed sports enthusiast, she argues that he thinks love of exercise can be a help or a hindrance to the philosophical life; it all depends on balance and measure. The longstanding *agōn* between philosophy and poetry as played out in the *Republic* is the subject of Guilherme Domingues da Motta's essay. He argues that Plato's opponents in this struggle are not only the poets, but also the (mis)interpreters of poetry, as represented by Glaucon's and Adeimantus's misleading speeches. Philosophy is the remedy to the abuse of poetry, not to poetry itself. Then, Marie-Élise Zovko's essay unravels the interlocking tapestry of *agōnes* in the *Symposium.* Set on the occasion of a dramatic contest, the contest of speeches constructs a deeper *agōn* between a human and a divine ideal of *erōs.* Zovko argues that the *Symposium* pits traditional Dionysian cult against a new form of erotic cult represented by Diotima.

A group of papers on method begins with Nicholas D. Smith arguing that Plato's Socrates uses shame agonistically, to push interlocutors emotionally toward rationally defensible beliefs. He says this process is compatible with Socratic "intellectualism" since it prepares people for rational decision-making while they are still subject to their emotions. Next, Jure Zovko argues that Socratic elenchos is fundamentally agonal in its structure and character, not just in the so-called early dialogues, but right through to Plato's later works. The dialectical analysis of language can teach us much about the good life, but to actually live it we need the kind of reasonable judgment that is cultivated through *agōn.* Gymnastic training inspires philosophical method in *Parmenides,* according to Lidia Palumbo and Heather L. Reid. They argue that the dialectical method called *gymnasia* in that dialogue not only resembles athletic training, it invites readers to wrestle with the relationship between universals and particulars.

That Socratic method can't be separated from its goals is demonstrated by the final set of essays. Daniel A. Dombrowski's article analyzes the four-term analogies in the *Gorgias*: beautification : gymnastics :: cookery : medicine, and sophistic : legislation :: rhetoric : justice. Emphasizing Plato's hylomorphism, Dombrowski concludes that the athletic life and the intellectual life in Platonic philosophy amount to the same thing. The key distinction is between "flattery arts" that seek pleasure and those, like gymnastics, that seek the good. Next, Lee M. J. Coulson contrasts the agonism inherent in sophistic eristic with that of Platonic dialectic. He claims that eristic aims arrogantly at triumph while dialectic aims at noble victory, noting that the latter precludes the former. In the concluding essay, Coleen P. Zoller argues that Plato's agonism does not imply acceptance of a logic of domination. He rejects the pleonectic approach of interlocutors like Thrasymachus and Callicles, and promotes a meritocratic hierarchy aimed at fostering goodness, harmony, and peace for all. Commentators who overlook this aspect of Plato's agonism, may have an impoverished understanding of *agōn* itself.

On the whole, these chapters show that the concept of *agōn* was central to Plato's thinking about philosophy: its method and aims, its people and places, and especially its rivalry with competing ways of life. If the contributors to this volume are correct, Plato's views throughout his career were shaped by his early years as a competitive wrestler. He saw a family resemblance between caring for the body and caring for the soul, and he saw the struggle of competition in every dimension of life in the *polis*. This struggle occurred in each person's soul, and it happened in the city as a whole, in a competition between ways of living. There was no greater contest in life, and Socrates invited all of us to take it up for ourselves (*Gorgias* 526e).

Gymnastics, Athletics, and *Agōn* in Plato

Heather L. Reid[1]
Plato's Gymnastic Dialogues[2]

It is not mere coincidence that several of Plato's dialogues are set in gymnasia and *palaistrai* (wrestling schools), employ the gymnastic language of stripping, wrestling, tripping, even helping opponents to their feet, and imitate in argumentative form the athletic contests (*agōnes*) commonly associated with that place. The main explanation for this is, of course, historical. Sophists, orators, and intellectuals of all stripes, including the historical Socrates, really did frequent Athens' gymnasia and *palaistrai* in search of ready audiences and potential students.[3] Perhaps they were following the example of Pythagoras, who may have been a boxing coach (*gymnastēs*) and was, in any case, associated with the extraordinary Olympic success of athletes from his adopted Croton—success so great it generated the saying that the last of the Crotonites was the first among all other Greeks.[4] After his visit to Western Greece, Plato famously established his school in or

---

[1] Heather L. Reid is Professor of Philosophy at Morningside College in the USA and Scholar in Residence at Exedra Mediterranean Center in Siracusa, Sicily. She is a 2015 Fellow of the American Academy in Rome, 2018 Fellow of Harvard's Center for Hellenic Studies, and 2019 Fulbright Scholar at the Università degli Studi di Napoli Federico II. As founder of Fonte Aretusa, she promotes conferences and research on Western Greece. Her books include *Athletics and Philosophy in the Ancient World: Contests of Virtue* (2011), *Introduction to the Philosophy of Sport* (2012), *The Philosophical Athlete* (2019), and *Olympic Philosophy* (2020).

[2] This paper was originally presented to the Society for Ancient Greek Philosophy in 2015. I thank Mark Ralkowski for suggestions on this revision.

[3] For an overview of philosophers' activity in Athens gymnasia, see John Patrick Lynch, *Aristotle's School* (Berkeley: University of California Press, 1972).

[4] Strabo (*Geog.* 6.1.12) reports the relationship in a story recounting the origin of the proverb. Stephen G. Miller discusses Croton's athletic success in *Ancient Greek Athletics* (New Haven: Yale University Press, 2006), 233 ff. Additional details on the link between philosophy and athletics in Croton can be found in Nigel Spivey, "Pythagoras and the Origins of Olympic Ideology," in Barbara Goff and Michael Simpson, eds. *Thinking the Olympics* (London: Bloomsbury, 2011) 21-39, and J-M Roubineau, *Milon de Crotone ou l'invention de sport* (Paris: Presses Universitaires de France, 2016).

adjacent to the Academy gymnasium in Athens, and he may have held the public office of Gymnasiarch there.[5] In this essay, I would like to argue that there are also symbolic reasons for Plato setting some of his dialogues in gymnasia. These dialogues *function* as virtual gymnasia in which readers are coached by the character of Socrates toward an innovative ideal of *aretē* (virtue, excellence).

Aretē and the Gymnasium

Taking the last claim first, we must remember that *aretē*'s oldest associations were with athleticism. Gods such as Zeus and Hermes, and heroes such as Heracles and Achilles, were endowed with the strength and beauty that athletes strove to emulate. Unlike mere mortals, however, gods and heroes never trained — their *aretē* derived directly from their full or partial divinity, and it was naturally accompanied by wisdom and eloquence. The beauty and athleticism of aristocratic mortals was likewise attributed to divine heredity and thought to require no special training. However, the rise of athletic festivals, the Olympic Games in particular, eroded such beliefs by revealing that athletic *aretē* could be acquired through training. Even as aristocrats employed professional coaches and gravitated toward equestrian events in the effort to defend their "natural superiority" using the weapon of their wealth, public gymnasia proliferated as places where *aretē* might be cultivated among all youth with the leisure to do so. In the beginning, these gymnasia were basically parks with little else besides groves of trees, shaded walking paths, open areas for exercise, a variety of religious monuments, and easy access to water for bathing.[6] Aristophanes's description of the Academy in *Clouds* (1005-1008) as a leafy park where "the plane-tree whispers

---

[5] The argument for this is made convincingly by Stephen G Miller, *The Berkeley Plato: From Neglected Relic to Ancient Treasure* (Berkeley, CA: University of California Press, 2009). Miller interprets "The Berkely Plato," a portrait herm of Plato adorned with athletic victory ribbons as evidence for his role as gymnasiarch.

[6] For an overview of the Greek gymnasium, see Jean Delorme, *Gymnasion: Étude sur les monuments consacrés à l'éducation en Grèce* (Paris: E. de Boccard, 1960).

to the elm" and where good young men go to exercise and socialize illustrates the early gymnasium of virtue well.[7]

As the idea took hold that even aristocratic young men needed some form of higher education to perfect their natural *aretē*, private, urban *palaistrai* were constructed to facilitate this. They were more convenient than the public gymnasia located on the periphery, and access to them could be controlled. It is just such a facility that Hippothales pulls Socrates into at the beginning of *Lysis*, as the philosopher is making his way between two public gymnasia, the Academy and the Lyceum (203a). Given that gymnasia and *palaistrai* were recognized as places for training *aretē*, it is no surprise that they attracted teachers of oratory and argumentation, since eloquence and debating skill were also considered signs of excellence. In *Antidosis*, the rhetorician Isocrates argues that *aretē* is achieved through parallel training in the "twin arts" of philosophy and gymnastics, which "employ similar methods of instruction and exercise."[8] By "philosophy," however, Isocrates intends the art of oratory, which imparts what he calls worthwhile *aretē*—in contrast with those who "profess to turn men to a life of temperance and justice…a kind of virtue and wisdom which is ignored by the rest of the world and disputed among themselves."[9]

---

[7] Aristophanes, *Aristophanes Comoediae*, ed. F.W. Hall and W.M. Geldart, vol. 2. (Oxford: Clarendon Press, 1907): ἀλλ᾽ εἰς Ἀκαδήμειαν κατιὼν ὑπὸ ταῖς μορίαις ἀποθρέξει/ στεφανωσάμενος καλάμῳ λευκῷ μετὰ σώφρονος ἡλικιώτου,/ μίλακος ὄζων καὶ ἀπραγμοσύνης καὶ λεύκης φυλλοβολούσης,/ ἦρος ἐν ὥρᾳ χαίρων, ὁπόταν πλάτανος πτελέᾳ ψιθυρίζῃ.

[8] Isocrates, *Antidosis*, trans. G. Norlin (Cambridge: Harvard University Press, 1980), 182: ἀντιστρόφους καὶ σύζυγας καὶ σφίσιν αὐταῖς ὁμολογουμένας, δι᾽ ὧν οἱ προεστῶτες αὐτῶν τάς τε ψυχὰς φρονιμωτέρας καὶ τὰ σώματα χρησιμώτερα παρασκευάζουσιν, οὐ πολὺ διαστησάμενοι τὰς παιδείας ἀπ᾽ ἀλλήλων, ἀλλὰ παραπλησίαις χρώμενοι καὶ ταῖς διδασκαλίαις καὶ ταῖς γυμνασίαις καὶ ταῖς ἄλλαις ἐπιμελείαις.

[9] Isocrates, *Antidosis*, 84. ἀλλὰ μὴν καὶ τῶν ἐπὶ τὴν σωφροσύνην καὶ τὴν δικαιοσύνην προσποιουμένων προτρέπειν ἡμεῖς ἂν ἀληθέστεροι καὶ χρησιμώτεροι φανεῖμεν ὄντες. οἱ μὲν γὰρ παρακαλοῦσιν ἐπὶ τὴν ἀρετὴν καὶ τὴν φρόνησιν τὴν ὑπὸ τῶν ἄλλων μὲν ἀγνοουμένην, ὑπ᾽ αὐτῶν δὲ τούτων ἀντιλεγομένην, ἐγὼ δ᾽ ἐπὶ τὴν ὑπὸ πάντων ὁμολογουμένην.

Isocrates's thinly-veiled reference to Socrates here should remind us that the Platonic understanding of *aretē* as a highly intellectualized "health of the soul" to be achieved through dialectical *agōn* must have been a radical innovation in its day. Isocrates, like many people, envisioned gymnastics as education strictly for the body and rhetorical education as sufficient for intellectual virtue. Plato's Socrates, however, explicitly rejects the former idea in *Republic*,[10] and attacks the latter with his own thinly veiled reference to Isocrates toward the end of *Euthydemus* as someone who fails to teach his students how to *use* their rhetorical skills, and thereby proving that "the art of speech writing is not the one a man would be happy if he acquired" (289d). This "art of happiness" is, instead, the Platonic idea of *aretē*, and Plato's gymnastic dialogues not only make the case—in opposition to his educational rivals—that there is a philosophical component of *aretē* which must be trained separately from (though not exclusive of) technical training in gymnastics, military arts, argumentation, and oratory, they also provide that training for their readers to some degree. Indeed some of them may have been written for the express purpose of being read and discussed in Plato's Academy.

The Philosophical Gymnasium

Reading and discussion would not have been the only activities taking place at Plato's Academy. In fact, the kind of building where such discussions usually took place, does not appear at the Academy until decades after Plato's school is established.[11] Rather, Plato would have directed all the traditional

---

[10] Socrates says, instead, that both *gymnastikē* and *mousikē* were established "chiefly for the sake of the soul," concluding further down: "It seems, then, that a god has given music and physical training to human beings not, except incidentally, for the body and the soul, but for the spirited and wisdom-loving parts of the soul itself, in order that these may be in harmony with one another, each being stretched and relaxed to an appropriate degree" (411e). This and all other English translations of Plato are taken from John Cooper, ed., *Plato: Complete Works* (Indianapolis: Hackett, 1997).

[11] Plato's school was inaugurated around 387 BCE. At the Academy, there is no archaeological evidence of a *palaistra* until the second half of the fourth

activities of the gymnasium toward the goal of improving the soul.[12] In Plato's dialogues, music, gymnastics, military training, and even erotic relationships are reinterpreted to promote Plato's philosophical understanding of *aretē*.[13] At *Republic* 410c, Socrates says specifically that the goal of music and gymnastics is to harmonize the soul[14]—a declaration that reveals two key assumptions behind Plato's gymnastic philosophy. The first is that the soul is the origin of human movement,[15] so moving the body

---

century BCE. See Ada Caruso, *Akademia: Archeologia di una scuola filosofica ad Atene da Platone a Proclo* (Athens: Scuola Archaeologica Italiana di Atene Pandemos, 2013).

[12] This is the general thesis of "Plato's Gymnasium" in Heather L. Reid, *Athletics and Philosophy in the Ancient World: Contests of Virtue* (London: Routledge, 2011), 66-68.

[13] Plato uses his own athletic analogy to provide a vivid illustration of the harmonious (and therefore just and virtuous) soul in another dialogue, *Phaedrus*. There, the tripartite *psychē* is likened to a two-horse chariot, the charioteer apparently representing the rational part of the soul, one good and noble horse the spirited part of the soul, and a second unruly horse the appetitive part (246ab). The chariot-soul's struggle for *aretē* is described as an upward climb toward truth and divinity that is especially difficult for humans because "the heaviness of the bad horse drags its charioteer toward the earth and weighs him down if he has failed to train it well" (247b). Keeping in mind the popularity of chariot racing in the ancient games, and noting the passage's use of athletic language such as *ponos* (effort) and *agōn* (contest), we might recognize a connection between the *psychē's* struggle for virtue and the athlete's struggle for victory. Both struggles, like the chariot, require the harmonization and cooperation of all the soul's parts in order to achieve their goals. Perhaps Plato is suggesting that the athletic struggle for victory can prepare one's soul for its lifelong struggle for virtue. For the full argument see H.L. Reid, "Sport as Moral Education in Plato's *Republic*," *Journal of the Philosophy of Sport* 34:2 (2007): 160-175, 163.

[14] At *Republic* 410c, Socrates says that both *gymnastikē* and *mousikē* were established "chiefly for the sake of the soul," concluding further down that "a god has given music and physical training to human beings not, except incidentally, for the body and the soul, but for the spirited and wisdom-loving parts of the soul itself, in order that these may be in harmony with one another, each being stretched and relaxed to an appropriate degree" (411e).

[15] In fact, for Homer, the *psychē* was life itself and the word for body, *sōma*, signified a corpse—a body lacking in movement because its *psychē* had

can actually train the soul. The second is that *aretē* (virtue, excellence) is understood as a kind of health and harmony in the soul, which, like bodily health, requires continual exercise or training (*askēsis*).[16] This exercise can be either physical or intellectual (ideally, it would be both). The issue is not so much the activity as its orientation. It needs to aim at Platonic virtue, which is to say at improvement of the soul, which is to say wisdom, which is to say philosophy.

In contrast with the conventional idea of a *kaloskagathos* (beautiful and good person), Plato's is an inside-out understanding of *aretē*, athleticism, and beauty. For him, even athleticism is a property of the soul—so much so that he imagines the athletic female Atalanta choosing to be reincarnated in a male body (*Republic* 620b). Socrates states clearly that a fit body does not produce virtue in the soul, but rather that the soul's *aretē* makes the body as good as possible (*Republic* 403d). Likewise, it is not victory that makes an argument valuable. And it is not mere eloquence that makes a speech admirable (*kalon*). Rather it is the *aretē* in a person's soul that renders all their actions—from argumentation to athletics—beautiful and good (*kala-kagatha*). The problem is that most people think, like Isocrates, that skill (*technē*) in athletics, argumentation, oratory, or whatever is sufficient for *aretē*. It is, after all, sufficient for Olympic victory, prevailing in lawsuits, and persuading large crowds. As Socrates argued in Plato's *Apology*, however, craftsmen's knowledge enables them to

---

escaped it at death. Plato uses the word *sōma* to signify living bodies and he considers the *psychē* to be the seat of reason, but he does not seem to have abandoned the idea that the *psychē*, and most specifically the spirited part of the soul, *thymos*, is what moves the body. For an excellent discussion of these terms and ideas, see Bruno Snell, *The Discovery of the Mind in Greek Philosophy and Literature* (New York: Dover, 1982), 8-22. For an update, see Brooke Holmes, *The Symptom and the Subject: The Emergence of the Physical Body in Ancient Greece* (Princeton, N.J.: Princeton University Press, 2010).

[16] Plato uses the virtue-as-health analogy in many dialogues. Here is one example from *Republic*: "Virtue seems, then, to be a kind of health, fine condition, and well-being of the soul, while vice is disease, shameful condition, and weakness" (444de).

perform their skill well, but it does not amount to *aretē* because it does not empower them to direct that skill toward the good (22d).

So a primary task of Plato's gymnasium, and of his gymnastic dialogues is to distinguish this innovative conception of *aretē* from its conventional association with athletic, oratorical, and argumentative *technē*. The health of the soul is the aim of every gymnastic activity and every gymnastic dialogue. The beginning of *Laches* even recounts a deliberation about this. A pair of fathers comes for counsel from two generals on educating their sons in military virtue. They are watching a demonstration of fighting in armor (presumably at a gymnasium), but all parties eventually agree that their goal is "a form of study for the sake of the souls of young men" (185de). They decide that worthy teachers would be "good themselves and have tended the souls of many young men" (186a). Socrates goes on to lament disingenuously that he lacked the money to be made *"kalon te kagathon"* by a sophist and says he is "unable to discover the art, even now" (186c). It turns out, however, that Socrates is exactly the instructor they need. Likewise, in the gymnastic dialogues, Socrates coaches readers by demonstrating his method, defeating dangerous views, and being an (unexpected) example of *aretē*. The dialogues also challenge readers to engage in dialectic and test their own understandings of *aretē*—which turns out to be a process that actually cultivates *aretē* in them.

Stripping and Exposure

Plato's gymnastic dialogues generally begin—as any visit to a gymnasium would—with stripping. Here, it is the metaphorical stripping of Socrates's sophistic opponents and the exposure of their *technai* as inadequate for achieving *aretē*. *Euthydemus* is actually set in the *apodyterion* (undressing room) of the Lyceum gymnasium.[17] Scholars call the process *elenchos*—which means to

---

[17] *Euthydemus* 272e. Socrates comments that Euthydeums and Dionysodorus joined him after making just two or three laps of the *"katastegnō dromō"* (273a). Since it was while walking around this covered walkway that philosophers worked out their theories (this may even be a specific

test, examine, refute, and even to shame. In the gymnastic dialogues it serves as consumer due diligence, since the sophists being examined are generally selling instruction in *aretē*. When Socrates asks Euthydemus what he teaches, the response is clear: "Virtue," he says, "and we think we can teach it better than anyone else and more quickly" (*Euthydemus* 273d). As Socrates counsels Hippocrates in *Protagoras*, however, "the sophist is really a sort of merchant or dealer (*kapēlos*) in provisions on which a soul is nourished," and just as vendors may hawk unwholesome food in the marketplace, sophists may be "ignorant which of their wares is good or bad for the soul" (313cd).[18] Socrates says in *Laches* that he was too poor to buy *kalokagathia* (186c), but the real point is that *kalokagathia* cannot be bought, it has to be trained—separately from skills like argumentation, rhetoric, and wrestling—through philosophy.

Socrates's stripping and exposure of the sophists does not imply that their skills are worthless, just that they are inadequate as education for *aretē*. Socrates demonstrates that Gorgias's *technē* of persuasion is achieved without understanding (454e-455a). And when Socrates points out that such skills may be abused, Gorgias defends himself with an athletic analogy:

> Imagine someone who after attending a wrestling school, getting his body into good shape and becoming a boxer, went on to strike his father and mother or any family member or friend. By Zeus, that's no reason to hate physical trainers." (*Gorgias* 456d)

It is, however, a reason to think that supplemental moral education is needed. The point is reinforced by the example of Euthydemus and Dionysodorus, who are described by Socrates as *pancratists* capable of fighting not only in athletic contests, but also in the battle (*agōn*) of the law courts. "They have become so skilled in

---

reference to the *peripatos* that eventually gave Aristotle's school its name), Socrates's comment may suggest that they are not "real philosophers" but are offering some quick and cheap substitute.

[18] W.R.M. Lamb trans., *Plato in Twelve Volumes* (Cambridge: Harvard University Press, 1967).

fighting in arguments," Socrates concludes, "[they can refute] whatever may be said, no matter whether it is true or false" (*Euthydemus* 271c-272b). Aristophanes had long since warned us of the danger of such skills. Just as the athlete needs a sense of the good in order to orient his skills toward virtuous action, skills in persuasion and argumentation need philosophical guidance.

The stripping and exposure of Socratic *elenchos*, like stripping for exercise in a gymnasium, should not be seen as an exercise in humiliation. As the myth in *Gorgias* shows, fair judgment of *aretē* requires psychic nudity—both for the judge and the judged. In that myth, Zeus puts a stop to bad judgment in the afterlife by requiring that both judges and judged be naked.

> Next, they must be judged when they're stripped naked of all [worldly adornments], for they should be judged when they're dead. The judge, too, should be naked, and dead, and with only his soul he should study only the soul of each person immediately upon his death, when he's isolated from all his kinsmen and has left behind on earth all that adornment, so that the judgment may be a just one." (*Gorgias* 523e)

The judgment takes place after death, because that is when the soul is stripped of its biggest adornment, the body (524d). Socrates believes that injustice and incontinence—in other words, lack of virtue—make the soul ugly (*Gorgias* 525a). *Aretē* is what makes souls beautiful, and like the athletic fitness that makes bodies beautiful, it requires gymnastic training that begins with stripping down.

Training with the Master

Socrates, for his part, says he'll "reveal to the judge a soul that's as healthy as it can be." He says he'll do this by disregarding the things that most people care about and by "practicing truth" (*Gorgias* 526de). The verb he uses, *askein*, is most properly applied to athletic training or exercise. "Practicing truth" or "practicing wisdom and virtue" (*Euthydemus* 283a) are both short, gymnastic answers to the very complicated question of how Socratic *aretē* might be achieved. They make it clear, however, that *aretē* is achieved in and through activity, and—like any skilled activity—they suggest that it must be learned through a kind of apprenticeship. It is not simply a matter of conventional knowledge, of memorizing formulas or recognizing terminology. As in the acquisition of a second language, we not only have to learn the vocabulary and grammar, we need to be able to speak, ultimately without effort and conscious calculation. And one of the first things we look for in learning this and other skills is a master, one who consistently demonstrates excellence in the desired skill.

In *Laches*, Socrates emerges as a master of virtue, first because "he is always spending his time in places where the young men engage in any study or noble pursuit of the sort you are looking for" (*Laches* 180c), and second because he has demonstrated his valor in battle, his *aretic* art has a recognizably excellent product. Says Laches, "He marched with me in the retreat from Delium, and I can tell you that if the rest had been willing to behave in the same manner, our city would be safe and we would not then have suffered a disaster" (181b). Laches observes that Socrates not only discusses virtue, his actions also demonstrate virtue. He compares this to a musical "harmony" that is "genuinely Greek" (188d). Socrates reinforces the harmony metaphor at *Gorgias* 482bc, noting he would rather have everyone disagree with him "than to be out of harmony with [himself]." Plato's depiction of Socrates in the gymnastic dialogues, and especially in the *Apology*, is clearly presented as an example to be imitated. He is a kind of *aretic* hero and his story as presented by Plato may be analogous to Achilles's story in the *Iliad*.

But Socrates's *aretē* is something different from Achilles's, and besides the heroic task of defeating sophistic monsters (a task he refers to as "labors" (*ponoi*), evoking Heracles, at *Apology* 22a), we might ask just how Socrates is actually "training" *aretē* in the gymnastic dialogues. The answer comes back to the issue of guidance and orientation. Like athletes and heroes, Socrates engages in dialectical struggle (*agōn*), but unlike *eristics* and rhetoricians, the goal of his *agōn* is wisdom. The subject of this *agōn*, furthermore, is *aretē*. And so there is a kind of double movement—it is by struggling to understand what *aretē* is that we cultivate it. The concept is illustrated in *Laches* with a metaphor about putting sight into eyes.

> Suppose we know that sight, when added to the eyes, makes better those eyes to which it is added, and furthermore, we are able to add it to the eyes, then clearly we know what this very thing sight is, about which we should be consulting as to how one might obtain it most easily and best. (*Laches* 190ab)

To put virtue into the soul, likewise, we must first strive to understand what virtue is. And it is through the attempt to understand what virtue is—the directing of our discussion toward wisdom—that we begin to achieve it.

Training One's Sights on Wisdom

In the gymnastic dialogues, virtue almost always turns out to be some kind of wisdom. In *Laches*, it is wisdom that makes "endurance of the soul" good and beautiful (*kalē kagathē*) (192c). Eventually, the argument leads to the hypothesis that courage amounts to the knowledge of good and evil (199cd). This is rejected, but only because it would imply that courage is no different from the other parts of virtue (i.e., justice, temperance, and piety) and they had previously agreed that courage could only be part of virtue (199e); but this is not Plato's considered view. In *Euthydemus* it is established that wisdom obviates any need for good fortune (280b) because it allows us to put goods such as wealth and health and beauty (and perhaps even skills like argumentation) to good use—to render them beneficial (281ab). Concludes Socrates,

> it seems likely that with respect to all the things we called good in the beginning, the correct account is not that in themselves they are good by nature, but rather as follows: if ignorance controls them, they are greater evils than their opposites, to the extent that they are more capable of complying with a bad master; but if good sense and wisdom (*phronēsis kai sophia*) are in control, they are

greater goods. In themselves, however, neither sort is of any value." (*Euthydemus* 281de)

The wisdom appropriate to *aretē* turns out to be a kind of art (*technē*), but it is a special kind that rules over the other arts — directing them toward the good. As Socrates tells young Clinias, "what we need, my fair friend…is a kind of knowledge which combines making and knowing how to use the thing which it makes" (*Euthydemus* 289b). In the end this is identified as a "kingly art" (*basilikē technē*) which rules all the products of the other crafts (291d). This metaphor of wise management will be perfected in *Republic*, but it is present in the gymnastic dialogues like *Gorgias* as well.

> The best way in which the excellence (*aretē*) of each thing comes to be present in it, whether it's that of an artifact or of a body or a soul as well, or of any animal, is not just any old way, but is due to whatever organization, correctness, and craftsmanship is bestowed on each of them. (*Gorgias* 506d)[19]

Ultimately, the *Gorgias* describes virtue as a kind of "helmsmanship, which saves not only souls, but also bodies and valuables from the utmost dangers." (511d).[20] Socrates's ability to "steer" his trial and execution, despite their apparent injustice, toward the ideals of virtue and justice is a paradigmatic example of this navigational *aretē*. By his example in the dialogue, furthermore, he guides not just his interlocutors, but also attentive readers toward the good.

---

[19] "ἀλλὰ μὲν δὴ ἥ γε ἀρετὴ ἑκάστου, καὶ σκεύους καὶ σώματος καὶ ψυχῆς αὖ καὶ ζῴου παντός, οὐ τῷ εἰκῇ κάλλιστα παραγίγνεται, ἀλλὰ τάξει καὶ ὀρθότητι καὶ τέχνῃ, ἥτις ἑκάστῳ ἀποδέδοται αὐτῶν: ἆρα ἔστιν ταῦτα;"

[20] The nautical imagery appears also at *Laws* 803a-b: "I'm trying to distinguish for you the various ways in which our character shapes the kind of life we live; I really am trying to 'lay down the keel,' because I'm giving proper consideration to the way we should try to live — to the "character-keel" we need to lay if we are going to sail through this voyage of life successfully."

Plato's Gymnastic Dialogues

Socrates not only theorizes his understanding of *aretē* as guidance toward the good, he demonstrates it like a good coach should, and even invites his charges to get involved. In *Euthydemus,* Socrates matches the argumentative skill of the "pancratist" brothers, defeating them repeatedly at their own game. The ultimate point is that argument must be more than just a game if it is to lead to wisdom and virtue. Socrates describes Dionysodorus picking up the argument "as though it were a ball" and aiming at the boy, Clinias (*Euthydemus* 277b). The philosopher also intervenes to encourage Clinias while "Euthydemus was hastening to throw the young man for the third fall," as in wrestling (277d). Ultimately Euthydemus and Dionysodorus fail not because they lack skill but because they aim at victory rather than wisdom. Their argument, says Socrates, has the old trouble of falling down itself in the process of knocking down others (288a). The misuse of argumentation for sport reduces it to child's play or frivolity (*paidia*) because, as Socrates puts it,

> even if a man were to learn many or even all such things, he would be none the wiser as to how matters stand but would only be able to make fun of people, tripping them up and overturning them by means of the distinctions in words, just like the people who pull the chair out from under a man who is going to sit down and then laugh gleefully when they see him sprawling on his back. (*Euthydemus* 278bc)

The frivolous *paidia* of Euthydemus and Dionysodorus contrasts starkly with their advertised goal of *paideia* (education).

Misdirection from lack of virtue not only prevents a *technē* from being beneficial, it can prevent the *technē* from truly being a *technē* at all. This is the thought behind Socrates's accusation in *Gorgias* that oratory isn't a craft, but merely a "knack" because all it really produces is gratification and pleasure (462a-c). He goes on to characterize it as "flattery" (*kolakeia*)—something that actively corrupts a true craft, the way cosmetics corrupts gymnastics and pastry-baking corrupts medicine.[21] Flattery "guesses at what is pleasant with no consideration for what is best" (464d-465c), thereby sacrificing what is truly good and noble in favor of a more easily achieved appearance of it. Socrates accuses oratory of flattering justice, whereas it and every other craft "is always to be used in support of what's just" (527c).[22] The tendency to engage in flattery is only exacerbated by the commercial pressures alluded to in *Protagoras*. If a teacher's goal is to make money, the temptation to aim one's craft at pleasure rather than truth can be strong. But the good man, as Socrates points out in *Gorgias*, always keeps his product in view (503de). That product for the craftsman of virtue is good and beautiful actions, which derive from *aretē*, which derives from the love and pursuit of wisdom (*philosophia*).

Readers Are Expected to Engage in *Aretic* Gymnastics

Philosophy turns out to be the "practice of *aretē*" and the gymnastic dialogues provide a "place" where the reader is invited to practice philosophy. The experience may be more analogous to an engaged spectator at a wrestling match than to actually competing in a wrestling match. But, like an engaged spectator, we learn to discern the most skillful moves and responses, and perhaps to anticipate them mentally as the dialogue goes forward. The *aporetic* nature of these works—the fact that no final answer to the questions they pose is given—invites us to continue the debate with friends or even in our own minds. We may be rooting for Socrates in the debate, but we are not supposed to imagine him having the answer. He is an experienced coach or guide, searching

---

[21] Socrates explains with an analogy between fitness in the body and fitness in the soul. Just as cosmetic may create the mere appearance of bodily fitness, which is properly gained through gymnastics, oratory may create the mere appearance of virtue in the soul, which is properly gained through philosophy (*Gorgias* 464a). See Dombrowski's essay in this volume.

[22] Socrates points to himself as an example of the proper use of oratory, which he calls the political craft: "I believe that I'm one of a few Athenians—so as not to say I'm the only one, but the only one among our contemporaries—to take up the true political craft and practice the true politics. This is because the speeches I make on each occasion do not aim at gratification but at what's best. They don't aim at what's most pleasant" (*Gorgias* 521de).

alongside us for wisdom: "For the things I say I certainly don't say with any knowledge at all; no, I'm searching together with you so that if my opponent clearly has a point, I'll be the first to concede it" (*Gorgias* 506a). Socrates even invites us readers, along with his interlocutors, to challenge his hypotheses. "Please don't falter in doing a friend a good turn," he says to Polus, "Refute me" (*Gorgias* 470c).

There is a sense that we, as readers, are competing with Socrates to understand *aretē*, but that is not the same as competing *against* him, and it is not for victory that we are competing. We are competing, like enlightened athletes, for the sake of mutual improvement, for the sake of *aretē*. Socrates says he is pleased to have met Callicles, who challenged him so fiercely, because the argument has functioned for Socrates's soul like a stone used to test the purity of gold (*Gorgias* 486de). "You love to win," Callicles says to Socrates, and the philosopher does not deny it. "But it's not for love of winning (*philonikia*) that I'm asking you," he explains, "It's rather because I really do want to know" (*Gorgias* 515b). We compete with Socrates not for *philonikia*, but rather for *philosophia*. And *philosophia*, because it is love of wisdom and not some perfected state of wisdom, can be practiced even with opponents who care only about victory, or opponents who are nothing more than characters in a dialogue. We become philosophers in the Socratic sense by thinking about and debating virtue, and like every skill, we get better through practice. As the *Gorgias* concludes,

> Nothing terrible will happen to you if you really are a *kaloskagathos*, one who practices excellence (*askōn aretein*). And then, after we've practiced it together [...] then we'll deliberate about whatever subject we please, when we're better at deliberating than we are now. (*Gorgias* 527d)

Even if the gymnastic dialogues fail to involve us in their debates, just as Socrates fails to get Theodorus to strip and wrestle with Theaetetus in the dialogue of the same name, it is enough that they inspire us to love wisdom—since it is that love that orients the "helmsman" of virtue, just as surely as the stars orient the helmsman of a ship. Socrates sets the example, commenting in *Gorgias* that just as lovers believe whatever their beloved says, he believes whatever his beloved, *Philosophy*, says, "and she's by far less fickle than my other beloved" [i.e., Alcibiades] (482a). In *Euthydemus*, the boy Clinias is exhorted that it is "necessary to love wisdom" (282d), "become wise and good" (282e), and to "practice (*askein*) wisdom and virtue" (283a). The argument with Dionysodorus has been an "incitement to virtue" (283b). Every gymnastic dialogue is likewise an incitement to philosophy, and therefore virtue. Most of them even end with a promise to continue the discussion—and most readers silently count themselves in on the promise. *Gorgias* ends with the good coach Socrates calling everyone "to this way of life, this contest (*agōn*), that I hold to be worth all the other contests in this life" (*Gorgias* 526e). And he exhorts us in *Euthydemus* to "pay no attention to the practitioners of philosophy but rather to the thing itself....to take it to heart, pursue it, and (*askē*) practice it" (307c).

Matthew P. Evans[1]
Architectural and Spatial Features of Plato's *Gymnasia* and *Palaistrai*

Classical Athens in the age of Socrates and Plato (mid fifth century to mid fourth century BCE) enjoyed several *gymnasia* and *palaistrai* as athletic training facilities. Fundamentally, a *gymnasion* was a place of nudity (*gymnos* in Greek), referring to the Greek practice of athletic nudity. Scant literary references depict *gymnasia* in Athens at this time as expansive parks, shaded by trees, with a natural water source, open-air running tracks, and few architectural features.[2] The earliest archaeological examples of *gymnasia*, dating to the second half of the fourth century BCE, include only a *palaistra* as an architectural feature: an enclosed building of varying size and layout, with an open-air, earthen courtyard framed by colonnaded porticoes and a few rooms (see figure).[3]

---

[1] Matthew P. Evans is a PhD candidate in the Department of Classics and Ancient History at the University of Warwick, UK. His dissertation examines the interrelationships between form and function of ancient Greek *gymnasia* using a sensory approach to space and the built environment. matthew.evans.2@warwick.ac.uk.

[2] For example, Aristophanes (*Clouds*, 1005-1008), Xenophon (*Hellenika*, 2.4.27; *On the Cavalry Commander*, 3.6), and Plutarch (*Life of Kimon*, 13.8) describe the Academy and Lyceum as expansive parks with running tracks (*dromoi*). In contrast, Old Oligarch/Pseudo-Xenophon (*Constitution of the Athenians*, 2.10), Xenophon (*Anabasis*, 7.8.1), Plutarch (*Life of Kimon*, 16.5), and Suda (s.v. "the wall of Hipparchus") suggest that *gymnasia*, including the Academy and Lyceum, consisted in some part of built structures.

[3] The earliest archaeological examples of *gymnasia* are at Amphipolis, Delphi, and Eretria. In the third or second centuries BCE, some *gymnasia* incorporated a covered running track (called a *xystos*) in the form of a *stoa* (an elongated building with a colonnade on at least one long side). For a detailed and relatively up-to-date discussion of the architectural development of *gymnasia*, see Christian Wacker, *Das Gymnasion in Olympia: Geschichte und Funktion* (Würzburg: Ergon, 1996); Christian Wacker, "Die bauhistorische Entwicklung der Gymnasien Von der Parkanlage zum 'Idealgymnasion' des Vitruv," in *Das hellenistiche Gymnasion*, ed. Daniel Kah and Peter Scholz (Berlin: Akademie Verlag, 2004). For a detailed and up-to-date analysis of

Matthew P. Evans

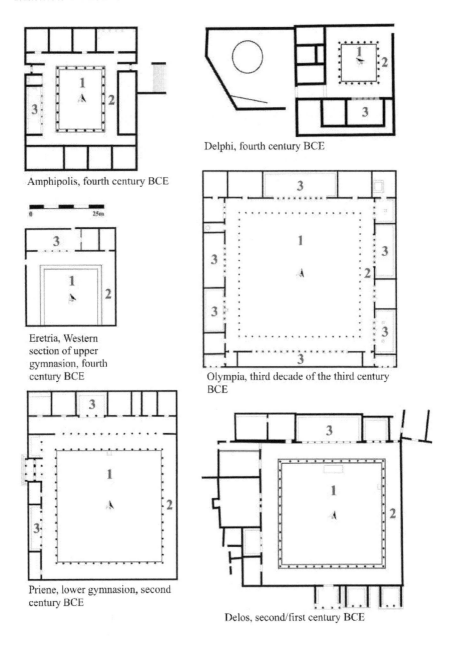

Amphipolis, fourth century BCE

Delphi, fourth century BCE

Eretria, Western section of upper gymnasion, fourth century BCE

Olympia, third decade of the third century BCE

Priene, lower gymnasion, second century BCE

Delos, second/first century BCE

the architectural development of *palaistrai* building types, see Burkhard Emme, "The Emergence and Significance of the Palaestra Type in Greek Architecture," in *Development of Gymnasia and Graeco-Roman Cityscapes*, ed. Ulrich Mania and Monika Trümper (Berlin: Edition Topoi, 2018).

Architectural and Spatial Features of Plato's Gymnasia

Palaistrai were places of wrestling (*palē*) that could exist either as facilities incorporated into *gymnasia*, as in the earliest archaeological examples, or as spatially—and institutionally—independent wrestling schools, which appear frequently in Plato (the term *"palaistra"* will describe independent wrestling schools in this paper unless otherwise stated).[4]

Both *gymnasia* and *palaistrai* were not limited to athletic training. In classical Athens, these facilities hosted philosophical activity by providing the perfect settings for intellectual discussion among the aristocratic men and (particularly) youths who frequented them in their leisure time. Plato, for example, describes the Lyceum *gymnasion* in Athens as a certain "haunt" of Socrates (*Euthyphro* 2a; *Symposium* 223d) and sets the Socratic dialogue *Euthydemus* within its grounds.[5] Plato sets a further three, if not more, of his dialogues within Athenian *gymnasia/palaistrai*: *Lysis* in a *palaistra* near the spring of Panops,[6] *Charmides* in the *palaistra* of Taureas,[7] and *Theaetetus* in an unspecified *gymnasion/palaistra*.[8] In each of these dialogues, Socrates seeks out beautiful and intelligent youths as his main interlocutors. Youths made the most suitable "sparring-partners" for Socrates's educational method of *elenchos* or question and answer (metaphorically represented in Plato as a type of philosophical wrestling)[9] as Theodorus, a relatively old man, states in *Theaetetus* (146b; cf. 162a-b):

---

[4] This terminology follows Plato's use of the terms *"palaistra"* and *"gymnasion."* For a discussion of the problematic terminology, see Stephen L. Glass, "The Greek Gymnasium: Some Problems," in *The Archaeology of the Olympics: The Olympics and Other Festivals in Antiquity*, ed. Wendy J. Raschke (Madison: University of Wisconsin Press, 1988), 155-173.

[5] Plato, *Euthydemus*, trans. Walter R.M. Lamb (Cambridge: Harvard University Press, 1924), 271a, 272e.

[6] Plato, *Lysis*, trans. Walter R.M. Lamb (Cambridge: Harvard University Press, 1925), 203a-204a.

[7] Plato, *Charmides*, trans. Walter R.M. Lamb (Cambridge: Harvard University Press, 1925), 153a.

[8] Plato, *Theaetetus*, trans. Harold N. Fowler (Cambridge: Harvard University Press, 1921), 144c.

[9] See Heather L. Reid, "Wrestling with Socrates," *Sport, Ethics and Philosophy* 4.2 (2010) for wrestling as a metaphor of Socratic *elenchos* in Plato.

...tell one of the youths to answer your questions [Socrates]; for I am unused to such conversation and, moreover, I am not of an age to accustom myself to it. But that would be fitting for these young men, and they would improve much more than I; for the fact is, youth admits of improvement in every way.

Perhaps it is due to the abundance of appropriate students that philosophers eventually set up schools within or near *gymnasia* in Athens, such as Plato's school at the Academy, Aristotle's at the Lyceum, and the Cynics' at the Cynosarges. Furthermore, in the Hellenistic period (323-31 BCE), *gymnasia* in *poleis* (city-states) across the Greek world increasingly served the intellectual and social development of male citizens alongside athletic (and paramilitary) training. By the late first century BCE, Vitruvius (*On Architecture*, 5.11) describes his ideal *gymnasion/palaistra* as a complex that catered equally to athletic and intellectual activity—a monumental realization of Plato's *gymnasia/palaistrai*.[10]

Plato, in setting his dialogues within *gymnasia* and *palaistrai*, reveals some of their architectural and spatial features such as walls, entrances, rooms, or other facilities. For archaeologists, these references provide valuable insights into the (pre-archaeological) *gymnasia* and *palaistrai* of classical Athens.[11] For historians and philosophers interested in Plato, on the other hand, these

---

[10] Vitruvius, *On Architecture*, trans. Ingrid D. Rowland (Cambridge: Cambridge University Press, 1999), 5.11. It should be noted that Vitruvius's architectural treatise on the *gymnasion/palaistra* is a typified ideal: no archaeological *gymnasion/palaistra* complex exactly mirrors Vitruvius's description, though Olympia's bears the closest resemblance.

[11] Plato's *gymnasia/palaistrai* appear to reflect real facilities available in Athens during his lifetime, familiar to his audience; there is little reason to suspect that they are fabricated or imaginary facilities. Archaeologists have not fully recognized the value of Plato as a source, with the exception of Jean Delorme, *Gymnasion: Étude sur les monuments consacrés à l'éducation en Grèce (des origines à l'Empire romain)* (Paris: E. de Boccard, 1960), who frequently references Plato in his seminal work on *gymnasia*.

Architectural and Spatial Features of Plato's Gymnasia

references are often considered nothing more than insignificant contextual remarks to the dialogue's setting. It has been recognized that the settings of *gymnasia* and *palaistrai* bear a philosophical significance for Plato: they are closely associated with competition (*agōn*), nudity, and the virtues of beauty and moral goodness.[12] However, the role of the specific architectural and spatial features as part of these settings remains as yet unexamined.

This paper, as a result, focuses on Plato's use of architectural and spatial features in *Lysis, Euthydemus, Charmides,* and *Theaetetus*. I argue that they function as carefully-selected metaphorical and dramatic devices that allow Plato to highlight and explore various philosophical ideas and methods in the dialogues and his broader philosophy. By examining both the exterior and interior features of *gymnasia/palaistrai*, I hope to demonstrate that Plato encodes philosophical meaning within the spatial fabric of his dialogue settings. We will begin with the exterior features.

Topography and Exterior Features

Lysis begins with Socrates describing his journey between two public *gymnasia*, "from the Academy straight to the Lyceum," when he comes across the recently-constructed private *palaistra* of Miccus on the road near the city walls of Athens and the Spring of Panops (203a). According to our topographical understanding of classical Athens, Socrates's route from the Academy to the Lyceum, in contrast to this account, is not the most direct. Socrates appears to have taken a considerable and intentional detour to bring him to this *palaistra*, though he claims to have been unaware of its existence.[13] A possible reason for Socrates's detour to this private *palaistra* is that he wishes to question younger boys than those he would usually find in public *gymnasia*; private *palaistrai*

---

[12] Heather L. Reid, "Plato's Gymnasium," *Sport, Ethics and Philosophy* 4, 2 (2010); Reid, "Wrestling with Socrates."

[13] Christopher Planeaux, "Socrates, an Unreliable Narrator? The Dramatic Setting of the "Lysis," *Classical Philology* 96, 1 (2001) convincingly argues that Socrates's visit to the *palaistra* was intentional.

hosted (at least in part) the elementary athletic education of young boys (*paides*). Conveniently, the day of Socrates's visit coincides with the day of the *Hermaia* (a festival celebrated in *gymnasia* and *palaistrai* throughout the Greek world), the only day of the year when young boys (*paides*) were permitted to mix freely with older youths and men in the *palaistra* (206d).[14]

The young age of Socrates's interlocutors, Lysis and Menexenus, is crucial in Plato's exploration of the dialogue's main theme: friendship (*philia*). At their tender age, they do not have a firm grip on what friendship is and answer Socrates's questions from their own experience as friends, in turn destroying their previous understanding of friendship and enhancing Socrates's educational method of *elenchos*.[15] The boys' interactions in the dialogue also demonstrate a childish and competitively-natured form of friendship, which is emphasized by the athletic, agonistic setting of the *palaistra*. It is enhanced further by the *Hermaia*, which involved athletic competitions as well as awards for the virtue (*eutaxia, philoponia*) and the physical condition (*euexia*) of the boys.[16] Without bringing Socrates to this private *palaistra*, therefore, Plato's philosophical discussion on friendship would be limited. The topographical detail of the *palaistra*'s location between two public *gymnasia* emphasizes the institutional differences of

---

[14] However, both Lysis and Menexenus are being closely watched by their personal attendants/tutors (*paidagogoi*) (208c, 223a-b). Socrates's youthful interlocutors in the other dialogues (*Euthydemus, Charmides*, and *Theaetetus*) are slightly older youths (*neoi, neaniskoi*) and could speak freely with older men like Socrates in *gymnasia* and *palaistrai*. For example, Socrates observes that if Charmides were any younger (for instance, as young as Lysis) he would be discredited for talking to him in the *palaistra* without the presence of his guardian (*Charmides* 155a).

[15] Hans-Georg Gadamer, *Dialogue and Dialectic: Eight Hermeneutical Studies on Plato*, trans. Christopher P. Smith (New Haven: Yale University Press, 1980), 11.

[16] See, for example, the provisions set out for the *Hermaia* festival at the *gymnasion* of Beroia in Macedonia (*Supplementum Epigraphicum Graecum* [SEG] 27.261, face b, lines 45-71). See also Nigel B. Crowther, "Male «Beauty» contests in Greece: The *Euandria* and *Euexia*." In *L'antiquité classique* 54 (1985): 285-291.

public and private facilities, which has further implications regarding the history of philosophical activity in these facilities.

Plato, in *Euthydemus*, juxtaposes the educational possibilities offered by public *gymnasia* and private *palaistrai*. Socrates, toward the end of the dialogue, advises the sophists Euthydemus and Dionysodorus to beware of public discussions before many people (like the one they have just completed in the Lyceum), where they risk receiving no credit for education. Instead, Socrates advises, they should talk privately between themselves, and charge a fee to anyone who wishes to join and listen (304a). Socrates then goes on to tell Crito, to whom he has been reciting the dialogue, that Euthydemus and Dionysodorus will teach their wisdom to anyone willing to pay them money (304c). Plato, as a philosopher, appears to be criticizing or jesting toward the sophists here, in that their aim is not purely the pursuit of knowledge and truth, as is the aim of philosophers, but, rather, the personal gain of reputation and money.[17] In this light, Socrates's advice perhaps reveals a motivating principle behind Plato setting up his philosophical school, which was exclusive but free to attend, within a public *gymnasion* (the Academy) rather than a private *palaistra*. In an explicit play on words in *Lysis*, Socrates calls Miccus, the owner of the private *palaistra*, a sophist (204a), thereby paralleling the paid, private gymnastic teacher with a sophist. *Gymnasia*, as public institutions, therefore provided more suitable facilities for philosophical education in comparison to private *palaistrai*.

The exterior architectural features of the *palaistra* in *Lysis* further emphasize its private nature in developing a juxtaposition with public *gymnasia*. Socrates, while standing outside of the *palaistra*, claiming to be unaware of what such a building is, describes it as "a sort of enclosure (*peribolos*) and a door (*thura*) standing open" (203b). The *peribolos* implies a non-descript, enclosing wall, similar to the exterior walls of the earliest

---

[17] Interestingly, Plato's *Sophist* (along with *Politicus*), which sets out the differences between philosophers and sophists, is probably set within a *gymnasion/palaistra* as a continuation of *Theaetetus* according to Stephen G. Miller, *The Berkeley Plato: From Neglected Relic to Ancient Treasure* (Berkeley, CA: University of California Press, 2009), 48 n. 122.

archaeological *palaistrai* (see figure). This enclosure (successfully) keeps the activities of the *palaistra* concealed from the gaze of people outside, justifying Socrates's claim of ignorance. The reference to the nearby spring of Panops (literally "All-Seeing") is ironic in this regard (203a). The enclosing wall as an architectural feature, therefore, affords the facility with a particularly private nature. Plato's choice to describe it here is probably to add an architectural element to the institutional contrast between private *palaistrai* and public *gymnasia*. However, the door (*thura*) standing open negates the *palaistra*'s privacy, penetrating the otherwise inaccessible enclosure and perhaps pointing to further significance.

The door, together with the enclosing wall, appear to metaphorically represent the basic tenets of Socratic *elenchos*. As Socrates demonstrates throughout the dialogues (especially in *Theaetetus*), the aim of his educational method of question and answer (*elenchos*) is to elicit the independent thoughts of his youthful interlocutors, and thus help them independently arrive at the truth, rather than attaining answers from others.[18] The enclosing wall, therefore, metaphorically represents a barrier to knowledge and truth. Socrates (typically claiming ignorance) asks Hippothales what the structure is and what happens inside, and gets his answer. However, to gain an independent understanding, Socrates must himself cross the barrier to knowledge facilitated by the door. Admittedly this metaphorical use of the exterior architectural features is highly speculative, but the interior spatial features of the same *palaistra*, at least, appear to continue the metaphor.

Interior Features

As Socrates enters the *palaistra* in *Lysis*, he emphasizes his revelation process by providing a particularly vivid description of

---

[18] Socrates, for example, reproaches Charmides for repeating a definition of *sōphrosunē* which he had learned from another philosopher (*Charmides* 161b-d). In *Theaetetus*, Socrates represents his method through the metaphor of midwifery, where he, as the midwife, aids youths to "give birth" to their own thoughts (150b-151d, 157c-d, 160e, 184a-b, 210b-d).

Architectural and Spatial Features of Plato's Gymnasia

the activities and spatial features that he discovers. The first thing he notices is that the boys inside had finished performing (presumably animal) sacrifices (206e), which would have required (and suggests the spatial feature of) an altar. The apparent proximity of this altar to the door of the *palaistra* perhaps has a philosophical significance in relation to the metaphor discussed above. Socrates's method of *elenchos* as a process of discovering the truth is closely associated with the Deity (*theos*). In *Theaetetus*, for example, Socrates claims his method is divinely ordained (150c, 210c) and that the Deity is equally responsible as he is in eliciting independent thoughts (150d): "But the delivery [of independent wisdom] is due to the god (*theos*) and me." Besides, the recipient of the sacrifices as part of the *Hermaia* in *Lysis* is Hermes. As a god associated with not only boundaries (relevant to the metaphorical use of the enclosing wall) but also with being a guide (most famously for guiding the souls of the dead to the underworld), the sacrifices to Hermes and the suggested altar emphasize Socrates's divinely-guided process of eliciting wisdom/truth. Furthermore, Hermes was a god associated with wrestling.[19] This not only explains why such sacrifices and festivals were dedicated to Hermes in the *palaistra*, but also provides a suitable deity with whom the Socratic method—represented in Plato as a kind of philosophical wrestling, mentioned above—could be associated.

Sacrifices to Hermes as a god of wrestling enhance the overall competitive/agonistic character of the *palaistra*, an effect which is continued by other interior architectural/spatial features in *Lysis*. The next spatial feature which Socrates notes as he enters is the "court out-of-doors" (*aulē exō*) (206e). Plato here seems to refer to an open-air, earthen courtyard similar to those of archaeological *palaistrai* (see figure, feature no. 1). The courtyard of a *palaistra* represents the space where the majority of athletic training would have taken place: athletes would prepare areas of sand or loosened earth with pick-axes, creating a surface soft enough to wrestle on.

---

[19] Hermes was related in some respect to the goddess Palaistra who is credited with inventing wrestling and thus providing an etiology for the *palaistra* as a place of wrestling.

In the scene described by Socrates, however, the boys play knuckle-bones in their finest attire within the courtyard. The fact that they are not wrestling in the nude does not necessarily diminish the enhanced competitive/agonistic character afforded by the courtyard as a spatial feature. On the one hand, the reference to the courtyard of the *palaistra* alone would have probably been sufficient for most of Plato's audience, who were acquainted with such spaces, to associate it with athletic training and wrestling (and, thus, with Socratic *elenchos*).[20] On the other hand, boys playing games in the courtyard has a philosophical significance, since Socrates often uses such games as metaphors. For example, he explains the format of *elenchos* to Theaetetus using the metaphor of a ball game between boys (*paides*) (*Theaetetus* 146a).[21] Moreover, Socrates uses a game specifically played in the courtyard of a *palaistra*, where one team has to drag the other over a line, to metaphorically represent his and Theaetetus's philosophical situation of being caught between two schools of thought (*Theaetetus* 180e-181a).[22] Thus, both the court as a spatial feature of the *palaistra* and the activities which take place within it are significant in enhancing the competitive/agonistic character of the setting and its relation to Socrates's method of philosophy.

Plato initially appears to reveal other types of spatial/architectural features associated with athletic training for the same effect. In *Euthydemus*, Socrates describes Euthydemus and Dionysodorus walking around the "covered *dromos*" (*katastegos dromos*) of the Lyceum (273a), while in *Theaetetus*, Theodorus notes that Theaetetus and his companions had been anointing themselves in the "outer *dromos*" (*exō dromos*) of the unspecified *gymnasion/palaistra* (144c). The term "*dromos*" suggests a track or

---

[20] Of importance here is that Socratic *elenchos* is a method more akin to training for improvement than competition for the sake of winning, as pointed out by Reid, "Wrestling with Socrates," 164.
[21] A ball game is also used in *Euthydemus* as a metaphor for the eristic method of Euthydemus and Dionysodorus (277b).
[22] This game is called the *dielkustinda* by the second-century CE writer Julius Pollux (*Onomasticon*, 9.112).

course for practicing running. More specifically, the "covered *dromos*" implies a *xystos*: a running track sheltered beneath a *stoa* (an elongated building with a colonnade on at least one long side), similar to those built at archaeological *gymnasia* in the third and second centuries BCE.[23] The "outer *dromos*," on the other hand, implies a simple outdoor running track like those described in other literary sources.[24] Theaetetus and his friends anointing their bodies with oil, an activity inherently associated with preparing for athletic training and competition, within the outer *dromos* emphasizes the competitive/agonistic nature of the setting, and perhaps acts as a metaphor for Theaetetus preparing to philosophically "wrestle" with Socrates. However, to accept that these *dromoi*, as architectural and spatial features, represent running tracks of different forms, and to consequently state that they are used by Plato to emphasize the competitive/agonistic character of their respective facilities, would be to disregard the architectural and functional issues which these features present.

Rather than running tracks, the *dromoi* more plausibly refer to porticoes around the courtyard of a *palaistra* (as seen in the archaeological examples of the figure, feature n. 2);[25] this interpretation would mean that *Euthydemus* takes place within an incorporated *palaistra* facility of the Lyceum *gymnasion*.[26] One

---

[23] This is certainly the interpretation of Delorme, *Gymnasion*, 55.

[24] For example, Xenophon, *On the Cavalry Commander*, 3.6; Plutarch, *Cimon*, 13.8; Pausanias, *Descriptions of Greece*, 6.23.1-2.

[25] This interpretation is presented in Walter R.M. Lamb, *Plato. Laches, Protagoras, Meno, Euthydemus*, Loeb Classical Library 165, (Cambridge, MA.: Harvard University Press, 1924), 385 n. 3 and also argued by Glass, "The Greek Gymnasium: Some Problems," 167.

[26] In fact, Eutychia Lygouri-Tolia claims to have found the *palaistra* of the Lyceum in 1996, not far east of modern Syntagma Square in Athens. The foundations of the building date to the last quarter of the fourth century BCE, chronologically aligning with an epigraphic reference (307/6 BCE) to building/reconstruction works at the Lyceum by Lycurgus (*Inscriptiones Graecae* [*IG*] II² 457b5-9). If this archaeological site is in fact a *palaistra*, and that of the Lyceum built by Lycurgus (none of which, I should note, is necessarily certain), perhaps it is a rebuilding of an earlier *palaistra* such as that in which *Euthydemus* is set. No traces of a *xystos* have been found at the

argument for interpreting the "covered *dromos*" as porticoes around a court rather than a *xystos*, is that Socrates can see Euthydemus and Dionysodorus walk around it from his seat in the *apodyterion* (the undressing room in a *palaistra*, discussed below, functionally equivalent to the locker room in current-day gyms). There is not a single archaeological example where someone in the *apodyterion* could see someone in the *xystos* due to the enclosed design of *palaistrai*. Other reasons for interpreting the *dromoi* as porticoes in a *palaistra* include: 1) the sequence of movement of Euthydemus and Dionysodorus from entrance to "covered *dromos*" (*Euthydemus* 273a) is consistent with archaeological *palaistrai* where the entrance leads into the porticoes around the court (see figure, feature n. 2) Euthydemus and Dionysodorus "walking around" (*peripateō, perielēluthote* from *perierchomai*) in the "covered *dromos*" (273a) suggests laps/circuits around a courtyard; 3) the distinction of the *dromos* in *Theaetetus* as "outer" perhaps refers to it being "outside" and thus around an unspecified courtyard rather than "out-of-doors" (although *peri*, not *exō*, would be the expected preposition); 4) Theaetetus and his companions going to the *dromos* to anoint themselves makes more sense if it is the porticoes around a courtyard, and thus near the *apodyterion* (undressing room), rather than a running track which would have been farther away; 5) finally, archaeological evidence for the architectural development of *gymnasia* demonstrates that they incorporated *xystoi* much later than *palaistrai*,[27] making the

---

site. For the preliminary archaeological report of the building, see Eutychia Lygouri-Tolia, "Excavating an Ancient Palaestra in Athens," in *Excavating Classical Culture: Recent Archaeological Discoveries in Greece*, ed. Maria Stamatopoulou and Marina Yeroulanou (Oxford: Beazley Archive and Archaeopress, 2002).

[27] At the *gymnasion* of Delphi, the *palaistra* dates to the third quarter of the fourth century BCE and the *xystos* around a century later to the middle of the third century BCE; at Olympia, the *palaistra* dates to the third decade of the third century BCE and the *xystoi* to second/first century BCE; at Delos, the *palaistra* was constructed before 280 BCE and the *xystos* around 200 BCE. Cf. Xenophon (*Oeconomicus* 11.15), writing at the same time as Plato, mentions walking about in a *xystos*, though this seems to refer to a "walking-place in

Architectural and Spatial Features of Plato's Gymnasia

existence of a *palaistra* with porticoes around a courtyard at the Lyceum and the facility of *Theaetetus* during the life of Plato much more conceivable than a covered running track. The ambiguity of Plato's terminology for these architectural/spatial features is perhaps the result of there being no established terminology for the porticoes around a court,[28] and a *dromos* can mean a course for walking as well as running.

The philosophical significance of the outer *dromos* in *Theaetetus* does not necessarily change as a result of its interpretation as the porticoes around a courtyard. If anything, porticoes merely provide a more suitable space, as compared to running tracks, within which Theaetetus could anoint himself with oil and metaphorically prepare to philosophically wrestle with Socrates (thus enhancing the competitive/agonistic nature of the setting). The reinterpretation of the covered *dromos* in *Euthydemus*, on the other hand, moves away from emphasizing the competitive/agonistic character of the dialogues' setting toward having a more dramatic function. In *Euthydemus*, Socrates sits alone in the *apodyterion* and, as mentioned above, watches Euthydemus and Dionysodorus enter and walk around the covered *dromos*/porticoes (273a) before he sees Cleinias enter the *palaistra* (273a). From the entrance (*eisodos*), Cleinias catches sight of Socrates sitting alone in the *apodyterion* and comes straight from the entrance to sit beside him (273b). Euthydemus and Dionysodorus, however, while they walk around the porticoes talking to each other occasionally glance toward Socrates and Cleinias before coming to sit next to them in the *apodyterion* (273b).

---

the ground of a private residence" (Henry George Liddell and Robert Scott, *A Greek-English Lexicon*, (Oxford: Clarendon Press, 1940), 1020. Plutarch (*Life of Cimon* 16.5), writing in the first-second century CE, mentions a *stoa* (basically a *xystos*) in the mid-fifth-century BCE *gymnasion* of Corinth, but this is probably an anachronism.

[28] A *gymnasion* inventory from Delos from c. 155 BCE mentions a peristyle (*peristōion*) and "enclosed stoai" (*exomenei stoai*) (*Inscriptions de Délos* [*ID*] 1417 A lines 119 (*peristōion*), 122-123, 133 (*exomenei stoai*)), both seemingly terms for the porticoes around a courtyard, while Vitruvius uses the term *diaulos* (*On Architecture*, 5.11.1).

Plato creates a sense of fluidity between the various spaces of the *palaistra* (*apodyterion*, entrance, covered *dromos*) through the spatial quality of inter-visibility (a two-way relationship of visibility between separate spaces). Such inter-visibility adds to the prelude of the dialogue by allowing Plato the opportunity to not only build tension but also introduce the relationships between Socrates and (those who will be) his interlocutors. Cleinias demonstrates his friendly acquaintance with Socrates by immediately joining him, while Socrates's fixed attention on Euthydemus and Dionysodorus and their glances toward him and Cleinias from a distance present a more hostile relationship fitting with Socrates's/Plato's views on sophists. The covered *dromos* and its inter-visibility with the *apodyterion*, therefore, function as dramatic devices. The fact that Plato does not highlight any inter-visibility between the outer *dromos* and the (presumed) *apodyterion* in *Theaetetus* is perhaps because the dramatic device is not required in the dialogue's prelude,[29] in turn, demonstrating its significance in *Euthydemus*.

The *apodyterion* is a significant spatial/architectural feature in Plato's dialogues set within *gymnasia/palaistrai*. In *Lysis*, Socrates reveals the size and design of the *palaistra*'s *apodyterion*. He describes that he had to sit on the opposite side of the room to the group of boys playing knuckle-bones in the corner in order to find somewhere quiet enough to talk (207a). The *apodyterion* must have been of considerable size for such an acoustic situation to be possible. In regards to its architectural design, at least one side of the room must have been open if we also consider the inter-visibility of the *apodyterion* in *Euthydemus*. A wide entrance would have provided such an opening, perhaps supported by columns/pillars (Socrates in *Euthydemus* refers to "the very

---

[29] Theodorus states that Theaetetus and his friends "were anointing themselves in the outer *dromos*" but now "seem to have finished" and are approaching him and Socrates (144c). The description here, unlike *Euthydemus*, does not suggest that Theodorus has watched them anoint in the outer *dromos* from his current seat. Instead, Theodorus appears to see Theaetetus and his friends approaching from another space, if not the same space as he and Socrates occupy (presumably the *apodyterion*).

Architectural and Spatial Features of Plato's Gymnasia

columns/pillars (*kiones*) of the Lyceum" (303b).[30] Such an architectural design resembles the large rooms of archaeological *palaistrai* (from the earliest *gymnasia* in the fourth century BCE to the third/second century BCE); these rooms have wide, columned entrances opening onto (and thus inter-visible with) the porticoes and courtyard, and often include long benches along their walls (see figure, feature n. 3).[31] Plato, in explicitly setting *Lysis* and *Euthydemus*, and probably (but not explicitly) *Charmides* and *Theaetetus* within the *apodyterion* of their respective facilities, reveals the historical significance of such spaces. It is within the *apodyteria* of classical Athenian *gymnasia/palaistrai* that philosophers like Socrates would have sat and held discussions among the relaxing athletes as they undressed before and dressed after exercise. *Exedrae*, as architecturally separate (from the *apodyterion*) and functionally specific spaces where "philosophers, orators, and everyone else who delights in study [were] able to sit and hold discussion" (Vitruvius, *On Architecture* 5.11.2), appear to have not been incorporated into *palaistrai* (and in turn *gymnasia*) until at least the third century BCE.[32] Plato's multifunctional

---

[30] As suggested by Glass, "The Greek Gymnasium: Some Problems," 166.

[31] Examples include Amphipolis, Delphi, Eretria (western section of the upper *gymnasion*), Olympia, Delos, and Priene. At Delphi and Eretria, these rooms are identified as the *apodyterion*: an inscription from c. 247/246 BCE mentions an *apodyterion* as being among the rooms of Delphi's *palaistra* (*Corpus des inscriptions de Delphes* [*CID*] 2.139 lines 19-21).

[32] Rooms resembling Plato's *apodyteria* at later archaeological *palaistrai* such as Delos and Olympia (early third century BCE), and Priene (second century BCE), which have two or more of these rooms (Olympia has five or six), are identified as *exedrae*, while the *apodyterion* is relegated to a smaller room with a narrow doorway. A *gymnasion* inventory from Delos, mentioned above (see note 28, lines 134, 138), appears to term the large, wide-entranced rooms *exedrae* (though this remains debated: see Jean Audiat, "Le gymnase de Délos et l'inventaire de Kallistratos," *Bulletin de Correspondance Hellénique* 54 (1930): pl.3; Georges Roux, "Á propos de gymnases de Delphes et de Délos," *Bulletin de Correspondance Hellénique* 104 (1980): 142-43). In fact, *exedrae* of later archaeological *gymnasia/palaistrai* assumed the architectural form of *apodyteria* in Plato's and early archaeological *gymnasia/palaistrai* (as noted by Delorme, *Gymnasion*, 55) and, more importantly, appear to have

apodyteria, therefore, represent a formative stage in the functional (and perhaps even the architectural) development of *gymnasia* and *palaistrai*.

The fundamental function of the *apodyterion* as, literally, the "place of undressing" the body (*apoduō*) in the *palaistra* (both as independent and incorporated facilities), also bears philosophical significance concerning nudity and beauty. Throughout the dialogues, Plato demonstrates the physical beauty of Socrates's youthful interlocutors as the objects of desire/love (*erōs*). Lysis, for example, is admired and loved by Hippothales (*Lysis* 204b-d) — in fact, Socrates showing Hippothales how to talk to his beloved provides a premise for entering the *palaistra* and engaging Lysis in a discussion (206c-d). When Socrates sees Lysis standing among the boys playing knuckle-bones in the *apodyterion*, he describes the boy's physical appearance as not only physically beautiful but also as imparting a sense of moral goodness (*kalos k'agathos*) (207a). Crito in *Euthydemus* also describes the appearance of Cleinias in this manner (*kalos kai agathos*) (271b) and, similarly, a group of lovers follows him (273a, 274b, 274c). Charmides is described as exceptionally beautiful, having "such a perfect beauty of form" (*Charmides* 154b, 154d). He has so many lovers that they both precede (153d-154a) and follow (154b) his entrance into the *palaistra* of Taureas; his entrance causes everybody in the facility to be struck with "astonishment and confusion" (154c) and to "gaze at him as if he were a statue" (154d). Such is his beauty that when Socrates glimpses his nude body beneath his clothes, he "catches fire" with desire for the youth and "could possess [himself] no longer," though he is eventually able to control himself (155d-e).[33] In each of these dialogues, as established above, Socrates is sat within the *apodyterion* (explicitly stated in *Lysis* and *Euthydemus*, and suggested in *Charmides*). As the place where these youths would strip and reveal their nude bodies, the *apodyterion* thus

---

inherited the philosophical function of Plato's *apodyteria*, at least in Vitruvius's ideal *gymnasion/palaistra* complex.

[33] Socrates's ability to restrain himself demonstrates his self-control, or *sōphrosunē*, which is the main topic of the dialogue.

represents a particularly suitable space within which Socrates could appreciate their physical beauty. In the case of *Charmides*, being in such a space (almost ironically) adds to Socrates's struggle against desire and temptation when he glimpses Charmides's nude body beneath his clothes.

The *apodyterion* also bears a metaphorical significance in developing a juxtaposition between the body and soul in relation to Socrates's educational method of *elenchos*, represented as a type of "undressing of the soul (*psychē*)."[34] Theaetetus, in sharp contrast to the youths of the other dialogues, is not physically beautiful. Theodorus tells Socrates, "lest someone should think that [he] was in love with [Theaetetus]," that "he is not handsome," having a "snub nose and protruding eyes" like Socrates (143e). Theodorus, instead, praises Theaetetus for his exceptional and "marvelously fine qualities" of intellectual ability and virtue (144a-b). Socrates explicitly contrasts the physical ugliness and intellectual beauty of Theaetetus by exclaiming (185e): "Why, you are beautiful, Theaetetus, and not, as Theodorus said, ugly; for he who speaks beautifully is beautiful and good (*kalos kai agathos*)." Beauty for Socrates, therefore, is realized through philosophical discussion. In essence, his educational method of *elenchos* strips away any corporeal aspects, whether beautiful or ugly, and reveals (or indeed undresses) the beautiful soul (*psychē*) beneath. Therefore, the setting of the *apodyterion* as the place of physical stripping, metaphorically emphasizes Socrates's *elenchos*.

Plato even directly compares Socrates's *elenchos* to undressing/stripping the nude body through metaphors. In *Theaetetus*, Socrates responds to Theodorus's refusal to engage in discussion with a metaphor of stripping in a Spartan *palaistra* (162a-b): "If you went to Sparta, Theodorus, and visited the *palaistra*, would you think it fair to look on at other people naked, some of whom were of poor physique, without stripping and

---

[34] Plato discusses the dualism of body and mind in relation to love (*erōs*) most comprehensively in *Symposium*. For further discussion of the conceptual link between *elenchos* and athletic nudity, see Reid, "Wrestling with Socrates."

showing your own form, too?" The almost voyeuristic Spartan principle referenced here, which is to "go away or else strip" (169a-b), metaphorically demonstrates that Socrates's method of undressing the soul was not a passive process that one could just watch, but a process that required active participation and cooperation. In *Charmides*, Plato makes the metaphorical significance of undressing the body particularly clear. Chaerephon, after Charmides has entered the *palaistra* but is evidently still clothed, states that "if he would consent to strip […] you would think he had no face, he has such a perfect beauty of form" (154d), to which Socrates replies (154e): "let us strip [his soul (*psychē*)] and view it first, instead of his form." Undressing the body to Chaerephon is a means of revealing the physical, exterior beauty of the exceptional youth. In contrast, Socrates—though he certainly appreciates Charmides's corporeal beauty, as demonstrated above (154b-d, 155de)—is more interested in the intellectual, inner beauty of Charmides. The *apodyterion*, therefore, provides a profoundly suitable spatial setting here. It is the place where the metaphorical undressing of the body would take place in the Spartan *palaistra* in *Theaetetus's* metaphor and the *palaistra* of Taureas in *Charmides*. Moreover, it is the space (suggested but not specified) in both dialogues in which Socrates's philosophical undressing takes place, revealing the soul (*psychē*) of his youthful interlocutors. Overall, Plato's *apodyterion*, as the spatial setting of the dialogues, bears a profound metaphorical significance in elucidating and emphasizing the aims of the Socratic method of education: to undress and examine the soul.

Conclusion

The architectural/spatial features of Plato's *gymnasia* and *palaistra* discussed in this paper do not merely add spatial context or depth to the settings of the dialogues. Plato's careful selection in what he chooses to describe reflects the significant function that these features play in the dialogues. The topography and exterior features of the *palaistra* in *Lysis* explore the institutional differences between public *gymnasia* and private *palaistrai* and their relation to philosophical education, which is, in turn, of historical significance regarding Plato's school at the Academy. The exterior architectural features of the *palaistra* in *Lysis,* along with the presumed interior spatial feature of the altar (sacrifices to Hermes), appear to provide a metaphor for Socrates's philosophical method of *elenchos*. The courtyard in *Lysis* and the outer *dromos* in *Theaetetus* enhance the competitive/agonistic nature of their settings through the activities which take place within them. The *dromoi* in *Euthydemus* (covered) and *Theaetetus* (outer) most plausibly refer to the porticoes around the courtyard rather than running tracks and, in turn, provide Plato with a dramatic device that utilizes inter-visibility with the *apodyterion* (at least in terms of the covered *dromos*). The *apodyterion* and its function as the undressing room emphasize the dualism of physical and intellectual beauty discussed in the dialogues and represent another metaphor for Socrates's educational method of "undressing/examining souls." The *apodyterion,* therefore, provides a profoundly suitable setting for the dialogues.

Overall, architectural and spatial features in Plato are worthy of examination and study. In the case study of *gymnasia/palaistrai*, archaeologists gain valuable insight into the architectural development of such facilities: in fact, by interpreting the *dromoi* as porticoes around a courtyard, Plato supports the archaeological inference that *palaistrai* were the first structures architecturally incorporated into *gymnasia*. Equally, the philosophical significance that Plato encodes within the architectural and spatial features of his *gymnasia/palaistrai* are of value and relevance to historians and philosophers. They not only explore and expand philosophical ideas and methods, but also reveal historical aspects of philosophical education in Athens. Given that *gymnasia/palaistrai* represent only a handful of Plato's chosen settings for his dialogues, there remains potential for further study. A more comprehensive study of the architectural and spatial features in Plato and their philosophical significance will certainly develop our understanding of their overall function in the dialogues as well as provide an insight into Plato's broader philosophy on architecture and space.

Erik Kenyon[1]
Socrates at the Wrestling School:
Plato's *Laches, Lysis,* and *Charmides*

Socrates was famously brought to trial for "corrupting the youth." In Plato's *Apology*, it takes Socrates little time to show this to be a trumped up charge. In fact, Socrates argues, the ease with which he can refute his accuser, Meletus, merely exposes Meletus's own "lack of care" (ἀμέλεια; 25c) and unjust meddling in important affairs. Later, Socrates explains his own activities as part of a divine mission (29d-31c): Apollo sent him to Athens, like a gadfly, to "refute" (ἐλέγχω; 29e) her citizens and make them "care for virtue" (ἐπιμελέομαι ἀρετῆς; 31b). Socrates recounts these refutations, as he looks to politicians, artists and craftsmen for moral knowledge and finds them all incapable of defending their views (21b-23b). It isn't obvious how conversations ending in perplexity (ἀπορία) will make anyone care for virtue. Judging by Socrates's track record in *Apology*, it tends just to make people angry (21c-23a). Nor is it clear in *Apology* what this caring amounts to or what value it has.[2]

We find a similar link between care for virtue and refutation in a group of Socratic dialogues set in or around wrestling schools. Each of these dialogues attempts to define a moral concept: bravery (*Laches*), friendship (*Lysis*), temperance (*Charmides*). Since each work ends in perplexity, we also find Socrates merely exposing problematic beliefs. Yet these works go beyond *Apology*

---

[1] Erik Kenyon holds a PhD in Classics from Cornell University with a research focus on philosophical dialogue. He is author of *Augustine and the Dialogue* (Cambridge University Press, 2018) and co-author of *Ethics for the Very Young: A Philosophy Curriculum for Early Childhood Education* (Rowman & Littlefield, 2019). From 2012 to 2020 he taught at Rollins College with courses in Classics, Philosophy and Humanities. His general education course, *Philosophy at the Gym*, grew out of interactions with Rollins's Powerlifting Club for which he served as adviser. Erik currently teaches Latin and Humanities at Friends Academy, North Dartmouth, MA.

[2] Greek terms based on the basic form μέλω are often translated into English as 'care,' 'concern,' 'give thought to' or (for lack of care) 'indifference.' The result is to obscure how frequently the term appears in Plato's writings.

Erik Kenyon

by situating refutation and care for virtue within the ancient wrestling school and the varieties of competition (ἀγών) that went on there. I argue that this constellation of ideas—competition, refutation, care for virtue—provides a view of Socrates's divine mission that is robust enough to show how refutation, in the absence of any positive conclusions, may lead individuals to care for virtue. It will also show what value this caring has. In reading these works, I will look to their narrative frame, inquiries into central moral concepts, and explicit reflections on the process of inquiry. To borrow a phrase from *Laches*, each dialogue explores the "harmony between words and deeds" (188d) as it presents individuals engaging with Socrates in philosophical inquiry.[3]

Laches

Laches opens as a group of men finish watching a demonstration of fighting in armor.[4] Lysimachus and Melesias, who have assembled the group, turn to two generals, Laches and Nicias, to ask whether fighting in armor is something their sons should "learn or train in so that they become good men" (179d). Fighting in armor, as presented, seems to be outside the normal course of studies. Nicias presents it as "no less useful than gym training (τὸ γυμνάσιον)" and draws parallels between the competition (ἀγών) of athletes (ἀθληταί) and of war (πόλεμος; 182a). Laches is more skeptical. He recounts a time when the practitioner they have just watched, Stesilaus, "demonstrated" the worth of his combination spear-scythe, which in actual combat only gets caught in things (183c-184b).

---

[3] Greek texts from John Burnet, *Platonis Opera*, vol. 3. (Oxford: Oxford University Press, 1903). All translations by the author. For detailed discussion, review of scholarship and English translations, see Rosamond Kent Sprague, *Plato: Laches and Charmides* (Indianapolis: Hackett, 1992); Christopher Moore and Christopher Raymond, *Plato: Charmides* (Indianapolis: Hackett, 2019); Terry Penner and Christopher Rowe, *Plato's Lysis* (Cambridge: Cambridge University Press, 2005).

[4] The setting for the work is not specified, yet the opening scene and discussion of training suggest an athletic context.

Socrates at the Wrestling School

The first layer of competition here is physical: contests of athletics and war. There is also competition *between* athletics and war as means of making men good. This leads into another form of competition, namely, of teachers for students. Nicias and Laches introduce Socrates on the grounds that he'd recommended a music teacher for Nicias's son (180d). But the current question is the "cultivation of the soul" (185d-e).[5] Were one seeking advice about gym exercise (ἀγωνία), Socrates argues, one would not take a vote but consult a competent trainer (184d-185b). So, too, in cultivating souls, one should seek out an expert. Since it is still unclear what making one "good in soul" means, Socrates makes a fresh start, asking what fighting in armor is supposed to accomplish (189d-190d). Laches responds that it should make young men virtuous and brave. Socrates asks, "What then is bravery (ἀνδρεία)" (190d)?

The inquiry into bravery that ensues (190d-201c) is actually shorter than the dialogue's opening frame (178a-190d). What ties these two halves together, I suggest, is questions of "care" (μέλω). Lysimachus and Melesias both had famous fathers, but neither of them has accomplished much himself. That's why they're seeking advice on caring for their own sons. Laches agrees that famous men often get wrapped up in public affairs and manage their sons "carelessly" (ἀμελῶς; 180b). Socrates asks Nicias and Laches whether they can recommend anyone who might care for their own sons along with those of Lysimachus and Melesias (187a). The implication is that the two generals, like Lysimachus and Melesias's fathers, might be too busy to care for their own children. Lysimachus takes the bait, replying that he went to these generals because "naturally" they would have cared about such things (187c). By this point in the discussion, Laches and Nicias have spoken at length about how to raise children. If the generals cannot explain what it means to raise a young man to be good, virtuous and brave, they will show themselves to be stuffed shirts and bad fathers. With this, the stage is set for the inquiry into bravery.

---

[5] "Cultivation" (θεραπεία) is treated as a general term (see 179b). After it is introduced, conversation slips freely between terms for learning (μανθάνω) and training (ἐπιτηδεύω). See 179d-e, 181c-182c, 185b, 186d, 190e.

Laches's opening definition of bravery is "standing one's ground on the battleline" (190e). Socrates points out that this is an example, not a definition. Laches regroups with "endurance of soul" more generally (192b). Socrates responds that bravery is a fine thing, but endurance of soul can be accompanied by folly. Laches specifies that he'd meant "wise endurance" (192d). Socrates points out instances when having more knowledge makes one less brave, e.g. by giving one a strategic advantage. At this point, Laches gets upset and hands the discussion over to Nicias.

Nicias picks up the idea that bravery and knowledge are related and suggests that bravery is "knowledge of the fearful and hopeful" (194e-195a). Socrates offers the counter-example of wild beasts, which seem brave but lack knowledge (196e). Nicias responds that animals, like children, are not brave but fearless through stupidity (197a-b). Since Nicias is adamant that bravery is linked to knowledge, Socrates spells out Nicias's initial definition as amounting to knowledge of future goods and bads (198c). This suggests a consequentialist calculus: brave actions are ones in which one must overcome a short-term bad for the sake of a greater, long-term good. Laches and Nicias, however, have each already agreed that bravery is merely one part of virtue (190c-d and 198a, respectively). Socrates argues that anyone with knowledge of future goods and bads will have knowledge of goods and bads in the past and present too. Such a person will avoid short-term goods for the sake of greater long-term goods and therefore be moderate. He will understand that advantages gained through crime are not worth it in the long run and therefore be just. Such knowledge seems simply to be wisdom. Far from being part of virtue, bravery ends up being the whole of virtue! With this, Socrates brings the conversation full-circle, and all admit defeat.

Laches's inquiry into bravery presents a third layer of competition: philosophical refutation. We can start drawing connections between this and care for virtue by looking at how Socrates's companions respond when they are reduced to perplexity. Laches, who is not familiar with Socrates's style of inquiry (188e), starts out with what seems to be the right attitude,

"Therefore, Socrates, I offer myself for you to teach (διδάσκω) and to refute (ἐλέγχω) as you wish" (189b). Once Socrates has finished refuting him, however, he gets "really annoyed" (ἀγανακτέω) and admits to being overcome with the "love of victory" (φιλονικία; 194a). After Nicias takes over the discussion, Laches keeps interrupting with petty snipes (195a-b, 196a-b, 197c, 199e-200a). Nicias's judgement is that Laches, having failed in his attempt to define bravery, just wants to drag him down too (195a-b, 200a-b). Nicias, by contrast, has dealt with Socrates before (187e). He knows that whatever it is they set out to discuss, if Socrates is present, he and Laches would eventually become the object of scrutiny (188c). Nicias even takes pleasure in having Socrates point out when he's wrong (188a-b) and makes plans to reconvene another day (200b).

What should we make of the contrast between these responses? Both generals present a reversal: Laches defines bravery as a form of endurance but abandons the search when he sees no way forward. Nicias defines virtue in terms of knowledge but eventually admits not knowing what bravery is. Both men seem to lack "harmony between their words and their deeds" (188d, 193e-d). Socrates, by contrast, disavows knowledge at the start, admits to being perplexed at the end, and tirelessly searches for answers throughout. He closes the discussion by flipping Lysimachus's opening speech on its head, saying "we will have to take care of both ourselves and the boys" (201b) by finding someone to instruct them in what bravery is. Meanwhile, the bravery Socrates showed in a military retreat at Delium is vouched for by Laches himself (181b). What then is bravery? Who can teach us about it? These questions go unanswered. Still, we're left with the impression that Socrates is our best bet in making any progress on them.[6]

---

[6] Francisco Gonzales, "Dialectic at Work in the *Laches* and *Charmides*," in *Dialectic and Dialogue* (Evanston, IL: Northwestern University Press, 1998), 19-61, argues that Socrates displays knowledge of bravery in *Laches* (37-38), albeit non-propositional knowledge, which straddles Nicias's intuitive yet naive awareness and Laches's sophistic yet vacuous understanding (21, 46-47).

What has been accomplished in *Laches* and how can it help us understand *Apology*? Broadly, we have seen a shift from *whether* to fight in armor to *why* to fight in armor. Today, if we don't expect our children to play soccer or the oboe professionally, why do we subject them to practice and rehearsal? This is a useful starting point for philosophical reflection. In *Laches*, Plato grounds Socratic refutation within the everyday life of an Athenian wrestling school. During this refutation, Nicias accuses Laches of trying to take him down with him in a negative way. Socrates, by contrast, takes others down in a positive, generative way, inviting them into his own perplexity and encouraging them, despite their advanced age, to seek a teacher. While these are mostly opening moves, we can infer that care for virtue is not merely for the young. What's more, it seems that one cannot care for another without also caring for himself. With this, we find the seed of a community. This alone is sufficient to start reorienting one's life, even in the absence of any robust moral knowledge.

Charmides

Charmides opens as Socrates returns home from a military campaign and heads straight for the wrestling school (παλαίστρα) of Taureus. His first question is about the state of philosophy and whether any young men are outstanding for wisdom, bodily beauty or both (153). Enter Charmides, Plato's maternal uncle. All heads turn. Older lovers (ἐρασταί) and boys (παῖδες) alike gawk at him as though at a statue (154c). Even Socrates is temporarily at a loss for words (ἀπορέω; 155c). Chaerephon says what perhaps

---

Gonzales contrasts this with readings which see Socratic refutation as primarily negative in outcome (37). While I am sympathetic to Gonzales's overall method, he seems to assume that the only positive outcome of a search for knowledge of bravery is to arrive at (some kind of) knowledge of bravery. By this reasoning, the real goal of *Meno*'s geometry lesson is to learn about geometry, which is clearly not the case. The positive outcome of *Laches*, I argue, is to draw Socrates's interlocutors into philosophy. Gareth Matthews, *Socratic Perplexity and the Nature of Philosophy* (Oxford: Oxford University Press, 1999), 29-30 likens this to the "wonder" which Aristotle cites as the beginning of philosophy.

Socrates at the Wrestling School

everyone is thinking: just wait till he strips naked (ἀποδύω; 154d)! Chief among Charmides's admirers is Critias, his uncle and guardian (ἐπίτροπος; 155a). To modern sensibilities, a caretaker who puts his teenage (μειράκιον; 154b) ward on display naked for men to admire is creepy, to say the least. The ancients, however, held regular competitions in "manly beauty" (εὐανδρία), which focused on bodily beauty and perhaps strength.[7] Socrates suggests looking instead at Charmides's soul "stripped naked" to see whether it too is well-formed (154e). Critias, who is responsible for Charmides's education, assures him that Charmides is a philosopher and a poet (154e-155a). While the most obvious contest here concerns Charmides's physical and moral beauty, it will become clear before long that it is Critias's competence as Charmides's guardian that is really on trial.

As a pretext for their conversation, Critias has Socrates pretend to be a doctor who can help Charmides with his morning headaches (155e-157d). Socrates cooks up an elaborate story involving an herb and incantation (ἐπῳδή; 155e), which he learned from Thracian doctors. These doctors treat patients (θεραπεύω; 156b)[8] holistically: not trying to cure (ἰάομαι; 155b) the eye apart from the head, the head apart from the body or the body apart from the soul. When Greek doctors fail to stop diseases—note the professional rivalry—it is because they do not provide holistic care (ἐπιμέλεια; 156e). Since health flows from the soul to the body, Socrates will start there. His incantation uses beautiful words (λόγοι; 157a), creating temperance (σωφροσύνη; 157a) in the soul.[9] This, in turn, creates health in the body. Critias assures Socrates that Charmides is outstanding in temperance (157d). Socrates replies that this is fitting given Charmides's good looks, ancestral history and all sorts of other things that Socrates will criticize Hippothales for singing about in *Lysis* (157e-158b).

---

[7] N. B. Crowther, "Male «Beauty» contests in Greece: The *Euandria* and *Euexia*." In *L'antiquité classique* 54 (1985): 285-291.

[8] Cf. *Laches*, where the same term is used for the young men's "cultivation."

[9] Moore and Raymond, *Plato: Charmides,* xxviii-xxxvii make a compelling case for translating σωφροσύνη as "discipline" in the context of *Charmides* (xxviii-xxxvii).

Erik Kenyon

Having fawned over Charmides sufficiently, Socrates asks whether he has temperance. Charmides's first response is to "blush" (ἀνερυθριάω; 158c). Socrates has him in a dilemma: if he says yes, this will seem intemperate; if he says no, he will accuse Critias of lying. Socrates is satisfied with this response. He gets Charmides to agree that if a person has temperance, he'll be able to talk about it (158e-159a). With this, Socrates proposes the question: what then is temperance? Charmides's first definition is "to do things calmly" (ἡσυχάω; 159b), i.e., quietly and slowly. As counter-examples, Socrates cites the "three R's" of Greek education: reading, writing, and wrestling (159c). Charmides tries again with "a sense of shame" (αἰδώς; 160e). But Socrates points out times when boldness is required, e.g. asking for help. Charmides responds with an idea he heard from "someone," viz. "minding one's own business" (τὸ τὰ ἑαυτοῦ πράττειν; 161b). Socrates suggests that this must be a riddle (αἴνιγμα; 161c). If raising crops is a farmer's business and making a plow is a blacksmith's business, then a farmer and a blacksmith who mind their own business would be unable to trade crops for plows. If we expand the point, this rules out all transactions and brings society to its knees. Admitting defeat, Charmides bats his lashes at Critias, who is clearly the "someone" who came up with this last definition.

At this point, Critias has been "struggling" (ἀγωνιάω) for some time. The Greek word straddles "compete" and "be distressed." Given that Charmides hasn't been performing well, Critias is "eager to gain honor" (φιλότιμος; 162c) in the eyes of those present, presumably to repair his reputation as Charmides's guardian. Socrates runs with it, claiming that Critias must have a care (ἐπιμέλεια; 162e) for such matters. Critias takes the bait and —in Sophistic fashion—attempts to salvage his definition by quoting poetry and splitting hairs, distinguishing between "making" (ποίησις), "doing" (πρᾶξις) and "working" (ἐργασία; 163b-c). Socrates brushes this all aside and gets Critias to agree that the temperate person does good things and not bad things (163e). But, Socrates replies, one can do good things without realizing it. Surely a doctor who "does not know himself, how he acted" (164c) has not been temperate. Momentarily flustered, Critias regroups and responds that this is "basically" (σχεδόν) what he said, i.e., that temperance is "to know oneself" (τὸ γιγνώσκειν ἑαυτόν; 164d). To save face, he even quotes the famous inscription at Delphi, "Know thyself" (γνῶθι σαυτόν), which is said "in an *even more* riddling way" (αἰνιγματωδέστερον; 164e).

While "self-knowledge" might sound impressive, Socrates points out that knowledge has to be "of something" (τινός; 165c). After a bit more wrangling, Critias says that temperance is "knowledge of itself and other knowledges" (αὑτῆς ἐστιν καὶ τῶν ἄλλων ἐπιστημῶν ἐπιστήμη; 166e), which Socrates glosses as "to know what one knows and doesn't know" (τὸ εἰδέναι ἅ τε οἶδεν καὶ ἃ μὴ οἶδεν; 167a). Socrates responds that temperance, so understood, is useless (169d-172d). If a doctor has first-order knowledge about the object of medicine, i.e., health, and a temperate person has second-order knowledge of medicine as a science (what we would call philosophy of science), then it is a doctor, not a temperate person, who can distinguish between the pretend doctor and the real one (170e). With this, worries about transactions, which Socrates raised against Charmides, return as worries about delegating tasks. Yet unless a leader has first-order knowledge of *every* task he oversees—which is surely impossible— he will not be able to delegate these tasks reliably. Critias pivots once again, responding that temperance does not consist in first-order knowledge of any particular craft; rather, it is knowledge of good and bad. But this idea has already been shot down (presumably at 164c)! Socrates accuses Critias of dragging him in a circle, and all are left perplexed.

Like *Laches, Charmides* presents multiple reversals. Charmides is praised as the product of two noble families—one including a renowned diplomat—but his understanding of temperance makes transactions impossible. Critias, as Charmides's guardian, is responsible for overseeing his education, but his definition of temperance makes delegating tasks impossible, which presumably involves choosing tutors. While Socrates critiques both men, Critias is his real target. For all his talk of self-knowledge, Critias's behavior shows more concern for how he appears in others' eyes.

Erik Kenyon

This is evident in two digressions on method. In the first passage (166b-e), Critias accuses Socrates of trying to "refute" (ἐλέγχω) him. The Greek can mean "shame," which Critias seems to have in mind. It can also mean "examine," and Socrates proceeds to say that if he, Socrates, is trying to refute Critias, he does so because he is "examining" (διερευνάω) himself for fear that he might think he knows something that he doesn't. In English terms, Socrates embraces perplexity as 'humbling,' while Critias avoids it as 'humiliating.' In the second passage (169c-d), Critias, as a man of good reputation (εὐδοκιμῶν), feels ashamed (αἰσχύνω) in front of the onlookers and "hides his perplexity by rambling" (ἔλεγέν τε οὐδὲν σαφές, ἐπικαλύπτων τὴν ἀπορίαν). Since Critias is unwilling to admit defeat, Socrates does it for him, claiming to be "really annoyed" (ἀγανακτέω; 175d-e) that, for all his good looks, Charmides's temperance and Socrates's incantation might turn out to be useless.

If *Laches* shows how refutation can spark individuals to care for virtue, then *Charmides* puts a caregiver to the test. Critias is quick to present Charmides as a poet and philosopher, thus bolstering his own reputation as Charmides's guardian. Yet when his competence in this role is challenged, he sets this reputation ahead of the reality of Charmides's upbringing. Critias's love of reputation, like Nicias's love of victory, presents an obstacle to caring for virtue. That's not to say that setting aside worries about reputation—whether for looks or virtue—is sufficient for attaining temperance. But it seems a step in the right direction. While Critias speaks in lofty terms about self-knowledge, by calling such talk into question, Socrates actually invites us to look within, stripping down our souls, not just our bodies. As Critias's response shows, such introspection is not always pleasant, as it calls us to sacrifice conventional goods.

In terms of making sense of *Apology*, Critias's account of temperance as knowledge of knowledge and the absence of knowledge introduces something akin to Socrates's account of human wisdom, i.e., "I don't think I know what I don't know" (*Apology* 21d). In this, *Charmides* connects the search for self-knowledge within another main activity of the ancient wrestling school: preparing young men to administer public and private business through delegating responsibilities. It also suggests an otherwise non-obvious connection within *Apology*, i.e., that it is human wisdom that bridges refutation and care for virtue: refutation brings about a level of epistemic humility, i.e., human wisdom, which throws conventional goods into question, thus bringing individuals to look deeper and turn within.

Lysis

Lysis opens as Socrates walks from one wrestling school to another when a group of young men invites him into yet another new wrestling school (203a). There are lots of beautiful young men there, Hippothales explains, who pass the time mostly in conversation (204a). This description turns out to be accurate. Entering the space, they find people engaged in conversations, a religious rite for Hermes, games of knucklebones, but no actual wrestling (206e-207b). Wrestling schools, it seems, were very chatty places.

Even if there isn't much literal wrestling going on, this is still a place for competitive games. At the top of the list is flirting. Hippothales is in love with the young Lysis.[10] Ctessipus teases him for writing love poetry, praising Lysis for his ancestors' victories in chariot races, his family's connection to Herakles and "other things that old crones sing about" (204c-205d). Hearing this, Socrates criticizes Hippothales for composing a victory ode (ἐγκώμιον) before he has won (νικάω; 205d): this only makes one's prey harder to catch (206a). Since the purpose of poetry is to soothe, Socrates concludes that Hippothales's behavior displays a lack of musicality (ἀμουσία; 206b). To show Hippothales the proper way to flirt, Socrates engages Lysis and his friend, Menexenus, in conversation. Along the way, he leads Lysis to

---

[10] Their age difference is unclear. Hippothales is introduced as a young man (νεανίσκος; 203a): maybe late teens or early 20's. Lysis is referred to as a young man (νεανίσκος; 204b), a boy (παῖς; 204e, 205b-c, 222a-d) and as belonging to a group of young men (νεανίσκοι) and boys (παῖδες; 106d & 207a). While Lysis is clearly younger than Hippothales, the difference does not seem huge.

Erik Kenyon

conclude that his parents don't love him (207d-210d) and that none of them, even though they are friends, can say what friendship is (223b). The lesson to be learned, it seems, is that when pursuing a potential boyfriend, one should "humble him" (ταπεινόω) and "cut him down to size" (συστέλλω; 210e).

The text is full of reversals. Hippothales writes poetry and gives Lysis a swelled head. Socrates sets up Menexenus as a clever (δεινός) debater (ἐριστικός; 211b-c) and fears being refuted by him (ἐλέγχω; 211b), yet it is Socrates who does the refuting. It's hard not to see parallels to modern card games. There are even 'tells.' When Socrates asks who the best looking in the wrestling school is, Hippothales "blushes" (ἐρυθριάω; 204b), showing that he's smitten. Later, when Socrates is talking with Menexenus, Lysis blurts out an answer to a question and "blushes," showing how closely he is listening (213d). At the end, when Socrates concludes that a lover must be loved by his boyfriend, Hippothales "beams every color" (222b), showing his pleasure.

Where there is competition, there is an audience. At the start, Ctessipus complains about listening to Hippothales's singing (204c-d). When Socrates agrees to demonstrate how to flirt properly, Hippothales says that it won't be hard to engage Lysis, since he is a lover of listening (φιλήκοος; 206c). Hippothales then hides so he can listen to their conversation (207b) and—like Critias in *Charmides*—"struggles" (ἀγωνιάω; 210e) as Socrates cuts Lysis down to size. Once Socrates has proven to Lysis that his parents don't love him, Lysis whispers in a boyish and friendly way (παιδικῶς καὶ φιλικῶς) to do the same to Menexenus so he can listen (211a-b). In short, this is philosophical refutation as a spectator sport.

The inquiry into friendship proceeds (212a-222e) as Socrates shoots down all possible options. Two people who love each other cannot be friends (φίλοι), since this would rule out the love of wine, gymnastic exercise and wisdom, none of which can reciprocate. One-sided love doesn't work either, as it requires loving enemies and hating friends. A bad person (κακός) cannot be a friend to a bad person, since they will act unjustly toward each other. A good person (ἀγαθός) is self-sufficient (ἱκανὸς...αὑτῷ) and will not need (δέομαι; 215a) other good people as friends. Similar people (ὅμοιοι) thus cannot be friends. Nor can unlike people, since good and bad people are "opposed" (ἐναντίος; 216b).

Socrates explores "neutral" people via a medical analogy (216c-222c): a human body is neither good nor bad but is a friend to medicine because of disease and for the sake of health. This "for the sake of" relationship sets up a regress, which eventually lands at a desire for "what one lacks" (ἐνδεής), i.e., "that which belongs to him" (τοῦ οἰκείου; 221d-e). Yet does this mean that "the good belongs to everyone" or "good belong to good, bad to bad and neutral to neutral" (222b-e)? The boys pick the latter option, and Socrates points out that they've already refuted the idea that friends are similar! Having argued in a circle, all are perplexed. Socrates declares that their discussion is "out of tune" (πλημμελής; 222c).

In the final analysis, is *Lysis* an exploration of friendship or a lesson in seduction? While its tortured dialectic might strike us as less than romantic, Lysis is captivated. We can connect the dialogue's frame and its content if we look to the "love of wisdom." This is first introduced with the silly claim that wisdom can't love one back (212d). It returns by placing philosophers into the neutral category (218a-d): If they were already good and wise, they would not love wisdom, because they would already have it. If they were bad and ignorant, they would not know enough to love wisdom. "Rather, they do not consider themselves to know things which they do not know" (218b). It is this middle state, which Socrates identifies as "human wisdom" in *Apology* (20d-23b), that leads them to love and pursue wisdom.

Awareness of their own ignorance is precisely what Lysis and Menexenus get out of their conversation with Socrates. And they find it attractive. Current ideals of equality within romantic relationships come closer to Aristotle's paradigm of friendship as two mature adults (*Nicomachean Ethics* bks. 8-9). Yet the *Lysis*'s playful reversals and good-humored banter create a context in which this process of being "cut down to size" is welcomed. If we can step over the erotic overtones—which are hardly pronounced in *Lysis* to start with—Socrates's tough love is most often found today in coaches who are hard on players for those players' own good. In either case, we find mutual affection in the joint pursuit of a good. While none of this amounts to a viable definition of friendship, *Lysis's* display of Socratic refutation provides rich fodder for further inquiry.

Conclusion

What should we make of dialogues in which men exercise naked in front of admirers but blush when personal details slip out in conversation? In them we find care for virtue and a willingness to admit one's own ignorance stacked against love of victory and reputation. All of this is infused with practices drawn from wrestling schools: competition, training in the nude, medicine and music. The last of these, music, plays out in harmony between words and deeds (*Laches*), out of tune conversations (*Lysis*) and holistic care of body and soul (*Charmides*). In the process of raising puzzles about different moral terms, the three dialogues form a kind of progression. *Laches* provides an entry point, as Socrates questions the goal of training practices and brings a group of fathers to care for virtue. In *Charmides*, he puts a caregiver, Critias, to the test and finds him wanting. In *Lysis*, he models what such care can look like.

When it comes to understanding *Apology*, these dialogues create a cumulative context for seeing how refutation, even in the absence of answers, leads to care for virtue through human wisdom. What's more, they show how these aspects of Socratic philosophy are interrelated. To say, "I don't think I know what I don't know" (21d) does not reflect a passive state of merely not claiming to know things. Socratic refutation brings characters to realize that they don't have a handle on matters that are vital to living their lives. Such perplexity demands a response. Laches and Critias get annoyed. Lysis and Menexenus become enamored. Characters in all three dialogues resolve to continue searching for answers. This searching has moral implications. *Laches* and *Charmides* frame this in terms of "care for virtue." Even when we can't define what the virtues are, simply recognizing this inability is enough to reorient our priorities. In *Laches*, old men—two of them successful by conventional standards—join their sons to seek a teacher. In *Charmides,* Socrates pushes beyond outward beauty and forces characters to look within. *Lysis* brings out the communal nature of such an undertaking. In short, epistemic humility about pressing issues provides the basis for a way of life that is egalitarian, critical, and collaborative.

On a practical level, such a life requires ongoing effort. This is where the gym setting resonates most clearly for readers in Plato's time and today. Getting in shape is not a goal to be accomplished and then set aside. As the pandemic quarantine of 2020 drove home, getting in shape for many of us is also a social undertaking. In setting dialogues in or around wrestling schools, Plato uses care for the body as a framework for thinking about care for the soul. The result is a community in which care for self and care for others coincide around on-going, purposeful and cooperative competition.

Christopher Moore[1]
Critias in Plato's *Protagoras*: an Opponent of *Agōn*?

Introduction

This paper begins addressing Plato's view of Critias of Athens, and its relevance to Plato's political-philosophical project.[2] This is the Critias who lived ca. 460–403 BCE, and was cousin of Plato's mother.[3] He is perhaps best known to contemporary students of ancient philosophy as an erstwhile friend of Socrates, or at least as one who shared an intellectual orbit. This was a fateful friendship for Socrates, since Critias's hated participation in the Thirty, the murderous oligarchy supported by the Spartans after the Peloponnesian War, redounded to Socrates, as his putative teacher.[4] But Critias was also a *littérateur*, a genre-spanning one, with sympotic poetry, studies of cities, rhetorical works, and lesser prose compositions to his name.[5] He is the first known Attic writer

---

[1] Christopher Moore is Associate Professor of Philosophy and Classics at the Pennsylvania State University. He is the author of *Socrates and Self-Knowledge* (Cambridge, 2015) and *Calling Philosophers Names: On the Origin of the Discipline* (Princeton, 2020), and with Christopher C. Raymond, of *Plato: Charmides. A Translation with Introduction, Notes, and Analysis* (Hackett, 2019). He has also edited or co-edited two volumes on the reception of Socrates (Brill, 2018 and 2019), and published many articles and chapters on topics in ancient philosophy.

[2] I thank Christopher C. Raymond for much fruitful discussion of this topic.

[3] Diogenes Laertius 3.1. For the extended family, see Debra Nails, *The People of Plato: A prosopography of Plato and other Socratics* (Indianapolis: Hackett, 2002), 106–11, though much scholarly controversy concerns the identity of his ancestors. The data is more neutrally and systematically presented in John S. Traill, *Persons of Ancient Athens*, vol. 10 (Toronto: Athenians, 2001), 583–88.

[4] Evidence especially in Xenophon's *Memorabilia* 1.2.12; Aeschines 1.173.

[5] For an overview of Critias's life and works, and an assessment of the scholarship, see Christopher Moore and Christopher C. Raymond, "Critias of Athens," *Oxford Bibliographies* (2019). Much of the material is collected in Hermann Diels and Walther Kranz, *Die Fragmente Der Vorsokratiker*, 6th ed. (Berlin: Weidmann, 1952), §88, with the best English translation to be found currently in John Dillon and Tania Gergel, *The Greek Sophists* (New York: Penguin, 2003).

of a "Constitution of the Spartans" and from what is likely his tragic poetry comes the famous "Sisyphus fragment" (DK B25), which presents religious belief as a socially useful fiction. So in Critias we have a central intellectual figure of the late fifth century BCE, of the Attic Enlightenment, among our very earliest political theorists, proximate to those later called *sophistai* and *philosophoi*, though less of a professional teacher or research specialist than either.

What is remarkable is that Critias appears in four authentic works of Plato: *Protagoras*, *Charmides*, *Timaeus*, and *Critias* (the latter two controversially but evidently).[6] He also appears in the spurious *Eryxias* and is alluded to in the *Seventh Letter* (324b–325a). Accordingly, nobody talks on more occasions with Socrates in the Platonic dialogues than Critias does. Each of the four authentic dialogues has politics as a core concern. There is even attractive evidence that the formulation for justice found in the *Republic*, "doing one's own things" (*to ta heautou prattein*, 433b), began as Critias's definition for a parallel (and easily conflated) virtue, *sōphrosunē* (*Charmides* 161a/162d = DK B41a),[7] and that Critias serves as backdrop for the *Republic* in other ways, including by having been author of Spartan constitutions, in which genre we can place the *Republic*.[8] He may even have had a special relationship with Glaucon, as conjecture from Schleiermacher to Mark Munn and Jacob Howland allows.[9]

---

[6] Nails, *People of Plato*, does not accept the identity of these Critiases, but I believe the evidence for that identity is overwhelming. I cannot argue this here, but note the most intriguing recent argument in favor: Antonio Aloni and Alessandro Iannucci, "Writing Solon," in *Iambus and Elegy: New Approaches*, ed Laura. Swift and Chris Carey (Oxford: Oxford University Press, 2016), 155–173.

[7] See, for instance, B.R. Donovan, "The Do-It-Yourselfer in Plato's *Republic*," *American Journal of Philology* 124.1 (2003):1–18.

[8] For the shared genre of Spartan constitution, see Stephen Menn, "On Plato's ΠΟΛΙΤΕΙΑ," *Proceedings of the Boston Area Colloquium in Ancient Philosophy* 21 (2005): 1–55.

[9] See Jacob Howland, *Glaucon's Fate: History, Myth, and Character in Plato's Republic* (Philadelphia: Paul Dry Books, 2018), following Mark Munn, *The School of*

Critias in Plato's Protagoras

The present research question concerns why Plato wrote as much as he did about Critias. To the extent the question arises, scholars usually give one of two opposing answers. The first, a near consensus for those who read the dialogues "dramatically," wanting to be sensitive to the characters, is that we are to read Plato with a heavy sense of historical irony.[10] Critias became a terrible tyrant, and Plato wants us to remember this. Critias is the anti-type of the *sōphrōn*, for example; he is an amoral atheist; he desires technocratic totalitarianism; he twists and instrumentalizes Socrates's ideas without understanding them. Plato's reason for recalling this to our mind is to show, repeatedly, that Critias brought on his own doom; though he once shared talk with Socrates, he is no chip off the old block. Plato has apologetic and, we might say, agonistic purposes to depict Critias as he does.

The second kind of answer—given most recently by Gabriel Danzig—notes a marked contrast between Plato and Xenophon.[11] Whereas Xenophon presents Critias as a terrible tyrant, in both the *Hellenika* (2.3-4) and *Memorabilia* (1.2.12–39), as craven, pleonectic, and rude, Plato is very far from doing so. Plato presents him as generally intelligent, engaged, creative, reasonable, even personable; he shows no strident disapproval. So Plato must actually have admired Critias, or at least wanted to defend his

---

History: Athens in the Age of Socrates (Berkeley: University of California Press, 2000). For Schleiermacher, see DK B75.

[10] Among many examples: W. Thomas Schmid, *Plato's* Charmides *and the Socratic Ideal of Rationality*, (Albany: State University of New York Press, 1998); Paul Stern, "Tyranny and Self-Knowledge: Critias and Socrates in Plato's *Charmides*," *American Political Science Review* 93.2 (1999): 399–412; Michael Eisenstadt, "Critias's Definitions of σωφροσύνη in Plato's *Charmides*," *Hermes* 136.4 (2008): 492–95; Laurence Lampert, *How Philosophy Became Socratic: A Study of Plato's* Protagoras, Charmides, *and* Republic (Chicago: University of Chicago Press, 2010), 147–240.

[11] See Gabriel Danzig, "Plato's *Charmides* as a Political Act: Apologetics and the Promotion of Ideology," *Greek, Roman, and Byzantine Studies* 53 (2013): 486–519. Earlier: Slobodan Dusanic, "Critias in the *Charmides*," *Aevum* 74 (2000): 53–63. With more nuance: Thomas M. Tuozzo, *Plato's Charmides: Positive Elenchos in a "Socratic" Dialogue* (Cambridge: Cambridge University Press, 2011).

family, of which Critias was a luminary. Again, Plato may have had apologetic but now non-agonistic purposes: Socrates did not corrupt Critias as is seen from the fact that Critias was not generally (or not until the end) a corrupt person.

Both camps could appeal to the *Seventh Letter* as a sort of corroboration. The Critias-as-tyrant view seems as fully supported by it as the Critias-as-inspiring-older-model view. Nevertheless, neither position seems sustainable to me. They do not track the evidence. I would argue, instead, the following view:

1. Plato judged Critias a significant forerunner in political thinking and an aficionado of discussion of a sort that helps build intellectual culture;

2. Critias's fall as tyrant is, in a sense, not Plato's sole or principal concern when writing about him;

3. Nevertheless, Plato judges Critias harshly, both for some of his ideas and for the way he dealt with his ideas. In doing so Critias brings into sharper relief the Socratic approach to politics, which involves revealing the *aporiai* of political leadership. In brief, Critias avoids *agōn* more than we might expect, with the result (or for the purpose) that he does not test his own ideas, and thus lacks important pieces of self-knowledge: the knowledge of his epistemic condition with respect to various important matters.

The relationship between Plato and Critias is complex, not least because they lived in different generations; indeed, Critias is dead before Plato's writing career takes off. Plato takes Critias seriously as an intellectual and as intellectual competitor, but he also leaves little question about Critias's decisive weaknesses. We as readers of the dialogues have to wonder about the relevance of those weaknesses to Critias's career—including his final months.

Of the multi-part view adumbrated above, this paper focuses only on the third part, and with only the smallest part of the evidence: Critias's role in the *Protagoras*. Yet I believe this is an important part of the evidence. I begin by discussing what Critias

Critias in Plato's Protagoras

says and does in the dialogue, which is rarely treated in detail, and it is here that we get Plato's mixed presentation of Critias as an intellectual who is curious and able but who lacks the impulse to self-examination and the rigorous submission to truth that Plato depicts as characterizing Socrates. I then respond to the few instances of scholarship on this passage, showing that their admittedly fascinating conjectures outrun the evidence. I do so at length because they are representative of scholarship in many fields that treats Critias one-dimensionally as a proto-tyrant. I then return to my positive picture by giving a brief corroboration with the *Charmides*. And then I conclude.

Critias's ameliorating speech in the *Protagoras*

The *Protagoras* probably takes place in 433/2 BCE, mostly in the courtyard of Callias, the richest man in Athens.[12] Early in the dialogue, the narrator Socrates names the luminaries already at Callias's home (314e10–315e10), and then notes that Critias enters with Alcibiades directly behind himself, and is thus the final guest (316a5–8). Socrates relates nothing Critias says until the dialogue's middle, after Socrates and Protagoras threaten to end their conversation (334c8–336b3); he presents Critias as the third of five speakers to encourage them to overcome their dialectical differences and continue their conversation (336b4–338b3). Why, we ask, does Plato write Critias into this dialogue, one that contains, apparently, the most elite intellectuals of the generation?

Formulating an answer starts by recounting Critias's speaking part:

---

[12] For discussion of the philosophical atmosphere of this meeting, see Christopher Moore, "Spartan Philosophy and Sage Wisdom in Plato's *Protagoras*," *Epoché* 20:2 (2016): 281–305, and Christopher Moore, *Calling Philosophers Names: On the Origin of a Discipline* (Princeton: Princeton University Press, 2019), 228–31. The dating is controversial: for this date, see Nails, *People of Plato*, 310–11; for an opposed view, that inconsistencies prevent us from being more specific than "the general period of the first decades [!] of the Peloponnesian War," see David Wolfsdorf, "The Dramatic Date of Plato's *Protagoras*," *Rheinisches Museum für Philologie*, 140:3/4 (1997): 223–30. The dialogue's date establishes, of course, the period of Critias's life being depicted.

> After Alcibiades, I think, Critias was the one who spoke: "Now, Prodicus and Hippias, Callias seems to me to be very much in favor of (δοκεῖ μοι μάλα πρός) Protagoras, while Alcibiades is always contentious about whatever he's cheering on (ἀεὶ φιλόνικός ἐστι πρὸς ὃ ἂν ὁρμήσῃ); but we ought not contend at all, neither for Socrates nor Protagoras, but instead join in begging of both not to dissolve the conversation in its middle (κοινῇ ἀμφοτέρων δεῖσθαι μὴ μεταξὺ διαλῦσαι τὴν συνουσίαν)." (*Protagoras* 336d–e)

Critias says that Alcibiades is being *philonikos* ("victory-hungry") for Socrates, whom he favors, and that Callias is simply on the side of Protagoras.[13] But they should not take sides, he implies, and certainly not with contentious vehemence; they should hope only for a continued discussion.

This is all Critias says; his is the shortest and the most verbally —and perhaps also programmatically—modest speech. He has made true observations, and to the extent that everyone wants the conversation to continue, even the parties to the dispute, he has made a reasonable suggestion. There would be little else to say about this speech were it not for its immediate context: four other speeches on the same topic, each of which, it would seem, hyper-characterizes its speaker, distilling into a short speech his signature methods or commitments. Prodicus, for example, synonymizes intensely; Hippias vaunts himself by congratulating the partygoers as wisest of anyone living. We might assume, then, that Plato is giving Critias a similar hyper-characterization. If so, what would it be?

---

[13] B.A.F. Hubbard and E.S. Karnofsky, *Plato's Protagoras: A Socratic Commentary* (London: Duckworth, 1982), 122, ask: "Is Critias right to accuse Callias and Alcibiades of taking sides in what he hints has become a contest?" Their question suggests they find a negative answer possible, but Alcibiades at least makes explicit his preference for Socrates; and this would seem "side-taking" unless "side-taking" means arbitrary partisanship and Alcibiades has good reason to judge Socrates superior, which he well may have. The contest-interpretation seems ensured already by Protagoras; Critias at most draws unsubtle attention to it.

Critias in Plato's Protagoras

Critias does not waste words, perhaps speaking with Laconic brevity. Indeed he may not really want to speak at all: it looks like he desires mainly to listen to the conversation between Protagoras and Socrates, and for this he desires that others help him to keep it going. We are overhearing a conversation about the nature of the virtue or skill that Protagoras says he teaches to up-and-coming citizens: the *politikē technē*. Critias understands the conversational dynamics heretofore, concerning rule-following and norm-breaking, as focused on something other than a continued conversation: probably, the reputation of Protagoras *vis-à-vis* current and prospective students gathered at Callias's house or those elsewhere but likely to hear reports about his performance there. He seems unimpressed by Protagoras's self-concern, but perhaps also by Socrates's righteousness; he just wants comity and a complete congress. This is no small thing, to be sure, and for this reason it is distinctive.

We do not know why Critias and Alcibiades came to Callias's house. Maybe Alcibiades wanted, like Socrates's young friend Hippocrates, to study with or at least learn about Protagoras, and Critias—an older mentor? also an *erastēs*? simply a friend from an earlier decade?—accompanied him, either as a way to introduce Alcibiades into this intellectual world of his elders, or as a way to insulate him from potential harms, in the fashion of Socrates with respect to Hippocrates (310b1–314c10). Then again, Critias could be the one intrigued by Protagoras—more likely him than Prodicus or Hippias, given the way he spoke to them—and wanted to enrich his friend Alcibiades's mental world. He seems not to have seen himself as a student or prospective student of any sophist, given his relative lateness to the affair. And he seems not to have expected Socrates's attendance—which is presented as having depended on Hippocrates's wish to attend—nor, given that Socrates does not say that they greeted each other, does Critias have a clearly visible relationship with him (yet).

Whatever his reason for attending the gathering, we might wonder whether one of Plato's reasons for including Critias is to give an origin-story to Critias's later associations with Socrates. We do not know the scale of those associations: the *Charmides* and the

Timaeus-Critias assume only that they have had periodic conversations, as do the criticisms of Socrates as teacher of Critias known from Xenophon and Aeschines. Anyway, we can be confident that they exist, and their existence suggests interests shared between Critias and Socrates. The presumed eventual dissolution of those associations also suggests something incompatible between the two men. I conjecture that this dialogue points at both: partial sympathy, partial difference. (Whether these men ever felt competitive with one another, in particular whether Critias ever desired to outdo Socrates in honor or intellectual influence, is impossible to know, even as one might wish to suppose it as an explanation for Critias's aggression toward Socrates as depicted by Xenophon in *Memorabilia* 1.2.29–31).

Critias has a number of similarities with Socrates—as I believe many of Socrates's interlocutors as portrayed by Plato do.[14] The most important similarity seems to be their avidity as listeners, as people who desire to hear the conversation reach its natural end. They treat the point of conversations as not to showcase the victory of one person or the vanquishing of the other, as Protagoras and his "sophistic" partisans may take it to be, but to allow an account of something to come into its fullness. This important similarity looks to be highlighted, or bolstered, by several dramatic commonalities. Critias and Socrates enter Callias's house at the same time. Remarkably, both have a relationship with Alcibiades, perhaps even an overlapping one. After all, the dialogue opens with Socrates's unnamed interlocutor noting Socrates's attentions to Alcibiades (309a2). Probably both admire this ambitious and brilliant young man; the historical record shows a continued, if ambiguous and eventually ambivalent, relationship between Critias and Alcibiades,[15] and the *Symposium* suggests a long one between Socrates and Alcibiades (213c1–223b2). Finally, of all the

---

[14] See, for two exemplary cases, Christopher Moore, "Socrates and Clitophon in the Platonic *Clitophon*," *Ancient Philosophy* 32:2 (2012): 257–78, on Clitophon, and Christopher Moore, "Charephon the Socratic," *Phoenix* 67.3/4 (2013): on Chaerephon.

[15] See DK B4 and B5, and, for example, György Németh, "Metamorphosis Critiae?" *Zeitschrift für Papyrologie und Epigraphik* 74 (1988): 167–180.

Critias in Plato's Protagoras

many named and unnamed characters in the dialogue, only Critias and Socrates (excepting Protagoras, Hippias, and Prodicus) are unaligned with a teacher; though both are open to hearing what others have to say, both also stand for a kind of self-sufficiency in such investigation.

For all the similarities, they also differ in at least one important way. While both listen, we see only Socrates challenging what he hears; only he presents himself as confused and seeking to understand; only he offers up his own perspective for investigation. Admittedly, we do not see Critias squirreling out of conversations, and he may well be respecting Socrates's holding of the floor in his conversation with Protagoras. But Socrates and Critias arrived at the same time, presumably with a shared purpose—to introduce Protagoras to their younger friends, or whatever—and yet only Socrates willingly addressed Protagoras, only Socrates put forward his suspicions about the teachability of virtue, only Socrates queried Protagoras at the close of the "Great Speech." And only Socrates could show how Protagoras's views, no matter how sensible and cool they seemed, could not hold up to analytic scrutiny. Socrates, therefore, is probably a better person for Hippocrates—or Alcibiades—to have around than Critias. When the topic of discussion concerns civic virtue and enculturation into it, and when one has actual or potential political influence, the cost of error, or complacency and inaction, is high. One could even wonder whether Plato hints that Critias serves somewhat as an enabler of Alcibiades, and to that extent absolving Socrates of the imputed responsibility for corrupting him.

Thus in the *Protagoras*, we learn of the centrality of Critias to intellectual-political culture, we see certain of his intellectual-conversational virtues, and we come to recognize his affinity with Socrates. But we also learn of Plato's negative diagnosis: because he does not enter into the competition of ideas, because he avoids submitting his views to the critical efforts of all comers, Critias cannot be sure of what he believes; and without this self-knowledge, his leadership and pedagogy cannot be wholly guided by what is truly so and truly good.

Christopher Moore

Alternative views

As I said above, very few commentators on the *Protagoras*, on which there is a massive secondary literature, have considered the role of Critias or the meaning of his presence in this dialogue.[16] Nicolas Denyer, author of the important Cambridge Classical Texts and Commentaries edition of the *Protagoras*, notes only that at his entrance, Critias "is appropriately paired with Alcibiades: they were the two most scandalously ill-behaved of all Socrates's associates," but he does not reflect on the relevance to the dialogue, or his speaking part more specifically.[17] Other editors also seem to see Critias as mainly a tyrant-to-be, but stop their interpretative work there, without pondering the reasons for his inclusion in the dialogue or finding that he acts in a particularly tyrannical or pre-tyrannical way.[18] All the same, there are two minor interpretative patterns where scholars of the dialogue give some attention to Critias.

---

[16] An interesting multi-decade slice of this scholarship is discussed in Jonathan Lavery, "Plato's *Protagoras* and the Frontier of Genre Research: A Reconnaissance Report from the Field," *Poetics Today* 28:2 (2007): 191–246.

[17] Nicholas Denyer, *Plato: Protagoras* (Cambridge: Cambridge University Press, 2008), quoting from 85 (ad 316a4–5); there Denyer adds that "one injury that [Critias] did to Athens was to arrange for the return of Alcibiades from one of his periods of exile," and that Critias was "leader of the Thirty Tyrants" (though in what respect he was *the* "leader" is uncertain). At the point where Critias does speak, Denyer observes that "unusually many people are now being drawn into the conversation" (140–41); the implication seems to be that the contributions show simply the pressures on Socrates's choreography of the conversation. Denyer mines Critias's speech only for the observation that Alcibiades is eager to come out on top.

[18] For example, Giovanni Reale, *Platone: Protagora* (Milano: Bompani, 2001), lxiv–lxv; Reale splits up his translation into sub-sections, and whereas the "interlude" speeches mostly get their own headings—i.e., for Callias, Alcibiades, Prodicus, and Hippias—Critias's does not (85, 222). C.C.W. Taylor, *Plato: Protagoras*, Clarendon Plato Series (Oxford: Clarendon Press, 1991), similarly provides analyses of Prodicus's and Hippias's speeches but does not even mention Critias's. Robert C. Bartlett, *Sophistry and Political Philosophy: Protagoras' Challenge to Socrates* (Chicago: University of Chicago Press, 2016), 23, refers to Critias simply as a "tyrant-to-be."

Critias in Plato's Protagoras

We can call the first the "proto-tyrant" view. Three recent attempts to read some or all of the Platonic dialogues in dramatic order, concerned to see a story about Socrates's maturation against an Athenian social and political background, fall into this pattern. Catherine Zuckert provides the largest-scale such reading. In an early chapter, given the *Protagoras*'s early dramatic situation, she comments on Critias's speech: "Displaying the desire for distinction that will lead him in later life to join the other oligarchs in overthrowing the democracy, Critias claims that he, Prodicus, and Hippias remain above the fray and can serve, therefore, as impartial judges."[19] Thus Zuckert sees Plato's inclusion of Critias here as a foreshadowing, a diagnosis of the crucial character flaw, a bit of historical irony—a trait unseen by Critias's fellow interlocutors but not lost on the fourth-century reader (or any subsequent reader). What looks initially as a salutary interjection proves, on (Zuckert's) reflection, to be a forewarning of future trouble.

Yet the text does not obviously underwrite Zuckert's interpretation. In Critias's brief statement, he does not say that he will judge anything. He suggests instead that he desires that he and the other notable persons in the audience encourage the conversation to keep going, at least until its proper end, whatever or whenever that may be. In suggesting this, he displays no distinctive "desire for distinction"—a *philonikia* or *philotimia*. It might be thought that he does display something of the sort by speaking up at all, advancing a view he thinks superior to those of Callias and Alcibiades, and indeed undermining the legitimacy of Alcibiades's view completely. But then all participants in the exchange about conversational dynamics, since all speak up and advance views as improvements on the previous, would deserve the same judgment, as "desiring distinction," and thus Critias would not be distinctive—and so this characteristic could not informatively foreshadow his later life. It might also be thought that his desire for distinction amounts to his desiring a longer

---

[19] Catherine Zuckert, *Plato's Philosophers: The Coherence of the Dialogues* (Chicago: University of Chicago Press, 2009), 224.

conversation for the sake of his continued presence in the public eye; but given that Socrates reports him to say nothing else for the remainder of the conversation, this supposition would be baseless.[20]

Indeed, it would be hard to link Critias's remark here at all to his membership in the democracy-overturning oligarchy three decades later unless we weigh heavily Zuckert's assertion that, just before Critias spoke, "Alcibiades suggests that they put the matter to a vote [...] thus impos[ing] a democratic process," and, in speaking, Critias rejects this suggestion. But Alcibiades does not obviously promulgate a democratic process. True, Alcibiades says that "each person ought to present his own opinion" (χρὴ γὰρ ἕκαστον τὴν ἑαυτοῦ γνώμην ἀποφαίνεσθαι, 336d5) even though he believes that Socrates seems to him to speak better (ἐμοὶ μὲν οὖν δοκεῖ ἐπιεικέστερα Σωκράτης λέγειν, d3–4); he presents himself as not having the decisive or authoritative position, and wishes for everyone else to speak up.[21] But this does not seem to be enough to gloss his suggestion as distinctly democratic. Alcibiades does not actually say that the majority opinion should win out. Socrates does not, when it is his turn to talk, endorse Alcibiades's view – and elsewhere he expresses discontent at a related procedure (at *Laches* 184d–e). And Critias, who is evidently well-acquainted with Alcibiades, judges Alcibiades as concerned more to win—to have *his* favorite prevail—than to foster the endurance of the community of which they are all part. Now, this *could* be a tendentious (or well-founded) criticism of partisan

---

[20] Bartlett, *Sophistry and Political Philosophy*, 53, actually presents Critias's being somehow more democratic than those preceding him as relevant: speaking of the scene's "comic touches," Bartlett observes that "the central speaker in these democratic deliberations is the future oligarchic thug Critias, who is critical of both Callias and Alcibiades for their zealous partisanship." As an interpretation this is difficult to assess, if the other speakers are hyper-characterized rather than contra-characterized.

[21] Maybe Zuckert is influenced by the note in translation of Robert C. Bartlett, *Plato: Protagoras and Meno*, Agora Editions (Ithaca: Cornell University Press, 2004) on Alcibiades's closing remark: "Here Alcibiades adopts the language of the resolutions of the democratic assembly and urges those present to cast their own votes" (35n103).

Critias in Plato's Protagoras

democracy, a political system organized by factional struggle rather than commitment to the common good. But Critias could just as well believe that Alcibiades has affixed himself to, and then tried to universalize for the group, the wrong norm, personal fealty or self-interest, one based, further, on the wrong vision of the event they are watching, as competitive rather than cooperative, zero-sum rather than accumulating in value—specifically, the value of understanding—as the discussion continues.

In any event, all we really see is Critias rejecting the idea that they should present their personal opinions. Maybe he suggests that Protagoras and Socrates should figure it out for themselves. This is far from Critias's offering himself, Prodicus, and Hippias as proto-oligarchic judges. Admittedly, at the end of Hippias's exhortation to good conversation, Hippias says that Protagoras and Socrates should "take my advice and choose a referee or moderator or supervisor who will monitor for you the length of your speeches" (338b1). But we must also admit that this is clearly not Critias's advice, nor even if it were is it a group self-nomination to be those referees, nor even if it were is it a recommendation that those referees judge relative success. Thus Zuckert's attempt to read an ambitious oligarchism into Critias is, while admirably directed by the desire to see dramatic continuity, inadequately founded.[22]

Laurence Lampert, around the same time and in a similar project, gives a relatedly cynical analysis.[23] Critias, "address[ing] only the leading men, [...] invites the wise to resolve the situation—Critias who will, as a future sophist, become an advocate of rule by experts and eventually take charge of Athens himself as the ruling expert who imagines he can solve its postwar

---

[22] Zuckert, *Plato's Philosophers*, 241–47, makes similar remarks about Critias in her reading of the *Charmides*. If those remarks are well-grounded, she may feel justified in retrojecting them onto the *Protagoras*; but they are not obviously well-grounded and, even if they were, there is no evident reason for reading the *Protagoras* in light of the *Charmides*; and, as I have shown, the specific claims look to be in tension with the evidence.

[23] Lampert, *How Philosophy Became Socratic*, 82 (with 83–84).

problems." Lampert assumes that Critias, now in his late twenties and not among the teachers celebrated at Callias's house, will join their ranks as a political or constitutional theorist: Lampert treats the Platonic Critias's analysis of self-knowledge in the *Charmides*, set four years later, as the "knowledge of knowledge" necessary for a flourishing city, as an expression of his burgeoning technocratic (or epistemocratic?) vision.[24] Lampert assumes that this vision underwrote Critias's decision to go into politics. And he assumes that Critias both thought he could go it alone, in an oligarchic fashion, and was mistaken in that thought (as the "who *imagines*..." snidely implies).

All these assumptions may be plausible, but are only doubtfully supported by the evidence available to the reader of the *Protagoras*. The "situation" to be resolved is the prospective dissolution of the conversation between Protagoras and Socrates; and the "resolution" is the encouragement of its continuation. There is no real decision to be made by a ruling expert, so it is hard to see the parallel with oligarchic "rule by experts." Post-war Athens was riven by animosity between democrats and others, and one could imagine a ruler advising that nobody flee into exile, that everyone just stick it out, keep talking, reconcile or prove to one another's content the superiority of one political vision over another. But this hardly reflects the sense of "rule by expertise" or the little we know about Critias's participation in the Thirty. To be sure, Critias's appeal to Prodicus and Hippias, as a group of three (ἡμᾶς... κοινῇ), does seem an appeal to those most likely or best positioned to weigh in on the course of the conversation, as the oldest, most eminent, and indeed explicitly invited as teachers or discussants to Callias's house. Everyone else seems to be a student. But then Critias's appeal hardly seems distinctively to "*only* the leading men" or to "the *wise*," as though he wishes to exclude anybody else from decision making. So here Lampert, like Zuckert, seems to be arguing tendentiously, perhaps influenced by the desire to see in any reference to Critias a foreshadowing of Plato's

---

[24] Lampert, *How Philosophy Became Socratic*, 162–234.

presumed denigration of his participation in the Thirty.[25] At least Lampert points at some relevance of Critias's speech to the dialogue as a whole, finding that, "at the center of his chronologically first dialogue, Plato allows Socrates's two most notorious associates to speak up together, each speaking on behalf of Socrates, each speaking characteristically."[26] The consequences are not clear, but the potential significance is well observed.

The third author in this recent interpretative tradition, Samuel Flores, presents himself as intending to take fresh look at the text but in fact just quotes and accepts Lampert's analysis. Flores adds only that the dialogue plays up Critias's merely apparent discipleship or partisanship of Socrates, and says that dialogues set dramatically later will show even greater distance between the two men.[27]

The second and smaller interpretative path (in contrast to the "proto-tyrant" view) we might call the "neutrality" view. We will see that it more closely approaches my own, without replicating it or hitting the same points. Patrick Coby observes that Critias seeks diminution of *philonikia* but "can offer no resolution of the quarrel that now detains them."[28] Critias wants to act as a fulcrum, balancing the equal weights of Callias and Alcibiades. But, Coby notes, those two views had already, as it were, cancelled themselves out. Critias fails to solve any problem: by merely

---

[25] Bartlett, *Plato: Meno and Protagoras*, 38, in his note on Critias's entrance at 316a, gives more than six of seven biographical lines to Critias's role in oligarchy. Admittedly Taylor, *Plato: Protagoras*, 63, does about the same; but at least he mentions that Critias "was a poet, dramatist, and prose writer."

[26] Lampert, *How Philosophy Became Socratic*, 82.

[27] Samuel Ortencio Flores, "The Development of Critias in Plato's Dialogues," *Classical Philology* 113:2 (2018): 162–88, at 166–67. The view that Socrates merely *appears* to enter Callias's house with a band of followers, Critias included, had already been made by Patrick Coby, *Socrates and the Sophistic Enlightenment: A Commentary on Plato's Protagoras* (Lewisburg: Bucknell University Press, 1987), 37.

[28] Coby, *Socrates and the Sophistic Enlightenment*, 91–92. Coby conjectures an explanation for Socrates's saying "I *think*" Critias spoke next as having nothing to do with Critias but only with Alcibiades having praised, and therefore distracted, Socrates.

encouraging the parties to continue their conversation, he overlooks their actual grievances, whether justified or not, that have inhibited their conversation. Not only that, but he himself hardly gives any positive encouragement; he puts the burden of so doing onto Prodicus and Hippias. What, anyway, are Prodicus and Hippias to say in encouragement, and what would make either of their views decisive? Thus Coby makes an appropriate observation: Critias's contribution is close to nugatory.

Perhaps, however, we should not imagine that Plato wrote in such a pointless Critias. On closer look we see that Critias did make a sequence of contributions. (i) He draws other sophists, who have not yet spoken, into the conversation and thereby constitutes an audience as a stakeholder to the conversation, a stakeholder with experience at conversations and a recognition of their value. (ii) He makes plain, without mincing words, that the two previous speakers failed as arbitrators because of their bald partiality, a partiality not for the wellbeing of the conversation—and thus of all interested stakeholders—but for a single friend. This *parrhēsia*, so to speak, shows some courage: Critias effectively assails his host, Callias, and his young upstart (and beloved?) Alcibiades, and seems to undercut the arguments put forth in favor of Protagoras and Socrates. That courage is in the interest of a broader community. (iii) Though engaging an audience of expert conversationalists, he does not propose that they tell Protagoras and Socrates what to do; he does not propose teaching. He instead advises helping them find a reason to go on. This manifests some epistemic humility. (iv) Critias cognizes the conversation as a complete event, one that has a proper ending; he sees it as something other than idle chat or a conflict that is to be contained or abridged.

Larry Goldberg, a few years earlier than Coby, proposed a richer neutrality view.[29] He recognizes a chiastic—and implicitly contestatory—structure in the five-person interlude: Callias (1)

---

[29] Larry Goldberg, *A Commentary on Plato's Protagoras*, American University Studies (New York: Peter Lang, 1983), 132–4; the whole analysis of the interlude is 131–44.

Critias in Plato's Protagoras

and Hippias (5) are pro-Protagoras; Alcibiades (2) and Prodicus (4) are pro-Socrates; Critias (3), at the middle and without partisanship, is the pivot point. This is not a static chiasmus, however; each speaker grows increasingly sophisticated with respect to justice. Critias, therefore, is halfway up the ladder of moral complexity. He "pleads, without argument, for a change from the partial or the contentious to the impartial or the agreeable"—and supersedes Alcibiades "not by superior argument, or, indeed, by argument at all, but by appeal to a higher norm." Alcibiades's defense of Socrates was inadequate, a matter of fulfilling his immediate desire. Critias's higher norm, it would seem, is something other than personal preference—it must be the preference of, or benefit to, the conversation overall. Thus Critias contributes to the interlude by nudging the debate toward a higher moral plane.

The spirit of this analysis sounds right, and seems of a piece with Platonic writing in general, as when, for example, Plato presents candidate definitions of virtues in ascending levels of moral significance – for example, drawing from the *Charmides*, "discipline" (*sōphrosunē*) as tranquility, then as shame, then as doing one's own thing, then as knowing oneself. But it leaves the connection between Critias and this third position undeveloped. Are we to infer that Critias has a moral insight superior to Callias and even Alcibiades, but inferior to Prodicus and especially Hippias? Maybe; it is provocative to imagine him as more morally insightful than "civilians" but less morally insightful than "sophists." Or are we not to generalize to overall moral insight but instead to see Critias as a partisan of impartiality and agreeableness? Is his participation in the *Protagoras*, and this interlude more specifically, explained by his culturally distinctive holding of this moral insight? Or might there even be an application of the norm of justice connected to impartiality and agreeableness that we are to see as decisive for his later career, even the last months of his life as member of the Thirty? I find these the really provocative questions; unfortunately, I suspect any answer would be wholly ungrounded, and thus prefer the more general position about Critias's commitment to intellectual discussion but disinclination to self-scrutiny developed in the previous section.

Corroboration by the *Charmides*

This has been a paper principally about Critias in the *Protagoras*, but we can find some corroboration for its tentative claims by looking at the *Charmides*. That dialogue, set several years after the *Protagoras*, provides the richest source for Plato's attitude toward Critias, and the most interpretative complexity. In that dialogue, we see that Critias has maintained his commitments to enthusiastic conversational participation.[30] When Socrates returns to the *philosophia* circle after a three-year absence on campaign in Potidaea, he discovers Critias having taken a central position in it (153c8). Critias encourages a conversation between Socrates and Charmides (154e10–155b1, 157c10–d10), and seems to enjoy listening. He takes over the definition of *sōphrosunē* only once Charmides, who in effect attributed it to him, could no longer serve as a productive interlocutor (162e5). When he finds himself refuted, he gladly enough rephrases his view and starts again, evidently to keep the conversation going (163e7–10, 164c8–d3, 165b1–5, etc.). He criticizes Socrates for, as he sees it, attempting to argue eristically rather than working to make sense of the subject at hand (166b7–c8). Even at the dialogue's end, he encourages Charmides's continued conversation with Socrates (176b6–8).

Just as Critias seemed invested in a conversation about political virtue in the *Protagoras*, Socrates shows that Critias's investment in the conversation about *sōphrosunē* in the *Charmides* depends on its being a political virtue. Twice Socrates creates thought-experiments about *sōphrosunē* that involve a political utopia, a city in which the rulers are wholly *sōphrōn*, in ways that give sense to Critias's elaboration of *sōphrosunē* as "the knowledge of knowledge." Critias probably did treat of *sōphrosunē* as *a* or *the* core political virtue, as the evidence from his "Spartan Constitution" and his first definition of *sōphrosunē* in this dialogue,

---

[30] For details and discussion, see Christopher Moore and Christopher C. Raymond, *Plato: Charmides: A Translation with Introduction, Notes, and Analysis* (Indianapolis: Hackett, 2019).

Critias in Plato's Protagoras

as "doing one's own thing," suggests. He probably also wrote about the norms of Athenian leadership, as the so-called "Athenian Constitution" fragments suggest.

For this paper's purpose, the particular tenor of the criticism of Critias is what matters most. He is not presented as traditionally lacking *sōphrosunē*: money-hungry, or excessive in his desires, or a drunkard, or anything else typical of the "tyrannical personality." The problem is just that he is not good enough at defending or explaining his views. He answers Socrates's questions with a view to keeping the conversation going rather than to keeping the criteria of knowledge in view, as Socrates seems to have suggested the *sōphrōn* person should do (172b1–c2)—and thus Critias favors impressive or appealing talk over rigorously scrutinized investigation. When Critias speaks expansively, he prefers cleverness over defensibility, enigma over clarity, and thus, to speak simplistically, appearance over reality. The *Charmides* concerns the virtue needed for political authority. *Sōphrosunē* is a good candidate, and Critias may fancy himself an embodiment of and expert in it. Thus he may fancy himself well-positioned for political authority. We do not learn that he has an especially villainous view of the virtue or that he would be an especially poor leader. But by contrast to Socrates, we see that he does not give priority to continued self-examination in light of rigorous epistemic norms. This, I think, is Plato's charge against Critias: not enough, or not withering enough, self-knowledge. What explains his diffidence about self-knowledge, Plato does not particularly reveal. Maybe it is an aristocratic hauteur that keeps him out of what he perceives as a hard-pressed competition, the competition necessary to get one's ideas examined; but this is only an idea.

Conclusion

I suspect there is a bigger story behind Plato's inclusion of Critias in the *Protagoras* than I have yet seen. That story, or much of it, may be forever obscured from us; most of Critias's literary production and biography is lost. Nevertheless, his inclusion ought not be forgotten, ignored, or hastily explained away. Critias's political thinking was plausibly a major influence on

Plato's own political thinking, from the *Protagoras* to the *Charmides*, from the *Timaeus* to the *Critias*, and even from the *Republic* to the *Laws*. His writings across genres may have themselves been influential, as one of the few fifth c. BCE authors we know to have success in both poetry and prose. It is conceivable that Critias, as a family-member of Plato's, was the occasion for Plato's meeting Socrates; at any event, Critias and Socrates led lives that would cross paths in various ways across their many decades.

The *Protagoras* is a remarkable dialogue, and a remarkable document about intellectual culture in the late fifth century. Plato presents Critias as one of the definitive figures of that culture, and one of the few Athenians worth depicting in conversation with Socrates. Critias's doom in 404/3 BCE should color our understanding of him but it is not all his life was, just as Socrates's death four years later colors our understanding of *him* but is not all his life was. Here is a dialogue introducing Socrates into popular intellectual culture: Critias, along with the sophists and Alcibiades, is someone in relationship to whom Socrates is to be understood.

Mark Ralkowski[1]
A Contest Between Two Lives: Plato's Existential Drama

He always ... makes me admit that my political career is a waste of time, while all that matters is just what I neglect: my personal shortcomings, which cry out for the closest attention ... I know perfectly well that I can't prove he's wrong when he tells me what I should do; yet, the moment I leave his side I go back to my old ways: I cave in to my desire to please the crowd ... I feel deeply ashamed, because I'm doing nothing about my way of life, though I have already agreed with him that I should. (*Symposium* 216a-b)

Several scholars have shown that for Plato, the *Gorgias*'s *agōn* between two lives (*Gorgias* 485e-486c, 489e, 500c-d, 506b-e) is a "battle" between two ideologies: one devoted to power and greed, which is defended by Thucydides's Athenians (Thucydides 1.76, 5.105) and Plato's Callicles (*Gorgias* 483c-484a), and a second devoted to justice and piety, which Plato defends in his portrait of Socrates as an exemplar of the "true political craft" (*Gorgias* 521d).[2]

---

[1] Mark Ralkowski is Associate Professor of Philosophy and Honors at George Washington University. He is the author of Heidegger's *Platonism* (Continuum, 2009) and *Plato's Trial of Athens* (Bloomsbury, 2018), the editor of *Time and Death: Heidegger's Analysis of Finitude* (Ashgate, 2005), and co-editor with Heather L. Reid of *Plato at Syracuse* (Parnassos Press, 2019).

[2] See R.B. Rutherford, *The Art of Plato* (London: Duckworth, 1995), 66-68; Simon Hornblower, *Thucydides* (Baltimore: Johns Hopkins University Press, 1987), 55; Jacqueline de Romilly, *The Life of Alcibiades: Dangerous Ambition and the Betrayal of Athens* (Ithaca, NY: Cornell University Press, 2019), 30-34, 186-90; Harvey Yunis, *Taming Democracy: Models of Political Rhetoric in Classical Athens* (Ithaca, NY: Cornell University Press, 1996), 34, 136-37, 137 n. 4, 142-145; Josiah Ober, *Political Dissent in Democratic Athens: Intellectual Critics of Popular Rule* (Princeton, NJ: Princeton University Press, 1998), 199; and David Gribble, *Alcibiades and Athens: A Study in Literary Presentation* (Oxford: Oxford University Press, 1999), 236. The *agōn* between two lives is one of the most important themes in the *Gorgias*, and it may well reflect a debate that was going on in Athens at the time (L.B. Carter, *The Quiet Athenian* [New York: Oxford University Press, 1986], 155-79). In addition to being explicit

Mark Ralkowski

This is the "war and battle" that the *Gorgias* refers to in its opening lines: "Who will form the future leaders of the polity, the rhetor who teaches the tricks of political success, or the philosopher who creates the substance in soul and society?"[3] Others have argued that the *Gorgias* is Plato's "second apology of Socrates"[4]: he was not the corruptor of the youth; the Athenian way of life was; Socrates spent most of his life trying to improve the souls of his fellow citizens. The point of this essay is to show that the *Symposium* is Plato's third apology of Socrates. The *Gorgias* makes the case against Athens, turning the tables on Socrates's accusers, and the *Symposium* shows us the stakes: the *agōn* between two lives was a battle being fought in the soul of every Athenian, and the "*polis* education" provided by the democracy and its empire was winning at great cost to the city.[5] Alcibiades is Plato's symbol of this problem. He was rationally persuaded that he should abandon his career in politics, but he could not follow through on his convictions because the "fair face" of the *dēmos* had already corrupted him (*Alcibiades I* 132a).

In what follows, I shall argue that Plato's depiction of Alcibiades's moral weakness in the *Symposium* serves at least three purposes. First, it adds to Plato's apologetic response to the trial of Socrates: he was the only true educator; he was not a corruptor;[6]

---

in the exchange between Callicles and Socrates, it is alluded to in the dialogue's many references to Euripides's *Antiope* (484e-486, 489e, 506b-e, 500c-d).

[3] Eric Voegelin, *Plato* (Baton Rouge: Louisiana State University Press, 2000), 24.

[4] See E.R. Dodds, *Plato's Gorgias* (Oxford: Oxford University Press, 1959), 28; cf. Theodor Gomperz, *Socrates and the Socratics*, v. 2, Bk. 4 of *Greek Thinkers: A History of Ancient Philosophy* (New York: Charles Scribner's Sons, 1905), 343-44.

[5] Kathleen Morgan introduces the concept of a "*polis* education" to capture the idea, shared by Plato and Isocrates, that the city's way of life was itself an educator ("The Education of Athens: Politics and Rhetoric in Isocrates," in Takis, Poulakos, and David Depew, eds., *Isocrates and Civic Education* [Austin, TX: University of Texas Press, 2004], 125-54).

[6] R.G. Bury, *The Symposium of Plato* (Cambridge: Cambridge University Press, 1909), xvii-xix and li-lii. Many scholars deny that the trial had a political subtext. For examples, see Tom Brickhouse and Nick Smith, *The Trial and*

second, it helps him shift the blame from Socrates to the Athenians by showing that Alcibiades, like Callicles in the *Gorgias*, was held captive by his love of the *dēmos*; and third, it provided him with a symbol of the soul's inevitable existential drama. As Proclus suggests in his commentary on *Alcibiades I*, "every human being is more or less clearly subject to the very same misfortunes as the son of Kleinias."[7] Socrates fails to improve the youth because he can not quite win their hearts back from the democracy and overcome these universal misfortunes.[8] Human nature proved incorrigible in the "*polis*-as-it-is"[9] — only radical reform could save the city from itself (*Republic* 492e).

The argument that I present in this essay has three steps. First, I present Alcibiades as a symptom of the social and political problem that *Alcibiades I*, *Gorgias*, and *Republic* diagnose and hope to solve. Second, I respond to the objection that Alcibiades is unimportant as a political symbol in Plato's dialogues by showing that Plato intended for us to see Alcibiades as a potential philosopher who was corrupted by the city's *polis* culture. Finally, I conclude by characterizing Plato's portrait of Socrates in his so-

---

Execution of Socrates: Sources and Controversies (New York; Oxford: Oxford University Press); Stanley Rosen, *Plato's Symposium* (New Haven, CT: Yale University Press, 1987); Anton-Hermann Chroust, *Socrates, Man and Myth. The Two Socratic Apologies of Xenophon* (London: Routledge), 174. For an overview of the debate, see Ralkowski, 2013, "The Politics of Impiety: Why Was Socrates Prosecuted by the Athenian Democracy?" in Nick Smith and John Bussanich, eds, *The Bloomsbury Companion to Socrates* (London: Bloomsbury Academic, 2013), 301-27.

[7] See Proclus: *Alcibiades I: A Translation and Commentary*, translated by William O'Neill (The Hague: Martinus Nijhoff), 4-5.

[8] *Alcibiades I* is not the only piece of ancient literature that contains these themes. Several Socratic authors contributed to "the whole 'Alcibiades literature'" (Chroust, *Socrates, Man and Myth*, 174), and they appear to have had some shared apologetic purposes (G.C. Field, *Plato and His Contemporaries: A Study in Fourth-Century Life and Thought* [London: Methuen & Co, 1967], 150), and literary strategies (Nicholas Denyer, trans., *Plato: Alcibiades* [Cambridge: Cambridge University Press, 2001], 5-6).

[9] I borrow this expression from Ober who contrasts "the *polis*-as-it-is" with "the *polis*-as-it-should-be, that is, the ideal state of the *Republic*," (*Political Dissent*, 212).

called "early" and "middle" dialogues. In this portrait, Socrates is depicted as the representative of a philosophical life that is at odds with Athenian political life. He tries and fails to convert the Athenian youth to philosophy because the democracy had already captured their hearts and turned them toward the ends of empire. This portrait of Socrates as engaged in a losing *agōn* with the city's ideology, values, and way of life allows Plato to turn the tables on Socrates's accusers and reflect more generally on philosophy's place in the city.

I. Athens on Trial: Turning the Tables on Socrates's Accusers

As a young man, Alcibiades was still open to philosophy, and he had not yet become an enemy of the state. He was proud and complacent, but also impressionable (*Alcibiades I* 135d), and so Socrates was able to seduce him into philosophy, away from his precocious ambitions. In *Alcibiades I*, the nineteen year-old Alcibiades is defeated in argument and shown that he lacks the self-knowledge he needs (*Alcibiades I* 105c-e, 124b-d); he realizes he is ignorant about the true nature of justice (*Alcibiades I* 106c-116e), having learned about it from the many (*Alcibiades I* 110d); and by the end of the dialogue, he has had his world turned upside down: he considers himself slavish and unready for a career in politics, and he ends up expressing a desire for justice and Socratic education (*Alcibiades I* 135b-e).[10]

As the dialogue concludes, Socrates tells Alcibiades he will not abandon him "unless the Athenian people make [him] corrupt and ugly." That is Alcibiades's "greatest fear" — that a love of the *dēmos* will "corrupt" him: "Many noble Athenians have already suffered this fate, for the *dēmos* of the great-hearted Erechtheus has a fair

---

[10] In the ancient world, no one doubted that Plato was the author of *Alcibiades I*; the Neoplatonists even considered it "the gateway to the temple," containing in outline the "whole of philosophy" (Denyer, *Alcibiades*, 14). It wasn't until the early nineteenth century that the dialogue's authenticity was first challenged by Friedrich Schleiermacher. For a recent discussion of the dialogue's authorship, see Jill Gordon, *Plato's Erotic World: From Cosmic Origins to Human Death* (Cambridge: Cambridge University Press, 2012), 146-83.

face" (*Alcibiades I* 131e10-132a5). When Alcibiades appears in Plato's *Symposium*, it is clear that Socrates's worst fears have been realized. Alcibiades was a gifted young man who showed unusual insight, intense passion, and even moral idealism and self-awareness,[11] but the city corrupted him. There is evidence of Alcibiades's potential in the contents of his speech at the end of the *Symposium*, and there is evidence of what went wrong: Alcibiades abandoned philosophy and turned his back on Socrates because he had a fragmented will. He loved philosophy, but not with a whole heart. His life was torn between "self-love and the love of philosophy, worldly ambition and appreciation of contemplative truth, reckless sensuousness and a deep admiration for Socratic self-control."[12] He was persuaded that he should change his life and abandon politics for philosophy, but he could not make this understanding an operational part of his life.

What happened to the young Alcibiades's love of philosophy and Socrates? What did the city do to "get the better" of him? Plato gives his full answer to these questions in the *Gorgias* and the *Republic*. In the *Gorgias*, he explains how the city turned its best men into slaves of the *dēmos* (*Gorgias* 481d-482c, 513c-d) and led them to misidentify the good with power (*Gorgias* 483e-484a) and pleasure (*Gorgias* 492b). And in the *Republic*, he argues that those who are born with the *phusis* to be philosophers are pulled away from philosophy by the "contrary education" they receive from the *polis* (*Republic* 489d-495c). This contrary education harmed the city in at least two ways. First, it wasted the potential of the city's best men by turning them into pandering *rhetores* who gratified the city instead of struggling against its *epithumiai* (desires) and practicing the true political craft (*Gorgias* 521d). Such men become experts at angering and placating the *dēmos*, but they never learn how to distinguish the true good from the apparent good (*Republic* 493b-

---

[11] See Gordon (*Plato's Erotic World*, 179), who points out that Alcibiades acknowledges his ignorance on numerous occasions (*Alcibiades I* 108e4, 112d10, 113b6-7, 116e2-3, 118a15-b3, 127a9-13).

[12] Gribble, *Alcibiades and Athens*, 251.

c). They become "servants to slaves,"[13] and it is as if they are "under Diomedean compulsion" to do only what "[the *dēmos*] approve" (*Republic* 493d). Second, because these men serve and gratify the *dēmos*, rather than struggling against it, the city is deprived of what would otherwise be its best bet for effective leadership; there is no order or wisdom in such a *polis*, and so it undermines itself in the pursuit of apparent goods, such as the Periclean *Archē*. This is how Plato understands what happened in fifth-century Athens. The most celebrated leaders of the past— Themistocles, Miltiades, Cimon, and Pericles—were not good at politics, judging by "results," because as they catered to the *epithumiai* of the *polis* they did not make the city better. They gave it a fever by satisfying all of its imperious desires (*Republic* 372e), and the city never fully recovered (*Gorgias* 515e-517c, 518e-519b). The *polis* itself became the "leaky jar" of the *Gorgias* (*Gorgias* 493a-c): it was "swollen and festering" with ambition and self-undermining greed (*Gorgias* 518e-519c). As Plato refutes Callicles, he is also criticizing the Athenian empire, the "tyrant of the Aegean," and the *pleonexia* (greed) it engendered.[14] His response to the trial of Socrates puts Pericles and his predecessors on trial instead: *their* ideology of power and *pleonexia* corrupted men like Alcibiades and his followers.[15] And so, Callicles's theory of the good life and skepticism about justice are refuted in theory and in

---

[13] Lawrence Lampert, *How Philosophy Became Socratic: A Study of Plato's Protagoras, Charmides, and Republic* (Chicago: University of Chicago Press, 2010), 339.

[14] See Arlene Saxonhouse, "The Unspoken Theme in Plato's *Gorgias*: War," *Interpretation* 11.2 (1983): 166. Saxonhouse describes the Athenians as victims of Alcibiades's oratory: *he* encouraged *them* to desire too much. The view I argue for here suggests a more complex picture: Alcibiades was a symptom, not a cause, of Athenian *pleonexia*; the Athenians taught *him* to desire too much, and he was a fast learner who soon became a "teacher"; cf. Yunis, *Taming*, 136-210; Ober, *Political Dissent*, 190-213; de Romilly, *The Life of Alcibiades*, 187; Catherine Zuckert, *Plato's Philosophers: The Coherence of the Dialogues* (Chicago, IL: University of Chicago Press), 546-56; and Steven Forde, *The Ambition to Rule: Alcibiades and the Politics of Imperialism* (Ithaca, NY: Cornell University Press, 1989), 12-67.

[15] Yunis, *Taming*, 142.

practice; Socrates defeats him in argument and points out the *real-life* consequences of taking his views seriously.

Of course, Socrates does not really win. Callicles's corrupted *erōs* resists Socrates's efforts to persuade him. He recognizes the logic of Socrates's argument, but he is not convinced (*Gorgias* 513c-d).[16] This is when he most resembles Alcibiades, who confesses to being even worse off than Callicles because he was persuaded but unable to act accordingly; he could not help but cave in to his "desire to please the crowd" (*Symposium* 216b). Plato diagnoses Callicles with a similar condition—they both are misled by their *erōs* for the *dēmos*, but in the *Gorgias* he also points to the social and political basis for this shared affliction. As Ober says, Callicles "has a bad case of the '*hoi polloi* disease.'"[17] His *erōs* has made it impossible for him *merely to process an argument*.

> Callicles: I don't know how it is that I think you're right, Socrates, but the thing that happens to most people has happened to me: I'm not really convinced by you.
>
> Socrates: It's your love for the people, Callicles, existing in your soul, that stands out against me. (*Gorgias* 513c-d)

The pessimistic conclusion of the *Gorgias* is that there cannot be any true politicians in Athens.[18] Philosophical persuasion is impossible in the city because the democratic structure of Athenian society enslaves the *rhetores* to the *dēmos*, and the tyranny of public opinion in the *polis* culture is too powerful for a philosopher to overcome. Men like Callicles cannot be persuaded because they do not understand that they are indoctrinated, and

---

[16] See Dodds, *Plato's Gorgias*, 352, who thinks this passage indicates that Plato believed "moral attitudes are commonly determined by psychological, not logical reasons;" cf. Terrence Irwin, *Plato: Gorgias* (Oxford: Clarendon Press, 1979), 233.

[17] Ober, *Political Dissent*, 208 n. 94.

[18] In the conditions of democratic Athens, the political expert "cannot establish his authority and cannot accomplish his educative goal," because he cannot persuade the citizens to "adopt courses that would improve them" (Yunis, *Taming*, 130-1).

they do not see that their *erōs* for the *dēmos* has turned them into "menial servants."[19] The *polis* culture must be completely reformed, as the *Republic* suggests, or philosophers like Socrates must learn to live in harmony with a city that is disordered and prepare for anything, including execution (*Gorgias* 521e).

II. The Case of Alcibiades

Plato's point in the *Gorgias* is a general one: Callicles is not a historical figure;[20] he represents his generation, and the *Gorgias* itself appears to take place during the full duration of Peloponnesian War.[21] Socrates's failure to persuade *him*, and Plato's diagnosis of that failure, explain what others have called the "Socrates and Athens problem": Socrates could not persuade the young men in fifth century Athens because they were slaves to the *dēmos*.[22] It is precisely because Callicles is *a type* of person, a representative cross-section of elite Athenian society, that Plato can use him, and especially the flaws with his arguments and attitudes, to critique his city more generally. The *polis* culture was the true educator in Athens because it required every citizen to take on the character of the regime (*Gorgias* 513a-c), which involved internalizing an ideology about what to say, what to value, how to live, and what kind of person one ought to be

---

[19] Ober, *Political Dissent*, 210.

[20] Dodds, *Plato's Gorgias*, 12-13; cf. Martin Ostwald, *From Popular Sovereignty to the Sovereignty of the Law: Law, Society, and Politics in Fifth Century Athens* (Berkeley: University of California Press, 1986), 245-7.

[21] They are in democratic Athens, "where there is more free speech than anywhere else in Greece" (461e), but Plato doesn't say exactly where. They are in an undefined space, "inside" (447c). The dramatic date is left ambiguous: Callicles says Pericles "died just recently" (503c), but Socrates says he served as *bouleutēs* "last year" (473e). These references point toward different dates: Pericles died in 429, and the *Apology* tells us that Socrates served as *bouleutēs* during the trial of the Arginousae generals in 406 — which means the dialogue is set in the 420s *and also* in the year 405 — among other dates. Dodds mentions five other possible dates (*Plato's Gorgias*, 17-18). Cf. Debra Nails, *The People of Plato: A Prosography of Plato and Other Socratics* (Indianapolis: Hackett, 2002), 326-27.

[22] Ober, *Political Dissent*, 165.

(*Republic* 492b-d). Alcibiades is Plato's case study. If Nietzsche is right that Plato's Socrates should be seen as "a physician," his Alcibiades is a "symptom" of the political problem that Socrates fails to "heal."[23]

Alcibiades was a polarizing figure in the ancient world.[24] For some, he was an Athenian Achilles or JFK, "the young prince who could take on the world and win big."[25] For others, he was an enemy of the state: banished from Athens in 415, recalled in 407, and banished again a few months later. As Aristophanes aptly wrote in his *Frogs*: "Athens longs for him, it detests him, but it wants to have him" (1425). By the time of his legendary death—his assassins set fire to his house and then killed him with javelins and arrows when he ran out to escape—Alcibiades had been exiled from Athens twice; he had overseen the slaughter of an island colony's male population; he had disrupted the fifty-year peace treaty with Sparta, and he was responsible for the disaster in

---

[23] F. Nietzsche (1871-79), "Introduction to the Study of the Platonic Dialogues," cited in Kaufmann, *Nietzsche: Philosopher, Psychologist, Antichrist*. (Princeton, NJ: Princeton University Press, 1950), 398.

[24] As Rebecca Goldstein put this point memorably, "imagine John F. Kennedy, Donald Trump, David Petraeus, Muhammad Ali, Julian Assange, Johnny Knoxville, Bernie Madoff, and Jude Law all combined in one" (*Plato at the Googleplex: Why Philosophy Won't Go Away*, [New York: Pantheon Books, 2014], 234). The ancient sources on Alcibiades's life are Thucydides's *History*, Xenophon's *Hellenica* and *Memorabilia*, Plutarch's *Life of Alcibiades* and *Life of Lysander*, Diodorus Siculus's *Biblioteca historica*, and Cornelius Nepos's *Lives of Famous Men*. Some scholars have wondered whether Alcibiades was one of Thucydides's sources for his *History*. For examples, see P.J. Rhodes, *Alcibiades* (Barnsley, South Yorkshire: Pen and Sword Military, 2011) and P.A. Brunt, 1952, "Thucydides and Alcibiades," *Review des etudes grecques* 65: 59-96. For modern sources on Alcibiades's life and disputed "genius," see Jean Hatzfeld, *Alcibiade* (Paris: Presses Universitaires de France, 1951); M.F. McGregor, 1965, "The Genius of Alcibiades," *Phoenix*, XIX: 27-46; Edmund F. Bloedow, *Alcibiades Re-Examined* (Wiesbaden: F. Steiner, 1973); Walter Ellis, *Alcibiades* (London: Routledge, 1989); Rhodes, *Alcibiades*; and de Romilly, *The Life of Alcibiades*.

[25] Barry S. Strauss and Josiah Ober, eds, "The Alcibiades Syndrome," in *The Anatomy of an Error: Ancient Military Disasters and Their Lessons for Modern Strategists* (New York: St. Martin's Press, 1990), 50.

Sicily.[26] Why is this self-serving, glory-loving playboy in Plato's *Symposium*? What does Plato want us to see in his character?

It turns out Alcibiades is a polarizing figure among Plato's commentators as well. Some say he is the "most brilliant" character in all of Plato's dialogues[27], while others argue that he did not understand Socrates *at all*. As Plochmann puts the point, Alcibiades provides us with a "clarification of what philosophy is *not*."[28] Blundell calls Alcibiades's antics a "hopelessly ill-conceived attempt to prostitute himself," and Blondell suggests that, at best, he confused Socrates with the Form of Beauty, the ultimate object of desire.[29] Nightingale develops this case against Alcibiades by arguing that he interprets the whole world, including his experience with Socrates, "in terms of an on-going struggle for power." He talks about feeling "enslaved" to Socrates (*Symposium* 219e3, cf. 215e6-7), and he mentions feeling "forced" to do whatever Socrates told him to do (216b3-4, 217a1-2, 218a6-7). The importance of this story, Nightingale thinks, is Alcibiades's "desire to conquer Socrates ... [He] sees the world in terms of winners and losers, victors and victims. Socrates's refusal to be manipulated is therefore interpreted by Alcibiades as an [...] attempt to dominate."[30] This contest for power, not a love of philosophy, is

---

[26] See Plutarch's *Life of Alcibiades*, 16.5 and 39.4, and Thucydides 5.44-46.

[27] de Romilly, *Life of Alcibiades*, 11-12, 188-89.

[28] George K. Plochmann, "Hiccups and Hangovers in 'The Symposium,'" *The Bucknell Review*, 11.3 (1963): 1-18.

[29] See Ruby Blundell, "Commentary on Reeve's 'Telling the Truth about Love: Plato's *Symposium*,'" *Proceedings of the Boston Area Colloquium in Ancient Philosophy*, 7 (1992): 123, and Ruby Blondell, "Where is Socrates on the 'Ladder of Love'?" In J.H. Lesher, D. Nails, and F. Sheffield, eds, *Plato's Symposium: Issues in Interpretation* (Cambridge, MA: Harvard University Press, 2006), 158. For similar criticisms, see G.R.F. Ferrari, "Platonic Love," in Richard Kraut, *The Cambridge Companion to Plato* (Cambridge: Cambridge University Press, 1992), 162; Stanley Rosen, *Plato's Republic: A Study* (New Haven, CT: Yale University Press, 2005), 237; and Reeve, "A Study in Violets: Alcibiades in the *Symposium*," in J.H. Lesher, D. Nails, and F. Sheffield, eds, *Plato's Symposium*, 141.

[30] Andrea Nightingale, "The Folly of Praise: Plato's Critique of Encomiastic Discourse in Lysis and Symposium," *The Classical Quarterly*, 43.1 (1993): 125.

A Contest Between Two Lives

the real basis of Alcibiades's attraction to Socrates. He wanted Socratic wisdom, but he did not want to change his life. If he wanted anything from Socrates, it was for his "private and political ends rather than those of philosophy."[31]

The point of this section is to show that this case against Alcibiades is inconsistent with many of the most important details of his speech: his insight into the beauty of Socrates's soul and arguments; his unusual *erōs* for Socrates's "divine words," which suggests he has learned to love the Forms through Socrates; his self-knowledge and moral idealism; his uniqueness in Plato's dialogues; and the respectability of his *motivation* in offering to exchange sex for Socratic wisdom. As we will see, the problem with the case against Alcibiades is that it treats the conflict in his soul as evidence against his potential instead of seeing it as an implicit critique of Athens. These points are crucial for our understanding of Plato's Alcibiades and the apologetic aims of the *Symposium*.

One of the most remarkable facts about Plato's Alcibiades is that he was able to see a transformative beauty in Socrates, despite Socrates's famously bad looks.[32] This is most evident when he compares Socrates to statues of Silenus and to Marsyas. Alcibiades uses the Silenus analogy to describe a "godlike" beauty he has seen in Socrates's soul and arguments (*Symposium* 216e-217a, 221e-222a), and he uses the example of Marsyas to describe the effect that Socrates's ideas have on him and others (*Symposium* 215b). These analogies show that Alcibiades had remarkable insight. Most people could not see beyond the surface-level appearance with Socrates, but Alcibiades did. He saw that Socrates's beauty

---

[31] Nightingale, "Folly of Praise," 125; cf. S. Schein, "Alcibiades and the Politics of Misguided Love," *Theta Pi*, 3 (1974): 158-67; and G. Scott, "Irony and Inebriation in Plato's "Symposium,"" *The Journal of Neoplatonic Studies*, 3.2 (1995): 26 n. 1, 33 n. 8, and 43.

[32] Frisbee Sheffield points out that the satyrs were a particularly apt "figuration of [Socrates's] ugliness" because they also were "bearded and goatish" (*Plato's Symposium: The Ethics of Desire* [New York: Oxford University Press, 2006], 189). Xenophon (*Symposium* 4.19) confirms Socrates's satyr-like appearances.

was psychological and intellectual, not physical—he and his arguments contained images of the gods that were of "great—no, of the greatest—importance for anyone who wants to become a truly good man" (*Symposium* 222a). Alcibiades's appreciation of this beauty suggests he has at least reached the third rung of Diotima's ladder (*Symposium* 210b), the stage at which one sees that the beauty in people's souls is more valuable than the beauty of their bodies.

As impressive as that was, the Marsyas analogy suggests that Alcibiades may have achieved even more than this. He may have glimpsed the Form of beauty in Socrates's "divine words" (*Symposium* 215c-e). Marsyas could transport people and cast spells over them with his music, revealing those who were ready for the god and his mysteries (*Symposium* 215c). Alcibiades says Socrates did something similar with his words, which elicited a "madness" and "Bacchic frenzy" that took possession of him and made him feel shame (*Symposium* 215c-216c, 217e-218b). As some commentators have pointed out, this reference to a "Bacchic frenzy" sounds a lot like Socrates's mystical account in the *Phaedrus* of the philosopher's state when he ascends to the intelligible world thanks to a sudden appearance of the Beautiful—it strikes like "a bolt of lightning" (*Phaedrus* 254b)—and remembers being lifted "up to what is truly real" (*Phaedrus* 249c) and initiated into "the most blessed of all" mysteries (*Phaedrus* 250b-c).[33] The *Symposium* does not provide conclusive evidence that Alcibiades reached the top of Diotima's ladder, at which point he would see "the great sea of Beauty" (*Symposium* 210d), but the *erōs* he feels for Socrates's *arguments* suggests that he got pretty close and started to recollect the Forms. That would explain the intensity of his *erōs*. It would also explain his shame and confirm his potential for philosophy. He had genuine insight; he had true passion, but he did not have sufficient power over himself to change his life.

Alcibiades's shame over his failures is supposed to stand out to us: Socrates upset him so profoundly that, as he says, his "very

---

[33] Richard Hunter, *Plato's Symposium* (Oxford: Oxford University Press, 2004), 106.

own soul started protesting that my life—*my* life!—was no better than the most miserable slave's" (*Symposium* 216a). This is an underappreciated moment of Platonic characterization.[34] Socrates's other interlocutors do not talk this way.[35] They do not confess to lacking wisdom or feeling shame; they are not inspired to follow Socrates on a path of goodness, and they do not have the self-knowledge or attraction to Socrates that Alcibiades shows in his speech (*Symposium* 216bc).[36] Even the characters who are portrayed as very sympathetic to Socrates (e.g., Crito, Cebes, Nicias, Agathon, Simmias, Glaucon, and Adeimantus) fall short. They have not appreciated that Socrates has the power to improve their characters, and they have not seen that Socrates has *in himself* and in his ideas "a beauty that is really beyond description" (*Symposium* 218d-219a). They do not confess to a "Bacchic frenzy of philosophy," the feeling of being snake-bitten (*Symposium* 218ab), and they do not reflect on the possibility that their lives are a mistake (*Symposium* 216ad). Alcibiades stands out in Plato's dialogues because he is the only character who appreciates Socrates's mission, its existential challenge and its conflict with Athenian *polis* culture. The fact that he had this reaction to

---

[34] Nichols (*Socrates on Friendship and Community*, 80) argues that Nicias is more advanced than Alcibiades because he uses one of Socrates's definitions of courage in the dialogue (*Laches* 187e-188a). This is mistaken for two reasons. First, Socrates refutes Nicias and shows that he is ignorant and self-satisfied. Nicias is like the soldier Stesilaus (*Laches* 183c8-184a7), who was too reliant on an acquired skill or art because he was too reliant on definitions and was therefore unequipped to engage in dialectic (Francisco Gonzalez, *Dialectic and Dialogue: Plato's Practice of Philosophical Inquiry* [Evanston, IL: Northwestern University Press, 1998], 22-41). Second, because Nicias thinks Socratic philosophy is fun (*Laches* 188b5), he shows that he doesn't understand its existential challenge.

[35] William Prior, "Why Did Plato Write Socratic Dialogues?" In M. McPherran, ed., *Wisdom, Ignorance, and Virtue: Essays in Socratic Studies* (Edmunton: Academic Printing & Pub., 1997), 117.

[36] Consider the difference between Alcibiades and characters like Euthyphro, Meno, and Callicles: Alcibiades is insightful and passionate; the others are resistant or obtuse (Gordon, *Plato's Erotic World*, 179; cf. Gribble, *Alcibiades and Athens*, 236 n. 67) and de Romilly, *The Life of Alcibiades*, 10-12.

Socrates—that he understood and internalized his message, and that he felt attracted to the transformative beauty he discovered in Socrates's soul, words, and ideas—makes him unique among Socrates's interlocutors. Plato goes out of his way to emphasize the point that nobody knew Socrates the way Alcibiades did,[37] and nobody else felt despair in knowing him.

Diotima would have understood some of Alcibiades's character flaws and mistakes. On her view, the love of wisdom begins when one falls in love with Beauty, and Socrates seems to have had this effect on Alcibiades. Socrates introduced him to a beauty that eclipsed all earthly beauties (*Symposium* 218e), and Alcibiades fell in love, albeit with Socrates rather than with the Beautiful.

Some commentators have suggested that this was a character-revealing mistake: Alcibiades fell in love with the wisdom-lover instead of wisdom itself.[38] But Diotima would not have counted this against Alcibiades's potential, because it is not a mistake to be excited erotically by philosophy. According to Diotima, philosophy *is* love. Alcibiades's mistake was to confuse his *erōs* for the Beautiful, which Socrates awakened in him, with *erōs* for Socrates the individual. But this kind of mistake was to be *expected*,

---

[37] Alcibiades tells us about Socrates's irony, wisdom, courage, endurance, self-control, uniqueness, erotic pedagogy, transformative beauty, and disdain for wealth, as well as his otherworldly powers of concentration and indifference to the effects of hunger, cold, wine, sleep, and physical *erōs*. As de Jacqueline de Romilly says, "In all of Plato's works, no text is more personal, or more profound, on the subject of the master" (de Romilly, *The Life of Alcibiades*, 11). Alcibiades's speech in the *Symposium* is second only to Plato's *Apology of Socrates* as a source of biographical information about the historical Socrates (Thomas C. Brickhouse and Nicholas D. Smith, *Plato's Socrates* [Cambridge: Cambridge University Press, 1994], 105 n. 5). See also: A. R. Lacey, "Our Knowledge of Socrates," in Gregory Vlastos, ed., *The Philosophy of Socrates: A Collection of Critical Essays* [Garden City, NY: Anchor Books, 1971], 43; Gregory Vlastos, *Socrates: Ironist and Moral Philosopher* [Ithaca, NY: Cornell University Press, 1991], 35; William Prior, "The Portrait of Socrates in Plato's *Symposium*," *Oxford Studies in Ancient Philosophy* 31 (2006): 161-63; and de Romilly, *The Life of Alcibiades*, 10.

[38] Ferrari, "Platonic Love," 262.

A Contest Between Two Lives

because Alcibiades was not fully advanced on Diotima's ladder. He had only taken the first few steps. He was "beside himself" with *erōs*, but his experience was "beyond his comprehension" (*Phaedrus* 250a), and so he did not see that his attraction to Socrates was really about his desire for the Good.

For related reasons, Alcibiades should not be faulted for trying to enter into a pederastic relationship with Socrates. He was not trying to "prostitute himself," as Blundell suggests; he was acting on a desire for moral improvement, an admirable motivation, in a culture where older men regularly offered wisdom to boys in exchange for sexual gratification, and the wisest man in Greece (*Apology* 21ab) flirted with him[39]: "what I thought at the time was that what he really wanted was *me*, and that seemed to me the luckiest coincidence: all I had to do was to let him have his way with me, and he would teach me everything he knew" (*Symposium* 217a). Alcibiades was wrong about this; Socrates was only pretending to have a sexual interest in him for pedagogical purposes.[40] But if Socrates intended for Alcibiades to fall in love with him as a first step toward falling in love with wisdom, how can we blame Alcibiades for taking the bait? In that case, he was merely doing what Socrates wanted him to do. Alcibiades wanted to acquire wisdom, and he thought Socrates was his golden ticket.

Plato goes out of his way to distinguish Alcibiades from Socrates's other interlocutors, and Alcibiades's most incriminating

---

[39] Jonathan Lear, *Open Minded: Working out the Logic of the Soul* (Cambridge: Harvard University Press, 1998), 161, describes Socrates as acting like "the camp queen" in the *Symposium*.

[40] Pierre Hadot calls this Socrates's "erotic irony," the aim of which, according to Kierkegaard, was to draw the Athenian youth into philosophy by causing them to fall in love. See Pierre Hadot, *Philosophy as a Way of Life: Spiritual Exercises from Socrates to Foucault* (Malden, MA: Blackwell, 1995), 159. See also the account provided by Kierkegaard, *The Concept of Irony, with Continual Reference to Socrates*, translated by H. V. Hong and Edna H. Hong (Pinceton, NJ: Princeton University Press), 213. Socrates calls himself Alcibiades's first, longest, and only true lover (*Alcibiades I* 103a, 104c, 119c, 131e, and 132a). He doesn't profess love to anyone else in the dialogues. Cf. *Gorgias* 481d.

mistake, his attempt to seduce Socrates and exchange his body for wisdom, is best seen as *understandable* confusion in his ascent up Diotima's ladder: he could not yet recognize the difference between wisdom and the wisdom-lover, and he had grown up in a culture that encouraged him to commoditize his beauty and acquire power. This last point explains the main weakness in the case against Alcibiades—it sees his disordered soul as evidence against his potential for philosophy instead of understanding it as a symbol of Athenian social and political dysfunction. We should not see Alcibiades as an example of what philosophy "is not"; he is an image of what philosophy could have been but wasn't in fifth-century Athens. If he is the referent in *Republic* 494c, as commentators have suspected since Plutarch in the first century CE, he is a symptom of the city's corruption and an example of how the democracy squandered its greatest talents and undermined itself.[41]

Plato's argument in this part of *Republic* VI (487e-500b) explains why philosophers are ignored—society is organized in a way that makes it difficult for people to listen to them (*Republic* 487e-489d), and philosophers are likely to be put to death for what they say (*Republic* 488c)—and it argues that those who are born with the philosophic *phusis* are corrupted by the "education" they receive from the city (*Republic* 489d-495c), especially in mass gatherings of people (*Republic* 492b-c). Alcibiades's speech in the *Symposium* (i) confirms that he had philosophical potential—arguably more than any other interlocutor—and (ii) shows that he struggled with living up to his aspirations because of his corrupted *erōs*; it (iii) suggests that his *erōs* was corrupted by the *dēmos*, and

---

[41] Many scholars have interpreted Plato's account of the philosophical *phusis* in the *Republic* as being based on the life of Alcibiades and his relationship with Socrates. 1902. James Adam, *The Republic of Plato*, 2 vols (Cambridge: Cambridge University Press), 25, notes that Plutarch draws upon Plato in developing his own account of Alcibiades's squandered talents (Plutarch, *Life of Alcibiades* 4.1). See also Desmond P. Lee, *Plato: The Republic* (London: Penguin Books), 290; David Gribble, *Alcibiades and Athens*, 219; C.C.W. Taylor, *Plato's Protagoras* (Oxford: Clarendon Press, 1976), 64; and Stanley Rosen *Plato's Republic*, 237-41.

A Contest Between Two Lives

(iv) it connects Socrates's relationship with Alcibiades to the trial: just as the *Gorgias* warns, Socrates is put to death for trying to educate people to virtue in a city whose way of life had no tolerance for him (*Gorgias* 521e-522c).

III. Socrates's Losing *Agōn* with the City

Thucydides is famous for saying that the Peloponnesian War revealed something essential about the human condition (Thucydides 1.22). Plato seems to have agreed with his general point about the enduring significance of fifth-century Greek politics, although for him this had less to do with the specifics of the War itself and more to do with the conditions that gave rise to it: the psychology and politics of democratic Athens, the ideology of power and *pleonexia*, and the ineluctable limits of philosophy in the *polis*-as-it-is.[42] Plato's representation of Alcibiades is a good illustration of this difference. Thucydides gives us an idea of how he spoke in the Assembly, why he was thought to be an aspiring tyrant, and how he betrayed his city during the Sicilian Expedition. Plato is more interested in how Alcibiades lived his private life and how he felt torn between politics and philosophy. For Plato, this inner conflict in Alcibiades reflects a larger struggle in the city, the *agōn* between two lives that Socrates fights and loses in the souls of *many* promising young men in Athens.

---

[42] Thucydides was also interested in the causes of the war, but he focuses on material conditions, such as the power differences between cities, and a theory of human nature that focused on fear, ambition, and self-interest (1.76). Hornblower speculates that Thucydides knew Socrates (*Thucydides*, 55). At the very least, Plato seems to have been influenced by Thucydides, either through Socrates or through carefully studying Thucydides's work. Rutherford, *The Art of Plato*, 66-68, sees connections between Plato and Thucydides regarding their criticisms of democracy, their depictions of demagogues, their characterizations of Alcibiades, their analyses of "imperial expansion and political-moral decline, and the ideology of power as expressed by Callicles and Thrasymachus in Plato and by the Athenians at Sparta and Melos in Thucydides." Their primary disagreement is in their assessment of Pericles's leadership. Cf. S. Schein, "Alcibiades and the Politics of Misguided Love," 158-67; Steven Forde, *The Ambition to Rule*, 10, 30; de Romilly, *The Life of Alcibiades*, 188; and D. Gribble, *Alcibiades and Athens*, 236.

Mark Ralkowski

In several of his dialogues, but especially in the *Gorgias, Symposium,* and *Alcibiades I,* Plato presents Socrates as a critic of culture who offered the youth of Athens a choice between two lives: the philosophical life and the political life. In Platonic existentialism, "the task of selfhood" begins with this choice. Plato's own life was shaped by it (*Seventh Letter* 326), and so was Alcibiades's: he was torn between two intractable desires—one for Socrates and the philosophical life, the other for politics and the *erōs* of and for the *dēmos*—as well as the corrupt *polis* education and *akrasia* that lead him to choose politics over philosophy against his better judgment.

The young Alcibiades chose Socrates and the philosophical life (*Alcibiades I* 135b-e), but the older Alcibiades revealed that he could not maintain his commitments (*Symposium* 216b). In the *Republic* (490e-500b) and *Gorgias* (481b-527e), Plato explains that the city was responsible for redirecting men away from philosophy and back toward the norms of Athenian *polis* culture. From the city's perspective, philosophy appears to be unmanly and useless, or even dangerous (*Gorgias* 485c, *Republic* 487c-d). And so, as Alcibiades was pulled back into the culture of empire building and unchecked ambition, he took on the "character of the regime" (*Gorgias* 513a-c), abandoned Socrates, and ended up embodying all of the vices of Athenian imperialism and narrow self-interest. For Plato, Alcibiades *is* Athens; his flaws are the city's flaws. That is what shows up at the end of the *Symposium*: Alcibiades doesn't interrupt Socrates and put him on trial for *hubris* and *hyperhania* (*Symposium* 219c-d); the city does, acting through Alcibiades. This moment foreshadows the actual trial of Athens in 399 BCE[43] *and also condemns* the city as the true corruptor of men like Alcibiades: he shows up late after drinking in the city with the *"agora* crowd"[44]; he missed the philosophical conversation *because the city got to him first.*

---

[43] Rosen, *Plato's Symposium,* 308.
[44] In the *Protagoras,* Plato associates flute girls with "the second-rate drinking parties of the agora crowd" (347c-348b), and so it appears that Alcibiades is late to Agathon's symposium because he has been attending a very different kind of party with a very different kind of crowd.

A Contest Between Two Lives

In 399 BCE, Socrates's accusers had grouped him with the sophists and argued that the sophists corrupted the youth. But the true corruptors of men like Alcibiades are the people who accuse the sophists, i.e., the citizens of the democracy (*Republic* 492a-b). The excitement of the *dēmos* stole Alcibiades's *erōs* away from philosophy (*Republic* 492c), just as Socrates worried it would (*Alcibiades I* 131e), and just as one would expect under the "present constitutions" of fifth-century BCE Greece (*Republic* 497b-c). There was little hope for Alcibiades to be educated to virtue in democratic Athens because the "contrary education" he received from the *dēmos* was all but impossible to counteract (*Republic* 492e). Alcibiades's dissolute life of self-aggrandizement and reckless imperial ambitions was the outcome Plato expected from his city's education. If anything about this is surprising, it is that Alcibiades made as much progress as he did. Alcibiades's critics fail to appreciate this because they do not look for the *causes* of his character flaws[45], all of which were part and parcel of the Athenian *polis* culture. In such an environment, "the philosophic nature fails to develop its full power and declines into a different character" (*Republic* 497b-c).

Thucydides saw human nature on display in the events of the War: the speeches, the battles, the conservatism of the Spartans, and the extraordinary daring of the Athenians. And he thought the decisive moment in the War was the death of Pericles, after which the empire lost its way, becoming harsher and more imprudent, more prone to strategic mistakes and overreaching. But until that time, Athens had been a site of human flourishing, in possession of a seductively brilliant character that he identifies with virtue and civic duty itself (Thucydides 2.43). It was Pericles's successors who were responsible for Athenian decline; they were the ones who abandoned Periclean principles and policy; if they had followed his advice to be moderate, they could have maintained the empire.[46]

---

[45] For an example of this, see Reeve, "A Study in Violets," 141.
[46] de Romilly, *The Life of Alcibiades*, 188.

Plato rejects Thucydides's adulation of Pericles and instead groups him with Themistocles, Cimon, and Miltiades as one of the founding fathers of Athenian vice. Plato saw human nature on display in the events of the war, just as Thucydides did, but his theory of human nature ran deeper. "The Four" were the original "true corruptors" of the youth because they created the empire whose principles organized the city *against philosophy*, making it impossible for Socrates to practice the "true political craft" and improve the souls of Athenians. Alcibiades embodies this problem more than any other character because he is represented as a person who had unusual philosophical insight and failed anyway. This is the real tragedy of the *Symposium*[47]: in the *polis*-as-it-is, there is an inevitable *agōn* between philosophy and society that philosophy cannot hope to win.

---

[47] Cf. Debra Nails, "Tragedy off Stage," in Lesher, Nails, and Sheffield, eds, *Plato's Symposium*, 179-207.

Stamatia Dova[1]
On *Philogymnastia* and its Cognates in Plato

The purpose of this paper is to examine Plato's terminology on love of exercise (φιλογυμναστία) and its significance for the balance between γυμναστική (athletics) and μουσική (music and liberal arts) in the context of philosophical pursuit. Through close readings of all relevant passages, I argue that Plato views fondness of exercise as potentially detrimental to philosophy and thereby subject to containment in the context of curricular design, character formation, and citizen training. While he prioritizes the cultivation of the soul,[2] and to that end emphasizes character formation through a liberal arts education, Plato does not fail to acknowledge the contribution of exercise toward the goal of sound personhood. His lexical choices, however, indicate a greater preoccupation with love of athletics than love of liberal arts: out of 1,053 compounds with the prefix φιλο-, thirteen pertain to φιλογυμναστία and its cognates, and only two to the adjective φιλόμουσος, η, ον, "loving music and the liberal arts," (*Phaedrus* 259b5, *Republic* 548e5).

As is often the case, examining words is the beginning of knowledge, to quote Antisthenes.[3] How does Plato refer to a

---

[1] Stamatia Dova is Professor of Classics and Greek Studies at Hellenic College in Brookline, Massachusetts, and the Associate in Hellenic Literature and Language at the Center for Hellenic Studies in Washington, D.C. Her books include *Greek Heroes in and out of Hades* (Rowman & Littlefield, 2012) and *The Poetics of Failure in Ancient Greece* (Routledge, 2020). Many thanks are owed to Heather Reid for her encouragement and feedback.

[2] According to Protagoras (*Protagoras* 326b6-c3), physical education aims at placing bodily fitness in the service of a sound mind, so that pupils may respond adequately, as citizens, to the future challenges of war and other similar duties. In the *Republic* (403d2-6), Socrates states that a fit body cannot counteract a deficient soul, while he considers the opposite quite possible. See Heather L. Reid, "Sport and Moral Education in Plato's *Republic*," *Journal of the Philosophy of Sport* 34:2 (2007): 160-75.

[3] "ἀρχὴ παιδεύσεως ἡ τῶν ὀνομάτων ἐπίσκεψις," fr. 38.9, F. D. Caizzi, *Antisthenis fragmenta* (Milan: Istituto Editoriale Gisalpino, 1966), 29-59.

person's love of exercise? His choice of terms is rather obvious, the verb φιλογυμναστέω, -ῶ, and its cognates, the action noun φιλογυμναστία (ἡ), the agent noun φιλογυμναστής (ὁ), and the adjective φιλογυμναστικός, ή, όν, all derived from the combination of the prefix φιλο-, "fond of" and cognates of the verb γυμνάζω, "I train naked."[4] It should be noted, however, that some of these terms are also available in a simpler form, without the prefix φιλο-; in those instances too, they are used to denote fondness of or skill in exercise. It is also interesting that while γυμνάζω and its cognates occur 120 times in the Platonic corpus, we have only thirteen attestations of φιλογυμναστέω, -ῶ and its cognates.[5] Therefore, we may well suppose that the prefix φιλο- is key to Plato's lexical choice, which, in turn, expresses his authorial intention to distinguish between "exercising" and "loving to exercise." At the same time, the difference between the two notions invites us to examine the context of the latter's attestations.

In Plato's *Symposium*, Pausanias discusses the laws of various cities regarding homoerotic relationships. After pointing out that the consummation of such a relationship "is considered shameful"

---

[4] Lidell-Scott-Jones, *Lexicon*. On athletic nudity in archaic and classical Greece, see P. Christesen, "Athletics and Social Order in Sparta in the Classical Period," *Classical Antiquity* 312 (2012): 193-255, esp. 241-246; Thomas F. Scanlon, *Eros and Greek Athletics* (Oxford: Oxford University Press, 2002), 211-212.

[5] Besides Plato, attestations of this group of words during the classical period are limited to the Hippocratic Corpus (φιλογυμνασταί τε καὶ φιλόπονοι, "lovers of exercise and toil," *Airs, Waters, and Places*, 1.20), Aristotle, (φιλογυμναστικαὶ [ἕξεις], "habitual fondness of exercise," *Eudemian Ethics* 1222a31), and Anaximenes (οἷον ἐκ τοῦ φιλογυμναστεῖν τὸ σῶμα ὑγιαίνειν, "the body enjoys good health as a result of practicing φιλογυμναστία," *Art of Rhetoric*, 3.3.1). The term φιλογυμναστία itself does not appear outside Plato with the exception of one attestation in the 6th century CE commentary on Plato's *Alcibiades* by Olympiodorus (166.20). Its antonym, ἀγυμναστία, does not occur in Plato and has only two attestations in extant Greek literature, one in Galen (*On the Natural Faculties* 5.91.3) and one in Porphyry (*On Abstinence* 1.36.1). The adjective ἀγύμναστος, "untrained," however, occurs seven times in the Platonic corpus, and is used mostly metaphorically, in the context of proficiency in virtue or lack thereof.

On Philogymnastia *and its Cognates in Plato*

(αἰσχϱὸν νενόμισται, 182b6-7) among the Ionians as well as "all those living under barbarian rule" (ὅσοι ὑπὸ βαϱβάϱοις οἰκοῦσιν, 182b7), he proceeds to strengthen his argument with an interesting commentary:

> τοῖς γὰϱ βαϱβάϱοις διὰ τὰς τυϱαννίδας αἰσχϱὸν τοῦτό γε καὶ ἥ γε φιλοσοφία καὶ ἡ φιλογυμναστία· οὐ γὰϱ οἶμαι συμφέϱει τοῖς ἄϱχουσι φϱονήματα μεγάλα ἐγγίγνεσθαι τῶν ἀϱχομένων, οὐδὲ φιλίας ἰσχυϱὰς καὶ κοινωνίας, ὃ δὴ μάλιστα φιλεῖ τά τε ἄλλα πάντα καὶ ὁ ἔϱως ἐμποιεῖν.[6]

> For in the eyes of the barbarians, on account of the despotic rule they live under, this [homoerotic love] as well as philosophy and love of exercising are shameful [αἰσχϱόν]. Clearly, it is not in the despots' best interests, if their subjects think lofty thoughts or form strong friendships and associations, which these activities, and especially [homoerotic] love, are likely to produce. (*Symposium* 182b7-c4)

According to Pausanias, states that approve of homosexuality are also unafraid of their citizens' free thinking and unhindered association with peers. Using political attitudes towards homosexuality as a criterion, Pausanias highlights the distinction between civic conduct governed by democratic ethos versus submission to a tyrannical regime (τυϱαννίς). Last but not least, Pausanias offers the example of the tyrannicides Harmodios and Aristogeiton as further (and definitive) evidence for the incompatibility of τυϱαννίς with powerful comradeship inspired by homoerotic love:

> ἔϱγῳ δὲ τοῦτο ἔμαθον καὶ οἱ ἐνθάδε τύϱαννοι· ὁ γὰϱ Ἀϱιστογείτονος ἔϱως καὶ ἡ Ἁϱμοδίου φιλία βέβαιος γενομένη κατέλυσεν αὐτῶν τὴν ἀϱχήν. οὕτως οὗ μὲν αἰσχϱὸν ἐτέθη χαϱίζεσθαι ἐϱασταῖς, κακίᾳ τῶν

---

[6] The text of Plato is quoted from John Burnet, *Platonis Opera* (Oxford: Clarendon Press, 1968 [1903]). All translations are my own.

θεμένων κεῖται, τῶν μὲν ἀρχόντων πλεονεξίᾳ, τῶν δὲ ἀρχομένων ἀνανδρίᾳ· οὗ δὲ καλὸν ἁπλῶς ἐνομίσθη, διὰ τὴν τῶν θεμένων τῆς ψυχῆς ἀργίαν.

And our tyrants here [in Athens] learned this lesson first hand; because it was Aristogeiton's love as well as Harmodios's reciprocal affection [φιλία], as this affection grew steadfast and strong, that overthrew the dictators. Thus, in places where the convention that it is shameful to please one's lover was established, it did so as a result of the moral deficiency [κακίᾳ] of its instigators, the greed of the rulers and the cowardice of the ruled. And in places where it became customary simply as something noble [καλόν], it happened so on account of the moral indolence [ἀργία τῆς ψυχῆς] of those who established it. (*Symposium* 182c4-d4)

We can only expect that Pausanias's analysis of responses to homosexuality is applicable to φιλοσοφία and φιλογυμναστία as well,[7] both of which he considers as cultural practices that pose equally serious threats to autocracy. As such, they are congruous with democracy,[8] and by extension, Hellenicity. Though arguably an Athenian construct, the connection between democracy and Hellenicity is enhanced by athletics, and especially by the role of the gymnasium in empowering citizens. Moreover, the pursuit of athletic excellence is showcased as a Panhellenic cultural trait in Herodotus, who employs the olive wreath awarded at the

---

[7] As Scanlon, *Eros and Greek Athletics*, 268 notes, "political order and freedom issue directly from a spirit of eros, taken in the widest sense, which is fostered in the gymnasium."

[8] Athenaeus (13.79.2) points out the hostile attitude of tyrants like Polycrates of Samos towards athletics and the homoerotic relationships—and opposition to tyranny—they are likely to foster. On the connection between sport and democratization in sixth and fifth century BCE Greece, see Paul Christesen, *Sport and Democracy in the Ancient and Modern Worlds* (New York: Cambridge University Press, 2012), 164-183. Cf. also Scanlon *Eros and Greek Athletics*, 264-269.

Olympics to explicate the difference between Greeks and Persians.[9]

In the context of Pausanias's speech in Plato's *Symposium*, the adjective "barbarian" is a synonym for "Persian," further evoking the confrontation between Athenians and Persians during the early fifth century BCE. With a dramatic date of composition placed at 416 BCE,[10] the year of Agathon's first drama victory, the *Symposium* looks back at a time when there was still hope for Athenian democracy and its leadership of the Greek world. The dialogue's actual date of composition, however, indicates otherwise, since by 385 BCE the lofty thoughts of free citizens fond of exercise and philosophy might have lost their glamour. Alcibiades's responsibility for this development is well known to all audiences of the *Symposium*, external and internal, even though his characterization in the dialogue does not echo any sentiments of resentment or disapproval over his subsequent conduct.[11] Well-known to Thucydides, Alcibiades's victories at the chariot race in the 416 Olympics,[12] and the way he tried to co-opt them for his self-promotion and election as general of the Sicilian expedition, bespeak the potentially uneasy relationship between sport and democracy. Alcibiades did not hesitate to combine his (aristocratic) version of φιλογυμναστία with his immense wealth and use it for political purposes while competing in a sport that bestowed on the victor considerable prestige without requiring

---

[9] In Herodotus's *Histories* (8.26.3), the Persian nobleman Tritantaechmes is astonished to hear that the Greeks compete at the Olympics for a wreath and not money. Cf. Donald Kyle, "Pan-Hellenism and Particularism: Herodotus on Sport, Greekness, Piety and War," *The International Journal of the History of Sport* 26:2 (2009): 183-211, 196-197; Truesdell Brown, "Herodotus's Views on Athletics," *The Ancient World* 7:1 (1983): 17-29, 28.

[10] On the dialogue's date of composition, see Kenneth Dover, *Plato: Symposium*. (Cambridge: Cambridge University Press, 1980), 10.

[11] Cf. Dover, *Plato: Symposium,* 164, and Ralkowski's essay in this volume.

[12] On the significance of Alcibiades's victories at the chariot race in the 416 Olympics see David Gribble, "Alcibiades at the Olympics: Performance, Politics, and Civic Ideology," *The Classical Quarterly* 62:1 (2012): 45-71.

any personal athletic engagement (ancient chariot victories went to the horse owners).

Therefore, we may wonder if the *Symposium* allows for an implicit reference to all that could—and did—go wrong with athletics as a means of political manipulation. As Alcibiades enters the banquet intoxicated, boisterous (212d3-e2), and adorned with victory ribbons (212e2),[13] we are given a glimpse into his world of self-satisfied revelry with all its disconcerting connotations of vanity and excess. One may also ask whether his demeanor is a possible result of the φιλογυμναστία and φιλοσοφία that Pausanias endorsed as Hellenic values a few moments earlier.

Yet, the love of exercising that fosters the kind of male camaraderie and civic ethos exemplified by Harmodios and Aristogeiton has nothing to do with ostentatious displays of wealth and power at the Olympics like the ones Alcibiades boasts about in Thucydides (6.16.1-2), only a few months after the dramatic date of the *Symposium*. So far, the *Symposium* presents two opposite versions of φιλογυμναστία, Pausanias's and Alcibiades's, and invites us to draw our own conclusions. While the former is openly described as robust and honorable, taking us back to the time of Hellenic civic self-definition through athletics and philosophy, the latter is left to operate as a dramatic subtext, warning us about the perils of extravagance. As we will see, Diotima's reference to φιλογυμναστία from a different perspective will complete the picture. For now, we are concerned

---

[13] In addition to 212e2, ταινία is associated four times with Alcibiades in the *Symposium* (212e7, 213a6, e1, e5), as he ends up sharing his ribbons with Agathon and Socrates. Alcibiades was also said to have crowned the Athenian triremes with victory ribbons on his way back to Athens (*Ath*.2,2.88.15, Eust.*Il*.3.876.17). The word, including its cognates, does not occur anywhere else in Plato. Stephen G. Miller, *The Berkeley Plato* (Berkeley: University of California Press, 2009), 53-55 convincingly argues that the ribbons on Plato's head in the 2nd century CE bust found at Berkeley denote the fulfillment of the philosopher's mission in analogy to an athlete's victory lap (περιαγερμός), where victory ribbons would normally be collected. Furthermore, Miller poses the very interesting question whether in his statue at the Academy Plato was depicted as a gymnasiarch (γυμνασίαρχος) and not as a philosopher.

On Philogymnastia *and its Cognates in Plato*

with Pausanias's praise of φιλογυμναστία as the antidote to political oppression, which he associates with the tyranny of the Peisistratids in Athens and the Persian rule over the Ionians. Thus, by contextualizing fondness of exercise within a civic space of male interaction, Pausanias also showcases the gymnasium's (or the palaistra's) potential to nurture exemplary bonds between citizens.

Central to such bonds is the concept of reciprocal friendship (*philia*), which Socrates sets out to examine in Plato's *Lysis*. He prefaces his inquiry with the statement that he values nothing better than a good friend (211d7-e8), whom he prefers to the best horses, dogs, quails, roosters, or even all the gold of Darius (211d7-e8). Arguing that reciprocity is the defining characteristic of true friendship, Socrates groups lovers of exercise (φιλογυμνασταί, 212d7) together with horse-, quail-, dog-, wine-, and wisdom-lovers in order to demonstrate that none of these can love in return and therefore be truly dear to the people who love them. Thus, Socrates identifies a kind of "one-way philia"[14] that will eventually point out the only true friend, the ultimate good. The dialogue takes place on the festival of Hermes, on the third day of the *Anthesteria*, the festival of Dionysus (206d1-2), at a new wrestling school,[15] the palaistra of Mikkon,[16] where Socrates has a once-a-year opportunity[17] to convert talented Athenian youths to

---

[14] I borrow the phrase from Terry Penner and Christopher Rowe, *Plato's Lysis* (Cambridge: Cambridge University Press, 2005), 236. As Penner and Rowe note, it is precisely this "one-way *philia*" that may cause a person to become attached to a potentially harmful entity, 236-243.

[15] As Heather L. Reid, *Athletics and Philosophy in the Ancient World: Contests of Virtue*. (New York: Routledge, 2011), 43, notes, "in *Lysis* Socrates is going from one gymnasium (the Academy) to another (the Lyceum) when he is pulled aside into [a] new wrestling school." On the palaistra as a space of philosophical debate in Plato's *Lysis*, see Clinton DeBevoise Corcoran, *Topography and Deep Structure in Plato: The Construction of Place in the Dialogues* (Albany: State University of New York Press, 2016), 133-35; cf. also Reid, *Athletics and Philosophy*, 56-64.

[16] Miller, *Berkeley Plato*, 48.

[17] On the festival of the *Hermaia* and its significance for the dialogue, see Christopher Planeaux, "Socrates, an Unreliable Narrator? The Dramatic Setting of the *Lysis*," *Classical Philology* 96:1 (2001): 60-68, 64-66.

philosophy by proving to them that sophistry is not their true friend. Although Socrates makes only a passing reference to φιλογυμναστία as an example of powerful yet one-sided attachment, the fact that he includes it on the list along with love of horses and wine indicates that it was a well-known occurrence. From this point of view, love of athletics constitutes a potential disruption in the search for the ultimate good, as it can mislead the individual into superficial and unproductive attachments.

The term, however, recurs in the *Republic* (535d3, 549a6), where the substantive use of the adjective φιλογυμναστής is paired with that of φιλόθηρος, "hunt-lover," to denote a man with a clear propensity towards physical activity that is out of balance with intellectual pursuits. From this point of view, the φιλογυμναστής is not the product of a well-rounded education. Indeed, he poses a risk to philosophy, as he may earn it a bad name (ἀτιμία, 535c6) on account of his overall unworthiness to undertake it (οὐ κατ' ἀξίαν, 535c8). Socrates opens this section very preoccupied with the bad reputation philosophy tends to get in his days, and identifies some ways to address it:

> Πρῶτον μέν, εἶπον, φιλοπονίᾳ οὐ χωλὸν δεῖ εἶναι τὸν ἁψόμενον, τὰ μὲν ἡμίσεα φιλόπονον, τὰ δ' ἡμίσεα ἄπονον· ἔστι δὲ τοῦτο, ὅταν τις φιλογυμναστὴς μὲν καὶ φιλόθηρος ᾖ καὶ πάντα τὰ διὰ τοῦ σώματος φιλοπονῇ, φιλομαθὴς δὲ μή, μηδὲ φιλήκοος μηδὲ φιλοζητητικός, ἀλλ' ἐν πᾶσι τούτοις μισοπονῇ· χωλὸς δὲ καὶ ὁ τἀναντία τούτου μεταβεβληκὼς τὴν φιλοπονίαν.
>
> First of all, I said, the person who aspires to philosophy must not be deficient in industriousness, committed to hard work for half of the tasks, yet indifferent in respect to the rest. This is the case when someone is passionate about exercise and hunting and loves any and all toil concerning the body but is not keen on learning or eager to listen to discourse or inquisitive, displaying a clear dislike for all these pursuits. Yet the man who has turned

On Philogymnastia *and its Cognates in Plato*

himself in the opposite direction is also deficient in his industriousness. (*Republic* 535c9-d8)

Embedded within the broader discourse of who is suitable to study philosophy and why, Socrates's primary concern is that the attributes of φιλογυμναστής and φιλόθηρος may signal a person's inability to focus on philosophy. This inevitably causes the underlying rivalry between γυμναστική and μουσική to resurface, reminding us that the balance between the two is solely responsible for producing a polity that is wholly good, as opposed to one that is a mixture of good and bad, as described by Socrates in his discussion of timocracy (*Republic* 548c3-5). It only follows that the citizens of such a state have had a rather lopsided education:

[...], οὐχ ὑπὸ πειθοῦς ἀλλ' ὑπὸ βίας πεπαιδευμένοι διὰ τὸ τῆς ἀληθινῆς Μούσης τῆς μετὰ λόγων τε καὶ φιλοσοφίας ἠμεληκέναι καὶ· πρεσβυτέρως γυμναστικὴν μουσικῆς τετιμηκέναι.

[...], having been educated not by means of persuasion but by force on account of their having neglected the true Muse, the one who attends to debate and philosophy, and of their having honored physical activity considerably more than intellectual pursuits. (*Republic* 548b7-c2)

As Socrates, Adeimantus, and Glaucon conclude (548e4-549a8), the citizen of such a state would still be fond of the arts (φιλόμουσον, 548e5) and of listening to discourse (φιλήκοον, 548e5), but would lack expertise in rhetoric, and would not aspire to be elected to government based on his oratorical skills. Instead, he would pursue his ambition to hold office "because of his bravery at war and his impressive military record, also being an accomplished athlete and huntsman" (ἀλλ' ἀπὸ ἔργων τῶν τε πολεμικῶν καὶ τῶν περὶ τὰ πολεμικά, φιλογυμναστής τέ τις ὢν καὶ φιλόθηρος, 549a6-8). Interestingly, this type of φιλογυμναστής is also φιλήκοος unlike the one we saw above (535d3-5), even though neither of them is intellectually inclined and therefore suitable for philosophy.

Thus, in the context of the *Republic*, φιλογυμναστία represents an imbalance. Even in its least detrimental manifestations, it inhibits a citizen's inclination to philosophy by overemphasizing the training of the body at the expense of the cultivation of the soul. Since, however, virtues such as focus, courage, and endurance are developed primarily through exercise, vigilance is required regarding the space granted to γυμναστική in the curriculum. The most effective way of preventing a curricular takeover by φιλογυμναστία is to enable φιλομαθία, "love of learning." In fact, as Socrates and his interlocutors in the *Republic* make clear, [18] being φιλομαθής is a highly desirable characteristic, as it demonstrates a person's promise in inquiry and thereby potential for open-mindedness and self-improvement. Not surprisingly, Plato uses the word φιλομαθία and its cognates twenty times in a variety of contexts, always with positive connotations, leaving no doubt that he considers it a virtue.[19]

---

[18] In the *Republic*, particular emphasis is placed on the functions performed by the part of the soul by which we learn: unable to affect learning without proper education (411d1), the φιλομαθές (neuter singular) uses intelligence and ignorance as criteria to determine what is familiar and what is not (376b6), is one and the same with the φιλόσοφον (376b9), and they together seek the truth (581b10). A person who is kind to his near and dear has to possess both qualities by nature (376c2), while neither belongs to a youth who is particular about his studies (475c2). A φιλομαθής (masculine) is attracted to truth from a young age (485d3), strives towards the true being (490a9), and is likely to be the product of the Attic climate (435e6). Finally, φιλομαθία is to be protected from slander (499e2).

[19] In the *Phaedo*, the masculine adjective φιλομαθής, always in its substantive use, is employed to describe a person who, thanks to his love of learning, is duly concerned with the purity of the soul (67b4), enjoys exclusive communion with the gods (82c1), has the privilege to let philosophy take charge of his soul and thus see it delivered from the oppression of the flesh (82d9 and 83a1), and is brave and well-behaved (83e5). In the spurious *Epinomis*, the feminine adjective, also φιλομαθής, modifies the soul (989c2). Moreover, in *Phaedrus* 230d3 Socrates applies the adjective to himself, while in *Laws* 810a3 a pupil who loves or hates studying is denoted by the participle of the verb φιλομαθέω and its (chosen for the occasion) antonym μισέω, to hate. In *Timaeus* 90b6, φιλομαθία occupies the mind of the sound intellectual who is ready for divine and immortal thoughts.

The inherent contrast between physical and intellectual ability applies to women as well:

> Ἦ οὖν ἀνδράσι πάντα προστάξομεν, γυναικὶ δὲ οὐδέν; Καὶ πῶς; Ἀλλ' ἔστι γάρ, οἶμαι, ὡς φήσομεν, καὶ γυνὴ ἰατρική, ἡ δ' οὔ, καὶ μουσική, ἡ δ' ἄμουσος φύσει. Τί μήν; Γυμναστικὴ δ' ἄρα οὔ, οὐδὲ πολεμική, ἡ δὲ ἀπόλεμος καὶ οὐ φιλογυμναστική;

> –Shall we therefore assign all pursuits to men, and nothing to women?

> –How could we?

> –But we shall say, I believe, that one woman is by nature inclined to be a physician, and another is not, and that one is musical by nature, while another is not.

> –Certainly.

> –Can we deny, then, that one woman is athletic [γυμναστική] and warlike by nature, and another unwarlike and not fond of athletics [φιλογυμναστική]? (*Republic* 455e2-456a2)

While the argument here is centered on gender, with some of the categories transferred from male-specific contexts, is it important to note that the adjectives γυμναστική and φιλογυμναστική are used interchangeably, and that the general connection between war and athletics is maintained.[20] Still, we should bear in mind that Plato appears markedly skeptical regarding the suitability of conventional athletic training for warriors, male or female.[21]

Furthermore, the element of natural predisposition enters the picture, and no distinction is made based on gender. Just as among men, passion for exercise is a gift with which some women are

---

[20] Cf. *Laws* 830d4-e2, *Republic* 547d5-9.
[21] Cf. *Republic* 404a1-b3, where the regimen of professional athletes is seen as unsuitable for soldiers, as it is too rigid and allocates too much time in sleeping.

born and some are not. The discourse on women and exercise seems to include an inquiry on gym etiquette, exploring what is socially acceptable at the *palaistra* for women—should they exercise naked, and if yes, both young and old? (*Republic* 452a10-b2).²² The potential for ridicule in such situations is compared to the one arising from the spectacle of "old men at the gymnasia pursuing their love of exercise even though they are full of wrinkles and not agreeable to look at" (ὥσπερ τοὺς γέροντας ἐν τοῖς γυμνασίοις, ὅταν ῥυσοὶ καὶ μὴ ἡδεῖς τὴν ὄψιν ὅμως φιλογυμναστῶσιν, 452b1-2). The verb φιλογυμναστέω is featured here in its natural environment, as the gymnasium is the locus of nurturing one's φιλογυμναστία par excellence.²³ And yet, this space seems to have been claimed by younger men, still unaffected by the ravages of time in respect to both appearance and, presumably, physical strength.

Are we to view this fondness of exercise as unnatural? Is a γέρων (old man)²⁴ expected to relinquish his φιλογυμναστία of previous years for the sole purpose of not offending the aesthetics of his fellow gymnasium users? Is the verb φιλογυμναστέω indicating a foolish inclination in this context, pointing to those elderly men's inability to accept that they don't belong to the gymnasium anymore?²⁵ Decidedly not. Socrates convincingly argues that women and, by extension, older men like himself have the right to exercise at the gymnasium, despite its implicit voyeurism.²⁶ In this context, φιλογυμναστία amounts to a good

---

[22] The answer is given in 457a3-7, where it is made clear that the wives of the guardians must strip for war, as they will be dressed in virtue instead of garments.

[23] Nevertheless, as Reid, *Athletics and Philosophy,* 5,7 notes, "Plato's gymnasium was designed to train beautiful souls in strong athletic bodies, and to dedicate them to a civic ideal of unity rather than strife."

[24] On old age in Plato, see Laetitia Monteils-Laeng, "Platon et la vieillesse: idéalisation du grand âge ou valorisation de l'ancien?," *Revue de philosophie ancienne,* XXXVII, no. 2 (2019): 153-178; on perceptions of old age in classical Greece see Robert Garland, *The Greek Way of Life: From Conception to Old Age* (Ithaca, N.Y.: Cornell University Press, 1990), 242-245.

[25] See also Reid, *Athletics and Philosophy,* 64-66.

[26] See note 23 above; cf. also *Laws* 879e6-880a3.

habit that promotes wellness and as such ought to become socially acceptable for all, regardless of gender and age.

The limits of exercise are also discussed within the context of φιλογυμναστία in Plato's *Lovers*. Despite the dialogue's questionable authenticity, its four attestations of φιλογυμναστία and its cognates merit consideration, if only to complete a comprehensive overview of the term in the Platonic corpus. The dialogue takes place in the grammar school of Dionysius, where handsome pupils of distinguished Athenian families are engrossed in a lively discussion of the work of the philosopher Anaxagoras and the astronomer Oenopides.

In the *Lovers*, the contrast between action and intellect is personified in the characters of two men who also happen to be competing for the affections of the same youth (ἀντεραστής, 132c5). One of them has been brought up in the liberal arts (περὶ μουσικὴν διατετριφώς, 132d1-2), while the other in athletic training (περὶ γυμναστικήν, 132d2). Socrates first attempts a conversation with the athlete of the pair, but ends up talking to his rival, an articulate young man with a clear predilection for philosophy. During his brief exchange with the athlete, whose take on the pupils' pursuits evokes Aristophanes's mockery of Socrates in the *Clouds* (132b8-10),[27] Socrates establishes his interlocutor's deep dislike for philosophy. It is the aspiring philosopher, however, who answers Socrates's question whether or not philosophy is a shameful thing, also taking the opportunity in the meantime to disparage his rival for his unrefined way of life: all he has been doing in his life is to practice the neck-hold, satisfy his hunger, and sleep (τραχηλιζόμενος καὶ ἐμπιπλάμενος καὶ καθεύδων πάντα τὸν βίον διατετέλεκεν, 132c8-9).

The next step is to reformulate the question, inquiring whether philosophy is not only a noble (καλόν, 133d1) but also a morally good (ἀγαθόν, 133d2) thing.[28] Receiving immediate

---

[27] Aristophanes, *Clouds*, 225-234.
[28] While both adjectives can mean "morally good," καλός, ή, όν has additional connotations of beauty; cf. Lidell-Scott-Jones, *Lexicon*.

confirmation, Socrates proceeds to ask the same question about love of exercise:

οἷον φιλογυμναστίαν οὐ μόνον ἡγῇ καλὸν εἶναι, ἀλλὰ καὶ ἀγαθόν; ἢ οὔ;

For example, do you consider the passion for athletics to be not only noble, but also morally good? Or not? (*Lovers* 133d6-7)

The inquiry goes on to explore the notion of measure in both athletics and philosophy. The aspiring philosopher fails to see any difference between πολυπονία,[29] much labor (133e3), and φιλογυμναστία, just as he considers πολυμαθία (ample knowledge, 133e5) to be one and the same with φιλοσοφία.[30] The (rather uneasy) duality φιλογυμναστία=πολυπονία versus φιλοσοφία=πολυμαθία inevitably leads to the *raison d' être* of φιλογυμναστία, the ultimate goal of exercise-lovers (τοὺς φιλογυμναστοῦντας, 133e6): "that which will get them into good bodily condition" (ὅτι ποιήσει αὐτοὺς εὖ ἔχειν τὸ σῶμα, 133e7-8). Of course, the phrase εὖ ἔχειν evokes the concept of εὐεξία, "good health" or "vigor," which was also "a kind of physique competition"[31] in classical and post-classical Greece.[32]

Nevertheless, Socrates seeks also an expert opinion, inviting the athlete back into the inquiry. This time he refers to him as ὁ

---

[29] The term occurs only here in Plato; the adjective πολύπονος, ον is also employed only once (*Laws* 633b9-c1), to modify the extreme hardship involved in the Lacedaemonian practice of *krupteia*.

[30] See also n. 37 below.

[31] H.W. Pleket and R.S. Stroud, "SEG-41-1749. Athletics. The Contests of εὐεξία, εὐταξία, φιλοπονία," *Supplementum Epigraphicum Graecum*, 2009.

[32] For a discussion of and epigraphic evidence on εὐεξία see P.L. Gauthier, "La Loi Gymnasiarchique de Beroia" (Athènes: Centre de Recherches de l'Antiquité Grecque et Romaine, 1993), 102-05; Nigel B. Crowther, "*Euexia, Eutaxia, Philoponia*: Three Contests of the Greek Gymnasium," *Zeitschrift Für Papyrologie Und Epigraphik* 85 (1991): 301-04 and "Male 'Beauty' Contests in Greece: The *Euandria* and *Euexia*," *L' Antiquité Classique* 54:1 (1985): 285-91. Along with εὐεξία, πολυπονία and [πολυμ]αθία, "much learning," were subjects of competition in ancient Greece (Crowther, *Euexia*, 301-04). Cf. also Scanlon, *Eros and Greek Athletics*, 205, 402 n. 24.

On Philogymnastia *and its Cognates in Plato*

φιλογυμναστής (134a3-4), making clear that he needs his support in light of his experience in athletics (διὰ τὴν ἐμπειρίαν τῆς γυμναστικῆς, 134a4). Indeed, the φιλογυμναστής hurries to endorse Socrates's point, agreeing that moderate exercise is best for the body (134c5-6), and takes advantage of the opportunity to point out, rather indelicately, his rival's softness, ignorance of all things sportive, and intellectual parity with a pig (134a9-b2). As φιλοσοφία and φιλογυμναστία become stepping stones toward the intended conclusion in favor of measure, it becomes evident that the *Lovers* is designed to host a schematic set of polarities. It is not a coincidence, however, that the inception of this pursuit is mediated by the pair μουσική-γυμναστική, the second of which tends to be confused with φιλογυμναστία, a notion, in turn, confused with πολυπονία. Yet πολυπονία may cause harm, as it is too much of a good thing. In this case, φιλογυμναστία too can be bad for one, and especially for a citizen of democratic Athens, who, nevertheless, is meant to be brought up with it. It would seem that we are going around in circles.

And, yet, since its inception in classical Greece, this argument has remained cyclical to a considerable degree. How much φιλογυμναστία is good for a pupil? For a citizen-soldier? For the state itself? Can love of sport get out of hand and stop contributing to the athlete's εὐεξία altogether? Is εὐεξία its own reward, or merely a step in the process of citizen training?[33] These questions form part of a broader *Problematik*, which seemed to preoccupy Athenian public discourse even before Plato's time. For example, in Pericles's Funeral Oration (Thucydides 2.35-46), the ability to keep sophistication within the limits of frugality and cultural enrichment and away from self-indulgence is praised as one of Athens' virtues:

Φιλοκαλοῦμέν τε γὰρ μετ' εὐτελείας καὶ φιλοσοφοῦμεν ἄνευ μαλακίας·

---

[33] As Scanlon, *Eros and Greek Athletics*, 210, notes, in ancient Greek athletics "[b]eauty was a highly desired and admired by-product of athletic pursuits, not an end in itself."

> For we indeed embrace beauty with thriftiness, and we pursue philosophy without becoming decadent.
> (Thucydides 2.40.1.1-2)

The speech constituted the ultimate praise for Athenian democracy, as well as its swan song. While Plato could not possibly have a personal recollection of the event, its cultural echo must have resonated with his generation of Athenians, the citizen-soldiers who witnessed the abysmal decline of the Athenian Empire and lived through its consequences.

Out of the four structural concepts of this sentence, only three occur in Plato: φιλοσοφία, whose attestations are understandably abundant (147 of the noun, 68 of the verb, and 136 of other cognates), εὐτέλεια (*Laws* 650b3, where it means "cheapness"), and μαλακία, "moral weakness" (*Laws* 836e1, *Republic* 398e6) or "softness" (*Gorgias* 410b4, *Republic* 410d1). The last occurrence is of particular interest for this discussion, as it showcases the antithesis between the adjectives ἄγριος, α, ον, "harsh," and μαλακός, ή, όν, a cognate of μαλακία, in the context of exercise:

> Ἔγωγε, ἔφη· ὅτι οἱ μὲν γυμναστικῇ ἀκράτῳ χρησάμενοι ἀγριώτεροι τοῦ δέοντος ἀποβαίνουσιν, οἱ δὲ μουσικῇ μαλακώτεροι αὖ γίγνονται ἢ ὡς κάλλιον αὐτοῖς.
>
> Indeed, he said [Glaucon speaking]. You mean that they who focus exclusively on physical training turn out harsher than necessary, while those who care only about music and the liberal arts become softer than is good for them. (*Republic* 410d3-5)

Thus, the balance between μουσική and γυμναστική, no matter how difficult to achieve, is credited with creating the proper mindset for responsible citizens.[34] Ideally, the role of φιλογυμναστία would be to contribute towards this balance by mitigating excessive attachment to music. Nevertheless, in the

---

[34] See also Reid, "Sport and Moral Education," 162-64.

absence of μουσική, φιλογυμναστία can take over and become its own end, potentially leading to obsession with exercise.

To negotiate the polarities between obsession with and dislike for exercise we need to return to Diotima's speech on love in the *Symposium*. Having explicated Eros's parentage and resultant characteristics, the mysterious priestess from Mantineia also sheds light on its multifaceted nature:

> τὸ μὲν κεφάλαιόν ἐστι πᾶσα ἡ τῶν ἀγαθῶν ἐπιθυμία καὶ τοῦ εὐδαιμονεῖν ὁ μέγιστός τε καὶ δολερὸς ἔρως παντί· ἀλλ' οἱ μὲν ἄλλῃ τρεπόμενοι πολλαχῇ ἐπ' αὐτόν, ἢ κατὰ χρηματισμὸν ἢ κατὰ φιλογυμναστίαν ἢ κατὰ φιλοσοφίαν, οὔτε ἐρᾶν καλοῦνται οὔτε ἐρασταί, οἱ δὲ κατὰ ἕν τι εἶδος ἰόντες τε καὶ ἐσπουδακότες τὸ τοῦ ὅλου ὄνομα ἴσχουσιν, ἔρωτά τε καὶ ἐρᾶν καὶ ἐρασταί.

> In general, the desire, in any form, for good things in life and happiness is love [ἔρως], most powerful and potentially treacherous for everyone; but the people who pursue it in various ways, including money-making, fondness of exercise, and philosophy, they are not called lovers, nor it is said of them that they are in love. However, those who seek one kind of love and focus on it, claim ownership of the entire group of words, love, and loving, and lovers. (*Symposium* 205d1-8)

By making φιλογυμναστία just another avenue towards personal fulfillment, Diotima also attributes to it the potential to bring happiness. As with all endeavors, it should be contained within the pursuit of happiness, we may assume, but Diotima is not concerned with that. She is mostly interested in identifying the ways in which love manifests itself in it, and, during this process, she ranks it next to philosophy, just as Pausanias had done earlier on in the dialogue. Therefore, φιλογυμναστία can be a good thing, just as its prefix φιλο- can indicate fruitful engagement with a person, object, or activity. This ability to engage bespeaks focus and commitment, both of which are attributes of ἔρως and prerequisites for the pursuit of the Good.

As in the case of poetry, Plato articulates two different views regarding the usefulness of love for exercise. In the third book of the *Republic* (386c3-7), Socrates censures the famous passage from *Odyssey* 11 in which the shade of Achilles declares that he "would prefer to be the hired worker of a serf with little property than rule over all of the dead" (489-91), thereby implying that he regrets his heroic death. In the seventh book of the *Republic* (516c7-e3), however, Socrates uses the same passage to express the former prisoner's aversion to the cave. As I have argued elsewhere,[35] eventually Socrates acknowledges the passage's depth and complexity by employing it to argue for the importance of education. Similarly, the *Symposium* looks at φιλογυμναστία as equal to φιλοσοφία, while the *Republic* and *Lysis* do not.

This pride of place, so to speak, that is granted to φιλογυμναστία is not accidental, as we see in the *Protagoras*. There, the question whether φιλογυμναστία or φιλοσοφία is the key to a successful state is examined within the framework of the antagonism between the civic ideologies of Athens and Sparta.[36] Despite appearances, Protagoras claims, the Spartan *modus operandi* relies on love of wisdom, not of exercise:

> γνοῖτε δ' ἂν ὅτι ἐγὼ ταῦτα ἀληθῆ λέγω καὶ Λακεδαιμόνιοι πρὸς φιλοσοφίαν καὶ λόγους ἄριστα πεπαίδευνται, ὧδε· εἰ γὰρ ἐθέλει τις Λακεδαιμονίων τῷ φαυλοτάτῳ συγγενέσθαι, τὰ μὲν πολλὰ ἐν τοῖς λόγοις εὑρήσει αὐτὸν φαῦλόν τινα φαινόμενον, ἔπειτα, ὅπου ἂν τύχῃ τῶν λεγομένων, ἐνέβαλεν ῥῆμα ἄξιον λόγου βραχὺ καὶ συνεστραμμένον ὥσπερ δεινὸς ἀκοντιστής, ὥστε φαίνεσθαι τὸν προσδιαλεγόμενον παιδὸς μηδὲν βελτίω. τοῦτο οὖν αὐτὸ καὶ τῶν νῦν εἰσὶν οἳ κατανενοήκασι καὶ τῶν πάλαι, ὅτι τὸ λακωνίζειν πολὺ μᾶλλόν ἐστιν φιλοσοφεῖν ἢ φιλογυμναστεῖν, εἰδότες

---

[35] Stamatia Dova, *Greek Heroes in and out of Hades* (Lanham, MD: Lexington Books, 2012), 141-47.
[36] Cf. Fritz-Gregor Herrmann, "Spartan Echoes in Plato's *Republic*." In: Paul Cartledge and Anton Powell, eds., *The Greek Superpower: Sparta in the Self-Definitions of Athenians* (Swansea: Classical Press of Wales, 2018), 185-215.

On Philogymnastia *and its Cognates in Plato*

ὅτι τοιαῦτα οἷόν τ' εἶναι ῥήματα φθέγγεσθαι τελέως πεπαιδευμένου ἐστὶν ἀνθρώπου.

> And here is the evidence, so you can see that what I say is true, and that the Lacedaemonians have the best education in philosophy and argument: if someone wishes to socialize with the least sophisticated of Lacedaemonians, for the most part he will find him inept in conversation. As their discussion progresses, however, that Lacedaemonian, like a master spearman, will drive the point home with a comment so brief and precise as to make his interlocutor look like a child. And so, this very fact has been observed by some of our contemporaries as well as by some of the people of old, that Spartan culture is much more about pursuing wisdom than athletics. For the people who noticed this also realized that the ability to speak so intelligently should be attributed to a perfect education. (*Protagoras* 342d4-343a1)

As Protagoras emphasizes, it is thorough training in arguing and reasoning that enables Spartans to excel over the rest of the Greeks, a fact they try to conceal at any cost in order to prevent their rival states from discovering the secret to their success. For this purpose, they keep to themselves and study philosophy in secret, also misleading their followers in other cities to imitate an entirely false image of Lacedaemonian ethos. They, dressed in Spartan capes, get all sorts of sports injuries in their overzealous practice of athletics (φιλογυμναστοῦσιν, 324c1), not knowing that to act like a Spartan is much more to be a philosopher than a super-athlete.

In conclusion, it can be said that Plato approaches the concept of φιλογυμναστία and its cognates with the citizens' best interests in mind. While assessing its efficiency as a component of character formation and citizen training, he also provides us with a kaleidoscopic view of its manifestations in state ideology, gender equality, and the pursuit of happiness. The value he attaches to it remains analogous to its potential to make citizens physically fit and morally sound, thus preparing them for φιλοσοφία, which is synonymous with the pursuit of the Good. In turn, just as its prefix suggests, its potential for good depends on the measure with which it is applied. Oscillating between "fondness for" and "obsession with" exercise, φιλογυμναστία in Plato can be philosophy's able associate or sizable antagonist. Well aware that it can prove too much of a good thing, Plato joins it with two other compounds of φιλο-, love of learning and of music and the liberal arts, to create a tripartite structure strong enough to support φιλοσοφία.

Guilherme Domingues da Motta[1]
The *Agōn* between Philosophy and Poetry

Introduction

In *Republic* 607b, in the context of justifying the exclusion of a certain kind of poetry from the city,[2] Socrates refers to an old quarrel between philosophy and poetry. In the *Laws,* the lawmakers consider themselves not only "poets" but rivals and competitors to the tragic poets because they consider their polity to be

> framed as a representation of the fairest and best life, which is in reality, as we assert, the truest tragedy. Thus we are composers of the same things as yourselves, rivals of yours as artists and antagonists [ἀντίτεχνοί τε καὶ

---

[1] Guilherme Domingues da Motta holds a PhD in Philosophy (2010) from the Universidade Federal do Rio de Janeiro (UFRJ). Currently Professor at the Universidade Federal de Ouro Preto (UFOP). His main research topics are Plato, Ethics and Education in Plato's dialogues. gmotta427@gmail.com.

[2] Namely, mimetic poetry: "τὸ μηδαμῇ παραδέχεσθαι αὐτῆς ὅση μιμητική· παντὸς γὰρ μᾶλλον οὐ παραδεκτέα νῦν καὶ ἐναργέστερον, ὡς ἐμοὶ δοκεῖ, φαίνεται, ἐπειδὴ χωρὶς ἕκαστα διήρηται τὰ τῆς ψυχῆς εἴδη," *Republic* 595a-b. As I have pointed out in "The Quantitative Restriction of *Mimēsis* in Plato's Republic" in *The Many Faces of Mimēsis:* eds. Heather L. Reid and Jeremy C. DeLong (Sioux City: Parnassos Press, 2018), 49-60, note 16, the fact that Socrates states here that it was right to reject mimetic poetry does not contradict what was said in Book III (396e) (where it was established that the guardian will use the form of elocution that contains simple narration and *mimēsis*), for, as Elizabeth Belfiore has shown, Plato here uses the word *mimētikē*—a technical term created *ad hoc* by Plato—to designate a person who imitates everything without restriction. The same term is used in book III (in 394e1 and 395a2) to refer to the type of poetry that will be banished from the city, the preference being instead for the type that employs both simple narration and *mimēsis* only of the good man. This accepted type is designated "the unmixed form" (397d) because it imitates only that which is proper for the good man, and not because it excludes *mimēsis* altogether. On that point see E. A. Belfiore, "Theory of Imitation in Plato's *Republic,*" *Transactions of the American Philological Association* (1984) 114, 126-127 and also G. Ferrari, "Plato and Poetry," in *The Cambridge History of Literary Criticism, i. Classical Criticism,* ed. G. A. Kennedy (Cambridge: Cambridge University Press, 1989), 114-115.

ἀνταγωνισταὶ] of the fairest drama, which, as our hope is, true law, and it alone, is by nature competent to complete.³

In this agonistic dispute, which involved harsh words from both sides,⁴ Plato himself played a significant role. The extensive restrictions that Socrates imposes on poetry in the *Republic* denounce the way Plato subordinates art to politics and clearly show that philosophy—not poetry—should have the final say when it comes to defining Greek education and morals. What makes this contest so particular is Plato's intention to reformulate poetry itself in order to serve his purposes, since he sees it as the best tool when it comes to promoting moral education.

A vibrant scholarly debate has recently shed light on the complexity of the theme and on the necessity of not dismissing Plato's arguments without trying to understand the context in which they were presented.⁵ Still, Plato's approach to poetry in particular, or art in general, remains one of the aspects of his

---

³ "[...] συνέστηκε μίμησις τοῦ καλλίστου καὶ ἀρίστου βίου, ὃ δή φαμεν ἡμεῖς γε ὄντως εἶναι τραγῳδίαν τὴν ἀληθεστάτην. ποιηταὶ μὲν οὖν ὑμεῖς, ποιηταὶ δὲ καὶ ἡμεῖς ἐσμὲν τῶν αὐτῶν, ὑμῖν ἀντίτεχνοί τε καὶ ἀνταγωνισταὶ τοῦ καλλίστου δράματος, ὃ δὴ νόμος ἀληθὴς μόνος ἀποτελεῖν πέφυκεν ὡς ἡ παρ' ἡμῶν ἐστιν ἐλπίς" *Laws* 817b-c. Plato, *Platonis Opera*, ed. John Burnet (Oxford: Oxford University Press, 1903); Plato, *Laws*, trans. R. G. Bury (Cambridge, MA: Harvard University Press; London, William Heinemann Ltd, 1967 & 1968), slightly modified.

⁴ For a brief review of this ancient quarrel, see William Chase Greene, "Plato's View of Poetry," *Harvard Studies in Classical Philology* 29 (1918): 1-75.

⁵ In this respect, see Arthur C. Danto, *The Philosophical Disenfranchisement of Art* (New York: Columbia University Press, 1986); G. Ferrari, "Plato and Poetry" in *The Cambridge History of Literary Criticism, i. Classical Criticism*, ed. G. A. Kennedy (Cambridge: Cambridge University Press, 1989), 92-148; C. Janaway, *Images of Excellence: Plato's critique of the arts* (New York: Oxford University Press Inc., 1995); E. A. Belfiore, "Theory of Imitation in Plato's Republic," *Transactions of the American Philological Association* (1984) 114, 121-146; P. Murray, *Plato on Poetry – Ion, Republic 376e - 398b9, Republic 595 - 608b10* (Cambridge: Cambridge University Press, 1996); P. Woodruff, "What Could Go Wrong with Inspiration? Why Plato's Poets Fail," in *Plato on Beauty, Wisdom, and the Arts*, eds. Moravcsik & Temko (Totowa, New Jersey: Rowman and Littlefield, 1982), 137-150.

thought to attract the most significant amount of criticism, alongside some of his political views.

It is not my aim in this paper is to deal with the rather broad issue of how Plato treats poetry in his work. I side with those who recognize the complexity of the question; I wish only to add to the discussion by focusing on a single point. I will specifically challenge the view that, in the *Republic,* Plato might be making Socrates twist the intended meaning of poetry, or having him quote it out of context as an expedient grounding for the restrictions he wishes to impose on it. In fact, in the agonistic dispute between philosophy and poetry, that would be a quite low blow from the likes of Plato, champion of philosophy.

I will begin by highlighting the importance of acknowledging that, in the *Republic,* before Socrates imposes any restrictions whatsoever on poetry, Plato registers Glaucon's and Adeimantus's initial speeches, which play a key but underrated role in understanding why Socrates "twists" poetry. A thorough reading of the brothers' speeches claiming to present the "majority's" views on justice will reveal that they, too, twist and interpret poetry so as better to present their case.

To present the brothers' speeches before Socrates's restrictions on the content of poetry seems to be Plato's strategy for making the reader understand that a distorted reading and even a cynical appropriation of the contents of poetry is what can actually happen if poetry is not purified of its ambiguities, precisely the sort of ambiguities that Socrates's restrictions aim to prevent. It is not possible to understand the *Republic*'s crucial role in the old *agōn* between philosophy and poetry unless one realizes that the contest there over restrictions on the content of poetry is not only between Plato and the poets but also between Plato and some contemporary interpreters of poetry.

Glaucon's and Adeimantus's Appropriation of Poetry

When one analyzes Socrates's arguments against traditional poetry, one serious accusation he seems vulnerable to is that of cherry-picking quotations and deliberately twisting their meaning, sometimes by presenting them out of context,⁶ and supposing that a regular hearer or reader would do the same.

The restrictions Socrates imposes on traditional poetry's content and form in the *Republic*'s first books are extensive, and among the various justifications for them, the main one is the deleterious influence that traditional poetry might have in shaping young people's beliefs and character (377a-378e; 383a-e; 386c387c; 388d-e; 389d-392a; 401b-402a). The main problem is how young people might interpret some verses which seem to be in contradiction with the values he intends to promote in his city. If poetry depicts gods or heroes, for instance, as prone to intemperance, violence, lying, disrespect for their parents, and the like, what would the young make of all that while forming their character? Would they interpret that the poet is endorsing these behaviors by attributing them to the best?

One could say that Socrates seems to be patronizing the audience of poetic works by assuming that they would interpret poetry most unfavorably, unable, for instance, to distinguish what is allegorical from what is not. Socrates is quite aware of possible objections to his restrictions. He recognizes that poets can be enigmatic (332b),⁷ and that even the passages he excludes might somehow be true (377e-378a) or allegorical (378d).⁸

The allegorical interpretation could "save" some of the proscribed myths because their allegorical sense, in contrast to the literal one, might be perfectly reconcilable with the morals intended for the city. But for Socrates, this strategy would not be sufficient to save them because it is children who are to be

---

⁶ On this point see David Bouvier, "Du frisson (*phrikê*) d'horreur au frisson poétique: interprétation de quelques émotions entre larmes chaudes et sueurs froides chez Platon e Homère," *Mètis* 9 (2011): 15-35.

⁷ Plato, *Platonis Opera*, ed. John Burnet (Oxford: Oxford University Press, 1903). On that passage, Shorey writes: "The poet, like the soothsayer, is 'inspired,' but only the thinker can interpret his meaning." To illustrate this point, Shorey appeals to *Republic* 331e and *Timaeus* 72a. See Plato, *Republic*, trans. Paul Shorey (London: Harvard University Press, 1994), v. 2, 23.

⁸ On the meaning of *hyponoia*, see Fulvia de Luise and Giuseppe Farinetti, "Hyponoia: L'ombre di Antistene" in *Platone – La Repubblica: Libro II e III - Traduzione e comment*, ed. Mario Vegetti (Napoli: Bibliopolis, 1998), 393-402.

educated by these myths (378a; 378d-e), and, like most adults, they would not be able to discern their "truth."

These are some of Socrates's explicit justifications for his restrictions on the content of poetry. There is also an implicit one, skillfully introduced into the text by Plato through the speeches of Glaucon and Adeimantus (357a-367e): most people (the *hoi polloi*) would not make a fair and thorough reading of the poetry; on the contrary, they would tend to interpret it in the manner most convenient to ground their own beliefs, "arguments," choices, and ways of life, even at the cost of removing it from its proper context, simplifying it, or twisting its meaning. Glaucon and Adeimantus's appropriation of poetry and presentation of what is supposed to be the view of the *hoi polloi* on justice illustrate precisely this risk. In the context of Socrates's restrictions on the content of poetry (376e-392c), Plato's opponents are not only the poets themselves but some contemporary interpreters of poetry. Many of the restrictions imposed on the content of poetry in the *Republic* are simply a collateral effect of this background struggle at play.

Glaucon's argument, according to which justice is good only because of its consequences, depends on one fundamental premise: men are fundamentally defined by *pleonexia* and by *epithumia* (359c). He uses, among other strategies to confirm his premise, the appropriation and reformulation of an already existent narrative to construct a myth.[9] The myth of Gyges, narrated by Glaucon, tells the story of a man who finds a ring that gives him the power to be invisible and engage in unjust actions of all sorts. According to Glaucon's interpretation of the myth, men would act on their desires without restriction if they were exempt from the punishments they usually receive for giving them free rein. It is only by weighing the disadvantages of acting like that or because of constraint that men who do not have such a ring refrain from indulging their desires. The myth is worth quoting:

---

[9] On the special character of Plato's myth of Gyges, see Francesca Calabi, "Gige," in *Platone – La Repubblica: Libro II e III - Traduzione e comment*, ed. Mario Vegetti (Napoli: Bibliopolis, 1998), 173-188.

> The license that I mean would be most nearly such as would result from supposing them to have the power which men say once came to the ancestor of Gyges the Lydian. They relate that he was a shepherd in the service of the ruler at that time of Lydia, and that after a great deluge of rain and an earthquake the ground opened and a chasm appeared in the place where he was pasturing; and they say that he saw and wondered and went down into the chasm; and the story goes that he beheld other marvels there and a hollow bronze horse with little doors, and that he peeped in and saw a corpse within, as it seemed, of more than mortal stature, and that there was nothing else but a gold ring on its hand, which he took off and went forth. And when the shepherds held their customary assembly to make their monthly report to the king about the flocks, he also attended wearing the ring. So as he sat there it chanced that he turned the collet of the ring towards himself, towards the inner part of his hand, and when this took place they say that he became invisible to those who sat by him and they spoke of him as absent and that he was amazed, and again fumbling with the ring turned the collet outwards and so became visible. On noting this he experimented with the ring to see if it possessed this virtue, and he found the result to be that when he turned the collet inwards he became invisible, and when outwards visible; and becoming aware of this, he immediately managed things so that he became one of the messengers who went up to the king, and on coming there he seduced the king's wife and with her aid set upon the king and slew him and possessed his kingdom. (*Republic* 359c-360b)

Glaucon departs from an already existing story, reshaping and adapting it in order to confirm a conception of man that is at the heart of his argument. Nonetheless, when contrasted to Socrates's conception of man, which will be presented in Book IV, it remains incomplete.

The Agōn *between Philosophy and Poetry*

Socrates rectifies Glaucon's myth by presenting a conception of man as not defined by desire alone; his own conception adds two other dimensions to the human soul: the spirited and the rational.[10] The prominence given to these elements, the description of their function and of the healthy interaction between them and desire— which is how he defines justice in the individual—is fundamental for Socrates's argument in defense of justice considered as a good in itself. Socrates's argument, much as Glaucon's, rests on a certain conception of man, but, in this case, on one that is fuller and richer.

If it is Glaucon's particular conception of man that grounds his praise of injustice and vituperation of justice, and if this conception is based on a model which he looks at, then it is understandable why Socrates, in seeking to defend justice, will characterize the search (*zētēsis*) that must be undertaken as one that demands sharpness of vision (368c9). This sharpness seems to be the *dynamis* that most people lack, including Glaucon, who rewrites and interprets a myth to suit his own purpose.

As I have shown in another text,[11] in Glaucon's myth of Gyges there are a number of elements that can be read as analogies, which in turn could potentially shed light on his model of man and on the risks his kind of interpretation of man might represent. One analogy the myth seems to allow for is the one between Glaucon's speech itself, as a possible cause of corruption and loss of moral values, and the hollow horse that ultimately caused the fall of Troy. If Glaucon can reshape a myth to better suit his own interests and does so as a representative of the "majority," Plato seems to be implying that anyone could do the same, which is why myths or poetry, in general, are matters to be watched very closely.

The shortsightedness of Glaucon, the constructor of myths, not to conceive a more comprehensive image of the human soul,

---

[10] For the tripartite nature of the soul, see *Republic* 435d-441c.
[11] See Guilherme D. Motta, "The necessity of philosophy. A Reading of Plato's *Republic* first books," in *Roses and Reasons: Philosophical Essays,* eds. Carlos Frederico Calvet da Silveira and Alin Tat (Bucharest: Eikon, 2020), 73-100.

also applies to his appropriation of Aeschylus when he chooses to use Amphiaraus, a character from *Seven Against Thebes*, to mock the idea of a just man who does not wish merely to seem but actually to be just. Glaucon, in the final analysis, explains justice or injustice as a result, respectively, of the repression or liberation of the same defining element of man, *epithumia*,[12] In comparing the lives of the perfectly unjust and perfectly just man, he cites Aeschylus's description of Amphiaraus as a "man who did not wish to seem but be good"(360e-361b). Indeed, Amphiaraus, in Aeschylus's tragedy, is described by the messenger as a notoriously moderate (*sophrōnestaton*) and brave (*alken*) man,[13] an exemplary combatant and seer, someone "exploiting the deep furrows of his wit/ from which there grows the fruit of counsels shrewd."[14]

If one notes that in the tripartite soul presented by Socrates in *Republic* Book IV wisdom (*sophia*) and courage (*andreia*) are the virtues of the two parts of the soul neglected by Glaucon in his speech—the *thymoeides* and *logistikon*—then he failed to see in Amphiaraus what could complement his picture of man so narrowly focused in the *epithymetikon*. Amphiaraus is the personification of the order that corresponds to the justice of the soul as understood by Socrates;[15] that of a man who submits his desires and interests to the order of reason and to a superior or divine order. He is, therefore, the counterpoint to Gyges, who is governed by desire. Where poetry admitted interpretation, Glaucon erred as an interpreter, at least by Platonic standards, for

---

[12] See Guilherme D. Motta, "The necessity of philosophy: A reading of Plato's *Republic* First Books," in Carlos F.C. da Silviera and Alin Tat, eds. *Roses and Reasons* (Bucharest: Eikon, 2020), 73-100.

[13] Aeschylus, *Seven Against Thebes*, with an English translation by Herbert Weir Smyth (London: William Heinemann, 1926), 568-569.

[14] Aeschylus, *Seven Against Thebes*, 593-594. I have cited the text as it appears in Shorey's aforementioned edition of *The Republic,* v. 1, 125.

[15] Socrates defines justice as the government of the rational element, with the aid of the *thymoeides* and the harmonious accord of the *epithymetikon*. Cf. *Republic* 442c-444a.

not seeing in Amphiaraus the image of man that could rectify the one he had just presented with the myth of Gyges.

It should also be remarked that in concluding his argument Glaucon proposes an inversion of the verse that, in the tragedy, describes Amphiaraus as he who desires not to seem but to be good. In this inversion, the verse would come to be applied to the unjust man who "desires not to seem but to be unjust,"[16] followed, as a finishing touch, by the same verse cited previously with reference to the good man: "exploiting the deep furrows of his wit/ from which there grows the fruit of counsels shrewd."[17] This is clearly a cynical appropriation of the verses to serve his purposes.

If even the portions of poetry that clearly portray the nobility of a character can be cynically subverted, more ambiguous passages would lend themselves easily to this. Plato seems to think this is something that can be avoided by the adoption of some restrictions on poetry. Glaucon's speech is intended to represent the views of the *hoi polloi* who would, like his own speech, manipulate the myths to substantiate their views. It is specifically this very questionable use of poetry that Plato seems to be worried about and against which he is ready to fight back when the time comes to present Socrates's restrictions on the content of poetry. The final part of Glaucon's speech, in which he cites Aeschylus, foretells Adeimantus's speech, who will take up where his brother left off and will mirror his shortsightedness and partiality.

Adeimantus's speech embodies a manner of appropriation and interpretation of poetry which Plato subtly seems to want to denounce and which signals the necessity of a deeper intervention, one that would ultimately exclude the very possibility of its utterance. By that I mean that Plato seems to imply that many—if not all—poetry quotations that Adeimantus (or, in any case, the *hoi polloi* he represents) uses to substantiate his interpretation would simply not be available had poetry been shaped so as to discourage such a spurious appropriation. That would be precisely, I contend,

---

[16] "οὐ δοκεῖν ἄδικον ἀλλ᾽ εἶναι ἐθέλειν," *Republic* 362a6-7.
[17] "βαθεῖαν ἄλοκα διὰ φρενὸς καρπούμενον, ἐξ ἧς τὰ κεδνὰ βλαστάνει βουλεύματα," *Republic* 362a8-b1.

the aim of many of the restrictions Socrates later imposes on the content of poetry. Again, Plato's struggle is not only with the poets themselves, but also with interpreters, poetry being the field of battle. The result of this battle is, of course, a level of intervention in poetry's contents that many have considered unacceptable. But, again, the aim of this paper is not to minimize the consequences of Socrates's restrictions on poetry, but rather to shed light on a single aspect of the struggle in the *Republic*.

Coming to the aid of his brother, Adeimantus aims to show, among other things, that exposure to traditional education, in which poetry has a fundamental role, can decisively contribute to arriving at the belief that justice is good only because of its consequences. His attempt to establish this view depends on a selective appropriation of poetry, in which interpretations of somewhat decontextualized and distorted poetic contents, emphasizing certain aspects to the detriment of others, are used to make the best case for himself. For Adeimantus, one of the reasons why people consider justice as pertaining to the class of goods that are valued because of their results is that, in all the education that is given to the youth, beginning with parents and arriving at the poets, there is no praise of justice that does not insist on the relation between the adherence to justice and other goods that follow (362e-363d).

What Adeimantus fails to see or prefers to omit is that if parents educating their children and poets composing their verses associate good consequences with justice, this does not necessarily mean that they do not also see justice as a good in itself. It is only natural that, if justice has good consequences, these are *also* remembered by the parents and by the poets.[18] To conclude that justice is good only because of its consequences seems, to say the least, unsound reasoning.

To stress how the poets indoctrinate people to relate justice with rewards given by the gods, Adeimantus also attributes to

---

[18] Note that for Socrates justice is a good in itself and for its consequences. See *Republic* 358a.

The Agōn between Philosophy and Poetry

Musaeus and his son "a more excellent song,"[19] according to which the gods reward the just and punish the impious and unjust in the afterworld. He makes a selective appropriation and a distorted interpretation of such contents to underline and mock the quality of the rewards: "a symposium of the saints, where, reclined on couches crowned with wreaths, they entertain the time henceforth with wine, as if the fairest meed of virtue were an everlasting drunk."[20] But this is clearly to turn upside down the poet's end, which was to emphasize that virtue is to be rewarded, stressing on the contrary a secondary aspect, one that might possibly be subject to allegorical interpretation: the quality of the rewards given to virtue.

Although some poets might say that the gods reward justice and punish injustice in the afterlife, there would be no reason, again, to interpret that justice is necessarily good only because of its consequences. An alternative interpretation would be that if the poets represent the gods rewarding the just it is because they consider justice as being a good having worth in itself. The same would apply to injustice: the gods punish it because of its evil nature.

Surprisingly, further on his argument, Adeimantus attributes to the poets the affirmation according to which the gods send misfortune and unhappiness to good men and the contrary to the wicked (364b). This seems to contradict what he had just said about the rewards the gods grant to the just person and the punishment they inflict on the unjust one. His whole argument is so characterized by an appropriation of poetry dictated by convenience that there is no concern to avoid presenting the poets

---

[19] "νεανικώτερα," *Republic* 363c-3. As Shorey (v. 1, 130) points out, "νεανικώτερα" is a word that has a humorous and depreciative use in Plato's works. In this case, the humorous and depreciative tone should be attributed to Adeimantus's choice of words to better convey the view that poetic education produces questionable moral beliefs.

[20] "συμπόσιον τῶν ὁσίων κατασκευάσαντες ἐστεφανωμένους ποιοῦσιν τὸν ἅπαντα χρόνον ἤδη διάγειν μεθύοντας, ἡγησάμενοι κάλλιστον ἀρετῆς μισθὸν μέθην αἰώνιον" (*Republic* 363c-d).

as conveying contradictory views, let alone any concern to try to reconcile them. Note that if in the first instance he said that, according to the poets, the gods reward the just and punish the unjust (362e-363e), in the second instance he says that the poets portray the gods attributing unhappiness and an unfortunate life to good men, and to their opposites, a contrary lot (364b).[21]

The way Adeimantus interprets the question of the unhappiness of the good and the happiness of the wicked is also the most simplistic and most favorable to his argument. An alternative interpretation, which is explicit in one of Socrates's *typoi* to be followed by the poets in his city, is that the gods cannot be the cause of evil (379b). He insists that whenever a poet says that the source of misfortunes to men are the gods, "they must devise some interpretation as we now require, and must declare that what God did was righteous and good, and they were benefited by their chastisement."[22] Later, in Book X, Socrates reinforces this view claiming that if the just suffer setbacks and the unjust are prosperous this does not mean that the setbacks of the former are not an apparent or lesser evil, or that the prosperity of the latter is an apparent or lesser and provisory good (613a-614a). But, once again, this is an interpretation that does not suit Adeimantus's case.

The same dubious attitude in interpreting the poets can be seen in another instance. Adeimantus remarks that poets and laymen agree on praising the beauty of temperance and justice, but they underscore the difficulty of acquiring such virtues. On the other hand, an intemperate and unjust life is easy to lead, its only enemies being reputation and the law (363e-364a). Once again, it is only by interpreting the poet's words in the most unfavorable manner that one can conclude that it is better to be unjust and

---

[21] On 364b, see Shorey's note (v. 1, 132) to the text: "The gnomic poets complain that bad men prosper for a time, but they have faith in the late punishment of the wicked and the final triumph of justice," which is coherent with Socrates's view in 613a-614a.

[22] "ἐξευρετέον αὐτοῖς σχεδὸν ὃν νῦν ἡμεῖς λόγον ζητοῦμεν, καὶ λεκτέον ὡς ὁ μὲν θεὸς δίκαιά τε καὶ ἀγαθὰ ἠργάζετο, οἱ δὲ ὠνίναντο κολαζόμενοι," *Republic* 380a-b.

intemperate than to seek justice and temperance, since, of course, it is not necessarily true that easier equates better.

Adeimantus also presents in a very insidious way the claim of certain begging priests and soothsayers who are said to be able, by means of payment, not only to purify men of their crimes but also to do evil to the enemies of the contractor, be they just or unjust. In order to maintain that evil is reaped with ease, he says that they cite Hesiod; in order to point out that the gods are flexible and that it is possible to purify crimes by means of sacrifices, they cite Homer, Musaeus, and Orpheus (364c-365b). The citation of Hesiod is clearly distorted and decontextualized,[23] just like that of Homer, which in the way it is used seems to warrant an interpretation that goes well beyond what could be rightly inferred from the poem.[24] Although it is not Adeimantus, but supposedly those begging priests who uphold an interpretation of Hesiod and Homer which sanctions their practices and beliefs, it is remarkable that there is absolutely no critique of an interpretation that ends up aiding charlatans. But this is appropriated because, in the end, it favors the argument presented by Adeimantus

Giving voice, hypothetically, to a gifted youth who was educated in the context of poetry as he describes it, Adeimantus argues that when deciding about how to live his life he would perhaps quote Pindar: "it is by justice or by crooked deceit that I the higher tower shall scale."[25] Although we have this poem in a

---

[23] A point noted by O'Connor, who denounces Adeimantus's omission in quoting the following verses, in which the poet says that the road is rough "only at first, but when we reach the top, then it's easy to travel, though hard before" See David K. O'Connor, "Rewriting the Poets in Plato's Characters," in *The Cambridge Companion to Plato's Republic*, ed. G. R. F. Ferrari (New York: Cambridge University Press, 2008), 291-292.

[24] Note that this view, according to which the gods would do *anything* in return for sacrifices, is not plausible. Anyway, Adeimantus does not refrain from borrowing it for the sake of rhetorical reinforcement of his point.

[25] "πότερον δίκα τεῖχος ὕψιον ἢ σκολιαῖς ἀπάταις ἀναβὰς," *Republic* 365b. The fragment cited by Plato is Bowra's 201; the translation is the one that appears on Shorey's edition of *The Republic*, v. 1, 135-137. See C. M. Bowra, *Pindar* (Oxford: Oxford University Press, 1964).

fragmentary state, from what is known about Pindar it is safe to assume that here again Adeimantus has quoted the poem out of context and maybe twisted it for rhetorical purposes.[26] When further on Socrates proposes extensive restrictions on what the poets can say in the city constructed with *logos*, some have discerned that the citations he makes of them are also often distorted appropriations and citations out of context.[27] Is Plato also guilty of placing in the mouth of Socrates a rewriting of poetry that is extremely biased in the interest of better sustaining the restrictions he aims to advance? What must be noted is that the unfavorable "rewriting" of Socrates only happens after the equally unfavorable rewriting of Glaucon and Adeimantus, which foreshadows that of Socrates.

Conclusion

The anticipations, in the speeches of the two brothers, of the distortions that Socrates will make in relation to poetry seem to have two functions. In the first place, they suggest to the reader that those distortions are not actually Socrates's (or Plato's), but rather examples of what someone having the opportunity would do, namely, to appropriate poetry as an instrument to confirm his own beliefs, "arguments" and choices.[28] In the second place, they have the function of showing that such appropriations would not be unlikely. Thus understood, the speeches of Glaucon and Adeimantus can be taken to be means to convey, among other things, an implicit justification for some of the restrictions imposed on poetry, which would aim to make it ultimately immune to this

---

[26] On this point, see Patrick Miller, *Pindar in Plato*, http://www.24grammata.com/wp-content/uploads/2011/12/Pindar_in_Plato-24grammata.com_.pdf

[27] On this point see Bouvier, "Du frisson," 15-35.

[28] One could produce many passages to illustrate Socrates's fear that portions of traditional poetry could influence people's character in a deleterious way: *Republic* 377e-378b; 383a-c; 386a-387d; 387d-388d; 389d-391d. But the most emblematic example of his fear that people could appropriate and quote poetry in a distorted way to justify their own choices and deeds is at 391c-392a. These are his final words on the necessity of restricting the content of traditional poetry. I would argue, notwithstanding, that the fear voiced there can be retrospectively applied to many of the passages cited above.

The Agōn *between Philosophy and Poetry*

kind of devious appropriation. This interpretation could shed some light on the nature of the *agōn* between Plato and the poets depicted in the *Republic* as a dispute which also aims at the interpreters of poetry and envisages a type of poetry that is ultimately immune to spurious appropriation by them.

In fact, what Socrates excludes or imposes in terms of content aims, among other things, to eliminate ambiguities that could be the source of spurious appropriation or interpretation. Of course, it seems to be an exaggeration to banish a myth that depicts the actions of Cronos towards his father for the fear that the young would interpret it as meaning that it is acceptable to commit violence against a father. Nevertheless, what Glaucon's and Adeimantus's use of poetry has shown is that twisting poetry to suit one's own ends and beliefs was not so unlikely. Plato, the literary genius, was aware of the need for illustrating the risk of the *pharmakon* before administering an antidote that he knew would seem harsh and hard to take.

Marie-Élise Zovko[1]
Agōn and Erōs in Plato's *Symposium*

That the *Symposium* involves a contest like that of the Dionysian festival has long been recognized. Opinion is divided, however, regarding its precise nature. Some commentators believe it is a contest of poetic skill between Agathon and Socrates; others, an example of the "ancient quarrel between poetry and philosophy" (*Republic* 607b). Robinson sees it as a "Contest of Wisdom between Socrates and Agathon,"[2] which Dionysos is called upon to judge (175e). In fact, it proves to be a contest between a human and a divine ideal of *erōs*. Diotima's instruction leads from preoccupation with physical beauty and limited attempts to make the good one's own forever, to what truly ensures immortality: "begetting upon the Beautiful in body and soul" (206b). Dionysos's role is thereby relativized; for the wisdom to be desired lies beyond his jurisdiction. Its ideal is "prudence, and virtue in general," and beyond these "the highest and fairest part of prudence," which "concerns the regulation of cities and habitations," namely "sobriety" (209a).

Both tragedy and philosophy hold forth on topics like piety, justice, and the object of religion. Tragedy, however, references traditional accounts, addressing the broader public. Diotima's

---

[1] Marie-Élise Zovko is a Senior Research Fellow at the Institute of Philosophy, Zagreb and doctoral advisor at the University of Zadar in Croatia. She was Fulbright fellow to Germany in 1981/82, visiting scholar at the Harvard Center for Hellenic Studies in 1999, visiting scholar at the Johns Hopkins Humanities Center in 2010, and visiting fellow at CRASSH/ Wolfson College, Cambridge, 2016. Her interests include Ancient Greek philosophy, Platonism/Neoplatonism, Spinoza, Kant, German Idealism, German Romantic philosophy, metaphysics, aesthetics and philosophizing in life contexts. Funding for her participation in the fifth Interdisciplinary Symposium on the Heritage of Western Greece was provided by the Croatian Science Foundation under the project "Relevance of Hermeneutic Judgment."

[2] Steven Robinson, "The Contest of Wisdom between Socrates and Agathon in Plato's *Symposium*," *Ancient Philosophy*, 2004, vol. 24 (1): 81-100.

discourse is addressed to the few, and as such parallels Dionysian *thiasoi*. However, Diotima's version of philosophical *erōs* is the antithesis of orgiastic Bacchic ritual. The path culminating in the vision of the Beautiful involves a transformation of *erōs* based on reason. The *agōn* of the *Symposium* is thus a contest between the Dionysian cult and a new form of erotic cult, and embodies an implicit challenge to the god of the festival and popular religious conceptions generally. The judge of the speeches will prove to be not Dionysos, but Diotima, permitting her to emerge as the unexpected victor.

A number of contests are taking place in the *Symposium* at the same time. There is clearly a contest between Agathon and Socrates as regards the task of providing an encomium to *erōs*.[3] The question is whether their contest is to be understood as a rivalry of poetic and rhetorical skill, a contest of wisdom, or a competition between poetry and philosophy (*Republic* 607b).[4] Both Socrates and Agathon are called *deinoi peri ta erōtika* (193e; cf. 207c), "masterful in love-matters," and also "conquerors in discourse," making them co-competitors on this account. Whereas Agathon, however, has won a single victory at the festival of tragedies, Socrates "conquers everyone" "always" with his method of argument (213e). In the contest of speeches and in love-matters, it is Socrates who will

---

[3] Gerhard Krüger drew attention to the ἀγών between Socrates and Agathon and its connection to Plato's critique of poetry, regarding whose wisdom Dionysos (and his counterpart, the drunken Alcibiades) was to be judge. Cf. Gerhard Krüger, *Einsicht und Leidenschaft. Das Wesen des Platonischen Denkens. Zweite durchsehene Auflage* (Frankfurt/M: Klostermann, 1948). Cf. Chris Emlyn-Jones, "The Dramatic Poet and His Audience: Agathon and Socrates in Plato's *Symposium*," *Hermes*, 132:4 (2004): 389-405.

[4] Cf. Robinson, "Contest of Wisdom," 81: "Some commentators...infer that Plato must be hinting at a contest of poetic skill analogous to the one Agathon had just won, but now with Socrates/Plato as his chief competitor...using this device to position himself as a poet (i.e., author of dialogues) in competition with the tragedians... Other commentators read it instead as a version of the 'ancient quarrel between poetry and philosophy' mentioned by Plato at *Republic* 607b .... For others, Plato has indicated no more than a comparison of the personal wisdom of these two characters."

Agōn *and* Erōs *in Plato's* Symposium

eventually win out. Alcibiades's encomium to Socrates at the close of the dialogue is an encomium to the philosopher as master speaker and lover *par excellence*.

Dionysos and his counterpart among the guests, Alcibiades, are the implied judges of the contest.[5] Dionysos, god of theatre and of ecstatic experience, is judge of the contest of tragedies from which Agathon stood forth as victor, and also of the wine-drinking contest which forms a ritual part of the traditional symposium. But the latter competition never takes place, removing implicitly the customary judge of the spectacle from the scene. Unlike the contest of the tragedians, which took place under the auspices of the god Dionysos, Plato presents us with a different kind of contest, to be judged according to different rules and principles.

Taking into account Plato's critique of poetry and of tragedy as discussed in the *Republic*, the *Symposium* emerges as an attempt to reframe the contest of the tragedians. It does this by presenting the ideal of what Spinoza called a "greater love."[6] This new ideal challenges the tragedians' monopoly of the emotions, by which they sway their audiences to identify in pity and love with characters of dubious ethical qualities, in particular with their suffering and fear in the face of death—and replace it with the philosophical ideal of an *erōs* governed by prudence and insight into the highest good.

The scene of the dialogue is itself a symposium, a private religious banquet with ceremonial drinking, organized by Agathon to celebrate his first victory at the Lenaea in 416 BCE.[7]

---

[5] Cf. 175e. Alcibiades appears at the end of the dialogue as a counter figure to Dionysos, crowning both Agathon and Socrates, but raising Socrates above the former as the true conqueror in *logoi*. On Alcibiades as image of Dionysos, see Robinson, "Contest of Wisdom," 81 n. 3, 82.

[6] Cf. Baruch Spinoza, *Short Treatise*, in: E. Curley, *The Collected Works of Spinoza* vol. I. (Princeton: Princeton University Press, 1985), ch. v, 104 ff. Marie-Élise Zovko, "Impassioned by Passion: Knowledge and Love in Plato and Spinoza," *Dionysius* 32 (2014): 140-171, 141.

[7] The festivals of Dionysos were 1) Lenaea, winter; 2) Anthesteria, spring; 3) Greater Dionysia, from ca. mid-6th century BCE, celebrated by public drunkenness and drama, from which came the plays of Aristophanes, the

Those present decide against a drinking contest since Pausanias, Aristophanes, Eryximachus, and Agathon agree with each other that they are in no condition due to the excesses of the day before, and with medical opinion, which states that drunkenness is harmful to humankind (176d; cf. 176a ff.).

Instead of wine-drinking, a contest of speeches (*logoi*) is decided upon. As Phaedrus points out, a hymn to Love, "so great a god," was never sung unto this day (177c). For this reason, each of the assembled is called upon to "honor the god" in turn with an encomium (177e), and to praise Love *as beautifully as he can* (177d). The latter becomes the talking point regarding which of the speakers will contend; the comparative beauty of the speeches is to be the measure of success. Socrates thereby has the advantage, professing to "understand nothing but love-matters" (οὐδέν φημι ἄλλο ἐπίστασθαι ἢ τὰ ἐρωτικά 177e).

The appearance of Diotima in Socrates's speech embodies a further contest, or further aspect of the same contest. Diotima's speech introduces intimations of an esoteric form of devotion, akin to the Eleusinian Mysteries, which contends with the civic (public or exoteric) ritual embodied in the Dionysia. Indeed, the speech of Diotima is imbued throughout with the language and symbolism of the Mysteries.[8] The new form of erotic cult proposed by Diotima

---

tragedies of Aeschylus, Sophocles and Euripides. Cf. Plato, *The Symposium*, trans. R.E. Allen, (New Haven/London: Yale University Press,1991), 21.

[8] On the Greek Mysteries, cf. Walter Burkert, *Ancient Mystery Cults* (Cambridge: Harvard University Press, 1987); Hugh Bowden, *Mystery Cults of the Ancient World* (Princeton University Press, 2010); George E. Mylonas, *Eleusis and the Eleusinian Mysteries*, (Princeton University Press, 1961). Besides Diotima's explicit references to the "lower" and "higher" mysteries, some of the elements of the Mysteries which appear are: pregnancy and birth (present in the cult of Despoina, a precurser to Persephone in the Mycenean period; cf. Pausanias 8.37.9), the striving for immortality (the desire "to elevate man above the human sphere into the divine and to assure his redemption by making him a god and so conferring immortality upon him," Martin P. Nilsson. "The Religion of Eleusis," in *Greek Popular Religion* [New York: Columbia University Press, 1947], 42-64), and the sudden apparition and vision of Beauty ("things shown") to the initiate.

constitutes an implicit challenge to the god of the festival and popular religious conceptions.[9]

Paradoxically, the path to the "higher mysteries," leading to the vision of beauty itself, is not secret, but remains open to all who undertake the "lower" ones. The latter require passage, under the guidance of reason, from desire for particular goods to desire for the good in a universal sense, and from love of the beautiful in a particular body to love of beauty in all bodily things; and thence to love of beauty in customs and laws, knowledge and virtue, and finally to the vision of beauty itself (210a-211d).

This complex opposition between different kinds and levels of love comes out in the contrast between the public wisdom of Agathon and the "secret" wisdom of Socrates. Whereas Agathon's wisdom is manifest to everyone, "shining forth" (*lampra*) "before an audience of more than thirty thousand Greeks," Socrates's wisdom is as "disputable as a dream" (175e). Socrates's wisdom is "like a secret that he alone possesses."[10] Socrates regrets that wisdom cannot flow from one to the other, as through a wick from a fuller glass to an emptier one (175e), and cannot be obtained by merely touching the sage (175c), but requires education in the path of virtue and dialectic.

The contest which unfolds in the individual speeches comprises, accordingly, a contest between human and divine love—but it is a divinity determined in a new, philosophical manner. Diotima's version of philosophical *erōs* challenges *both* civic and private devotion, Dionysos and Alcibiades, and involves a transformation of public *and* private veneration of Eros into new

---

[9] In Euripides's *Bacchae*, the story of Pentheus, prince of Thebes, Dionysos appears as more terrible than his typical depiction as wine-god, "...portrayed as powerful, effeminate, pitilessly cruel, licentious, and specifically in respect to Pentheus and Agave, who oppose him, moved by motives of humiliation and revenge." Agave, Pentheus's mother, tears apart her own son due to temporary madness, i.e., possession by the god (cf. Plato, *The Symposium*, trans. R.E. Allen, op. cit. 22f.; cf. ibid. 20-24).

[10] Robinson, "Contest of Wisdom," 84. Agathon admits that testing by Socrates requires a greater deal of composure than to stand up at the assembly in the theatre: for "an intelligent speaker is more alarmed at a few men of wit than at a host of fools." (*Symposium* 194a).

form of erotic cult. Her cult represents the antithesis of orgiastic Bacchic ritual. It is a path culminating in the vision of the Beautiful, which entails a transformation of *erōs* based on *reason*, not unquestioned convention or irrational mania. The new aspect of *erōs* introduced by Diotima is this relationship to rationality. Far from implying any kind of repression, the proper relationship of desire and reason sought by the philosopher is meant to bring about liberation from servitude to the emotions and desires caused by inordinate consignment of oneself and one's powers to the dictates of physical need and uncontrolled lust.

The *agōn* between Socrates and Agathon clearly aims to showcase the opposition between popular and philosophical conceptions of love, as well as "between popular and philosophical conceptions of the divine."[11] The critique of epic poetry and tragedy in the *Republic* further highlights this problematic. In the *Republic*, the tragedians and the heroes of Homeric poetry are criticized for arousing fear of death, when in fact the aim of human *aretē* should be to habituate us to "fear slavery more than death."[12] Tragedy arouses emotions, like the need to feel pity and weep at the fate of the hero. Such emotions are not in themselves evil, but they are not necessarily in accord with reason and virtue. This contrast is now carried over to highlight the difference between human and divine love.

---

[11] Robinson, "Contest of Wisdom," 87.

[12] This is a central point of Plato's critique of poetry (cf. *Republic* III, 386a ff.). The ideas "concerning the gods" which Homeric epic and Greek tragedy imbue are opposed to a system of morality based on principles of reason. Plato's censure of narrators of tales aims to correct mistaken ideas about death, to free the guardians from irrational fear, and to instill in them instead self-sufficiency, a constant love of true freedom, and a fear of slavery to the desires and emotions. Along with "unworthy representations of the gods" subject to changeable emotions, images of famous men "weeping and wailing" (387d) are to be replaced by the conviction that "for a good man" death is not "a terrible thing" (387d-e). Their "lamentations" and frenzy will be replaced by "the greatest equanimity" in the face of misfortune. In this manner, the youth will be taught to have shame, self-control, moderation, endurance.

Agōn *and* Erōs *in Plato's* Symposium

Erōs originally meant "desire in all its forms."[13] As Diotima explains, all humans love the good for the sake of happiness (205a). But though all people love the good in this sense, not all are true lovers; rather, "some people love and others do not." Diotima takes the fact that "Love loves the good to be one's own forever" as indicative of the universal human desire for immortality, and as an occasion to investigate the ways in which humans attempt to achieve this goal. As Aristotle puts it, "we desire something because it seems good to us, rather than it seeming good because we desire it." The "starting-point," either way, is rational thought (*noēsis*) (*Metaphysics* 1072a29). And it is the connection to rational thought which determines whether desire is transformed into love of true beauty and desire for what is genuinely good.

In the Greek tragic tradition, the "dark side of Eros" was "associated with madness, wrongdoing, destruction."[14] The competition of tragedies which formed an integral part of public cult showcased the fate of infamous humans who aimed too high, and were doomed to suffer destruction because of their *hubris*. The *Symposium*, however, replaces the ambivalence of Dionysiac cult with a doctrine of love as the "steadfast and coherent pursuit of beauty and goodness that culminates in the contemplation of Beauty itself."[15]

Herein lies the connection of the dialogue to the *Republic*. According to *Republic* 403a, *right erōs* is "by nature a temperate and cultivated love of good order and beauty." As Allen notes: "the account of Beauty itself at 210a-212a anticipates the account of the Good in *Republic* VI, 506b-509b," although beauty has a different role to play than the good in the achievement of human excellence.[16] The attraction to beauty awakens a need for a

---

[13] F.M. Cornford, "The Doctrine of Eros in Plato's *Symposium*," in G. Vlastos. *Plato II. A Collection of Critical Essays. Ethics, Politics and Philosophy of Art and Religion* (Univ. of Notre Dame, 1978), 119-131; 121. Cf. Allen, *Symposium*, 7.

[14] Allen, *Symposium*, 8.

[15] Allen, *Symposium*, 26.

[16] Although many scholars operate on the basis of the conviction that the idea of Beauty itself which forms the pinnacle of the philosopher's ascent in the

Marie-Élise Zovko

formation of desire, whereas right formation of desire depends on true knowledge of its objects.

In Plato's eyes, desire is essentially for the good; but desire in the sense of *pothos*, unsatisfied longing, is akin to drunkenness and is itself a source of madness. It is the master passion of the tyrant, which incites him to oppress and exploit others, and eventually succumb to servitude to his own passions and lusts (572e, 573a-b, d cf. 586c). *Phaedo* 81a speaks in this sense of "fierce loves," from which the philosopher must be freed by the practice of death. *Phaedrus* 265a-b, meanwhile, speaks of love as a kind of madness inspired by Aphrodite and Eros, dividing it into a "left-handed" and "right-handed" part, the first "rightly reviled," the second, "divine" and "author of our greatest goods" (266 a-b). *Laws* 836e chastises the cowardice of one who always yields to pleasures, and distinguishes love between opposites, which is "terrible and fierce and seldom reciprocal" (837b), from true friendship, *philia*, based on similarity, which is "gentle and reciprocal throughout life," as well as from a third kind arising from a mixture of the two, which drags one in opposite directions, that of bodily desire, on the one hand, and longing for soul, on the other. The latter favors "the kind of love which belongs to virtue," regarding "bodily satisfaction… as an outrage," and "reverently worshipping temperance, courage, nobility, and wisdom," desiring "to live always chastely with the chaste object of his love" (837c-d).

In each of the speeches of the *Symposium*, some element of true, divine *erōs* is highlighted, but each time compromised or weighted down by aspects of earthly, merely human or bodily *erōs* opposed to that ideal.

Phaedrus (178a-180b), who makes Eros the "eldest" of the gods except Chaos, highlights *erōs*'s connection to virtue by highlighting "the shame we feel for shameful things, and ambition

---

Symposium is identical with the idea of the Good in the *Republic*, this is, in fact, not the case. The fact that the beautiful and the good "go together" no more implies that they are interchangeable, "than the fact that equiangular and equilateral go together in Euclidean geometry means that these are the same." F.C. White , "Beauty of Soul and Speech in Plato's *Symposium*," *The Classical Quarterly*, 2008, vol. 58 (1): 69-81.

for what is noble" without which it is impossible for any city or individual to perform high and noble things (178e). The *erastēs* or lover is ashamed to appear "ugly" (*aischros*) or cowardly to his beloved (*erōmenos* or *paidika*), and wants to appear "beautiful" (*kalos*) by performing bravely and nobly in public and private life, ready even to die for his beloved. A city or army of lovers and their favorites would "make even a little band victorious over all the world," since a lover would sooner die than have "his favorite see him forsaking his station or flinging away his arms" (179b).

Pausanias (180c-185c) raises the bar philosophically with his ascertainment that *erōs* in itself is neither noble nor base, but determined by its object and aim. He distinguishes two types of *erōs*: vulgar or popular *erōs*, and noble or heavenly *erōs* (cf. 184d). For Pausanias, vulgar love concerns women and young boys, body more than soul, and is as inconstant as its object, doing everything haphazardly. His position, however, proves self-contradictory, when he asserts that, while the aim of love is noble friendship (*geneaia philia* 184b) and to make one better in respect to wisdom and virtue, it is also permitted to deceive in order to do so.[17] As Allen notes, Pausanias's model is further opposed to Diotima's speech, where intercourse between a man and a woman is portrayed as a divine thing, an immortal element in the mortal creature (206c), and the relationship of an older man to a younger is portrayed to be for the sake of education, not sexual gratification (209b-c), comprising "a stage in the ascent to beauty itself" (211b).[18]

Eryximachus (185e-188e) echoes Pausanias's division with a variation, when, from a medical standpoint, he introduces the idea of good and bad *erōs*, orderly and disorderly love, as two universal natural or cosmic forces, making a distinction between desires which should and should not be satisfied. *Erōs* is understood thereby as an attraction, universally present in animals, plants and "practically everything that is," to a great variety of things (186d).

---

[17] Cf. Allen, *Symposium*, 20.
[18] Cf. Allen, *Symposium*, 18.

Eryximachus thus anticipates Aristophanes's treatment of the healing power of human love as a natural force (189d, 193d).[19]

In his famous myth on the human condition, Aristophanes ventures to portray our original nature as three kinds of spherically shaped creatures, male, female, and man-woman, with four arms, four legs, two faces looking in opposite directions etc., walking or tumbling round at will, and *erōs* as a natural healing force (*hē toū erōtos dunamis*, 189d-190b). These creatures are sliced in two when they become proud and overbearing, conspiring against the gods. Love expresses itself here as their striving to be restored to their primal state.

Agathon, victor at the festival of tragedies, shows the nearest understanding for the philosophical approach to *erōs* when he expresses his aim, instead of "felicitating humanity on the benefits bestowed" by *erōs*, to show "the nature of the benefactor himself" (194e). He goes on, however, to provide only accidental characteristics of love, depicting Eros as the youngest god, singing hymns to love's effects, and praising the god's beauty, goodness, temperance, and valor (196c).

Agathon's failure to portray the essence of love provides the occasion for an encapsulated contest with Socrates, a miniature *agōn*, so to speak (194a), for the sake of which Socrates conducts a brief *elenchos*, from which he emerges as victor over Agathon.

With his "customary irony," Socrates regrets ever having claimed to be "an expert in love-matters" (198d), since he thought this meant to speak the truth, which he takes to mean not merely *appearing* to praise love, by ascribing to it the highest and fairest qualities, but truly praising love. As in the *Apology*, Socrates admits he is ready to provide his encomium to *erōs* only if he will be permitted to speak "the mere truth" in his own way, and "*not to rival*" the previous discourses, and so make a laughing stock of himself (199b). He requests the permission of Phaedrus to question Agathon, and secures Agathon's agreement to the thesis "Love is desire of what one lacks" (199e). It follows that if love is love of

---

[19] Cf. Allen, *Symposium*, 28.

beautiful things, love itself must lack beauty. This is the point of departure for Socrates's own speech.

What follows is a speech within a speech, and an *agōn* within an *agōn*, the central contest of the dialogue between Socrates and Diotima, which turns out not to be an encomium like the previous speeches, but to embody the initiation of Socrates, the other speakers and ourselves into the "mysteries" of love itself. This device permits Diotima to carry the day by refuting Socrates's mistaken views, as well as those of the other speakers, and emerging as true victor of the competition.

According to his customary method, which is that of dialectic and philosophy, Socrates seeks to determine *who* and *what* sort of being love is, and what its works are (τίς ἐστιν ὁ Ἔρως καὶ ποῖός τις, ἔπειτα τὰ ἔργα αὐτο, 201d-e). Like Agathon, Socrates thought Love was a great god, beautiful and good; but, in fact, he has confused lover and beloved. Not the lover, but the beloved, the object of love, is beautiful (204c). Love itself is neither beautiful nor good (201e). It is not therefore ugly or bad, but something in between: between ignorance and wisdom, gods and mortals, a *daimon* (202d-204b), born of Resource (*Poros*), his father, and Poverty (*Penia* 203b), his mother, himself lacking but endlessly conspiring to acquire wisdom, beauty, and the good.

Here, no less than in the previous speeches, the attempt to define *erōs* assumes the thing it wishes to define ("love is *love* of...", viz. the good, the beautiful, immortality; "love loves the good to be one's own forever," 206a). The reason for this logical inconsistency is the ineffability, that is, the impossibility of expressing the highest things in predicative speech. For this reason, speech about love, beauty, and the good demands a circuitous, indirect method of showing the reality of the thing sought, one first made explicit in the central analogies of the *Republic*.

What love aims for is "begetting upon the beautiful" (*tokos en kalōi*, 206b), an activity constituting "something divine and immortal in mortal nature." All humans are "pregnant" in body and soul, and on reaching a certain age, desire to beget. This they cannot do "in what is ugly, but only in what is beautiful." The lover "approaches one who is beautiful" (206d) in order to give birth. The beautiful is incidental to the process of becoming immortal, not itself the object of love.

Though all love the good, not everyone can be said to truly *love*. Diotima compares this to the distinction of various kinds of creative productivity (*poiēsis*) from poetry *per se*.[20] Similarly, while love is the generic name for desire for good things and being happy, not every lover deserves the title in a proper sense. Those who pursue money-making or incline to sports do not deserve to be called lovers in the same way as the philosopher. Nonetheless, "all those who pursue [love] seriously in one of his several forms obtain, as loving and as lovers, the name of the whole" (205c).

Love competes with love, then, rivalling for the title of true lover, and the method by which one pursues the good and strives to make it one's own forever determines how truly one loves. If love is not of the beautiful, but of "engendering on a beautiful thing by means of body and soul" (τόκος ἐν καλῷ καὶ κατὰ τὸ σῶμα καὶ κατὰ τὴν ψυχήν), then the question of the beauty of the object will determine the genuineness of the love. Those who are pregnant in soul more than in body seek one who is "fair and noble and well-endowed" with whom to discourse on virtue and beget virtue, the "highest and fairest part" of which concerns "regulation of cities and habitation" and is called sobriety and justice (209b).

Taking in hand the other's education, the philosopher "brings forth" with him "his long-felt conception" and together they share "the nurturing of what is begotten." In this form, engendering and bringing to birth is truly "a divine affair... an immortal element in the creature that is mortal." In Diotima's view, these are the true "poets." Lovers like these enjoy a "far fuller community with each other" than that which comes with physical children, and "a far surer friendship, since the children of their union are fairer and more deathless."

---

[20] "But still...they are not called poets: they have other names, while a single section disparted from the whole of poetry—merely the business of music and meters—is entitled with the name of the whole. This and no more is called poetry; those only who possess this branch of the art are poets" (205c).

Agōn *and* Erōs *in Plato's* Symposium

This is the beginning of the ascent to the vision of Beauty. The initiation into these "preliminary mysteries" opens the avenue to the "final, highest rites and revelations" (τὰ δὲ τέλεα καὶ ἐποπτικά, 210a). Diotima bids Socrates to follow if he can, advancing from association with beautiful bodies, to love of a particular beautiful body, in which one engenders not physical children, but beautiful *logoi* (210a), at the same time not remaining tied to a particular body, but recognizing that beauty in any body is cognate (*adelphon*) to beauty in all (210b). From here, one must "set a higher value on the beauty of souls than on that of the body" (210b), "bringing forth ...such converse as will tend to the betterment of the young" (210c). Next, one must contemplate the beautiful as it appears in observances and laws, from there advancing to beauty of the branches of knowledge, and, "looking thus on beauty in the mass," escape "from ...slavery of a single instance," turning instead "towards the main ocean of the beautiful." By contemplating this, one may "bring forth ...many fair fruits of discourse and ...a plenteous crop of philosophy." Passing then "from view to view of beautiful things, in right and regular ascent," such a one will "suddenly ...have revealed to him ...a wondrous vision, beautiful in its nature ... the final object of all those previous toils."

With this object of love no other can compete, since it is incommensurable with any other, and not subject to particular differences or limitations:

> First of all, it is ever-existent and neither comes to be nor perishes, neither waxes nor wanes; next, it is not beautiful in part and in part ugly, nor is it such at such a time and other at another, nor in one respect beautiful and in another ugly, nor so affected by position as to seem beautiful to some and ugly to others. Nor again will our initiate find the beautiful presented to him in the guise of a face or of hands or any other portion of the body, nor as a particular description or piece of knowledge, nor as existing somewhere in another substance, such as an animal or the earth or sky or any other thing; but existing

> ever in singularity of form independent by itself, while all the multitude of beautiful things partake of it in such wise that, though all of them are coming to be and perishing, it grows neither greater nor less, and is affected by nothing. (210e-211b)

Ascending thus by right method and induction into love matters, the philosopher lays hold of the final secrets, the vision which enables her to produce true examples of virtue and, winning the friendship of heaven, to become immortal herself (cf. 212b).

In a dialogue determined by contests, the primary contest is between limited forms of human love, directed as they are towards particular goals, whether conventional or private, and a new form of erotic cult, which challenges both conventional and popular views of love and religious conceptions which fail to embody the true character of divinity and divine love. The *agōn* at the center of the *Symposium* embodies a struggle which differs fundamentally from the contest of the tragedians which is its occasion. It is a contest of desire vs. desire, erotic vs. a "greater love." Desire for the good and the beautiful must be joined to reason in order to enable advancement to the greatness and beauty of the soul which culminates in immortality. The judge of the discourses on love is not Dionysos, but Diotima. At the close of the dialogue, the "Lord of the symposium" is no longer Dionysos, nor any other "man in the house," but Diotima, a woman, in full possession of her powers, like her protégé Socrates, who departs as the last of the guests, unaffected by their drunken revelry.

Nicholas D. Smith[1]
Socrates's Agonistic Use of Shame

Introduction

In a path-breaking paper, "Socrates and the Irrational," Woodruff argued that Socrates's sense of shame, as well as his shaming of his interlocutors, indicated a rejection of what Woodruff calls "the fifth-century rationalist project." In place of what has become known as "Socratic intellectualism" about morality, Woodruff presented a Socrates who is "guided by an inner moral sense that affects him through shame," which Woodruff contends is "irrational (*alogon*) in Socrates's terms because he cannot support its results on his model of rational knowledge."[2]

In this paper, I want to agree—but also disagree—with Woodruff's assessment. That is, I propose to agree that Socrates's own sense of shame and also his uses of shame with his interlocutors engage a psychological process that is etiologically non-rational. But I will then go on to characterize the way in which Socrates conceives of shame in terms that make it entirely compatible with what has come to be known as "Socratic intellectualism." In that sense, while accepting the basic insight of Woodruff's important paper, I will try to show that the insight itself does not alter the various ways in which Plato, in his early dialogues, has Socrates characterize either virtue or human motivation.

---

[1] Nicholas D. Smith is the James F. Miller Professor of Humanities in the Departments of Classics and Philosophy at Lewis & Clark College in Portland, Oregon, USA. He is the author of *Summoning Knowledge in Plato's Republic* (Oxford: Clarendon Press, 2019), and the co-author (with T. C. Brickhouse) of a number of books, articles, and book chapters on Socrates, including *Socratic Moral Psychology* (Cambridge University Press, 2010), *Plato's Socrates* (Oxford University Press, 1994), and *Socrates on Trial* (Oxford and Princeton University Presses, 1989).

[2] All above quotations from P. Woodruff, "Socrates and the Irrational," in *Reason and Religion in Socratic Philosophy*, eds. N. Smith and P. Woodruff (Oxford: Oxford University Press, 2000), 130.

I will develop my argument in stages. First, I will remind readers of what Woodruff's own arguments were, and why he supposed that this was in conflict with Socrates's purported "intellectualism" about virtue and motivation. I will then briefly review what I take to be the general form of so-called "Socratic intellectualism," also noting differences in the scholarly reports of precisely what this "intellectualism" involved. I will end with an application of an account of "Socratic intellectualism" that I have developed with Tom Brickhouse over the course of many years, and show why I think that account can render Socrates's sense of shame, as well as his shaming of certain interlocutors, in a way that is fully consistent with his intellectualist views of virtue and motivation.

Irrational Socrates

According to Woodruff, the Socratic rejection of fifth-century rationalism involved both a religious aspect and also a psychological/ethical aspect. It is the latter aspect I take up herein. This psychological/ethical aspect itself has two parts, in Woodruff's view:

> (1) [T]he naïve hope that human beings can be readily moved by moral considerations, and (2) the traditional view that people ought to be moved by fear of shame and the desire for honor. The Platonic Socrates resists such rationalism on both points, actively defending irrational elements in ethical motivation and rehabilitating both shame and honor.[3]

Woodruff regards as "one of the unsung triumphs of the fifth century, the idea that certain procedures enable people to make rational decisions without a basis in knowledge" and cites the Sophists' encouragement of contrasting argumentation as an exemplar of such a procedure—one recognized at the time and also recognizable now as the kind of procedure we find used in

---

[3] Woodruff, "Socrates and the Irrational," 131.

courts of law.[4] But according to Woodruff, "Socrates rejects this entire approach"[5] and promotes in its stead a paradigm of *technē* or expertise, which "allows only knowledge-based procedures to count as rational and raises the standards for knowledge so high that no one—not even Socrates—is found to satisfy them."[6] The result, according to Woodruff, is that any examples of human success in the moral domain cannot be explained in terms of cognitive success; since there is essentially none of that to be found. Instead, Woodruff argues, any such success must be accounted for by appeals to "factors outside of what counts as rational,"[7] including fear of shame.

Plato makes a model of Socrates, as one we should strive to emulate in spite of being immersed in lives that are filled with ignorance and a lack of expertise in what Plato has Socrates call "the most important things" (*Apology* 22d). Plato's Socrates urges us all to lead examined lives (*Apology* 38a), and he claims to deserve Athens's highest recognition for his contributions to his fellow citizens, saying that "the Olympian victor makes you think yourself happy; I make you be happy" (*Apology* 36d). So while it may not be that Socrates can make such claims in terms of his extraordinary achievements in the *technē* of living well, whatever Socrates does believe about his own or our prospects for success, Plato does seem to me at least to represent Socrates as one we would *reasonably* seek to emulate. So the question is now: is Woodruff right in insisting that Socrates can serve as a paradigm for us *only* because of some non-rational factor(s)?

Woodruff's account seems to me to make the mistake of assuming what I would call an "all-or-nothing" conception of the *technē* that Socrates holds as a kind of aspirational ideal. Recall Woodruff's analysis that Socrates "allows only knowledge-based procedures to count as rational and raises the standards for

---

[4] Woodruff, "Socrates and the Irrational," 131.
[5] Woodruff, "Socrates and the Irrational," 131.
[6] Woodruff, "Socrates and the Irrational," 131.
[7] Woodruff, "Socrates and the Irrational," 131.

knowledge so high that no one—not even Socrates—is found to satisfy them."[8] This seems to me to be an overstatement not just as a representation of Plato's Socrates, but also as an understanding of what the model of *technē* actually provides. Let me take these up in reverse order.

The standard examples of *technē* that Plato has Socrates provide (when he engages in what scholars often call the "craft analogy") are fairly common skills widely recognized and practiced commercially in Socrates's day: such things as playing the flute, piloting a ship, serving as a military commander, carpentry, and so on (all examples taken from *Euthydemus* 279e-280c). These examples are not well conceived in all-or-nothing terms. Those who develop these skills obviously do so in stages, over fairly lengthy periods of time, during which their actual levels of skill will increase gradually (at least if they are diligent in their pursuit of the skill). But if this is so, Socrates's appeal to *technē* as a model for rational action allows one's actions to be more or less rational: more insofar as we become more skilled, and less insofar as we do not make sufficient efforts to become skilled. Socrates does—as Woodruff quite rightly claims—identify rationality with skill, and also identifies the skill that really matters for us as wisdom. But he does not, as Woodruff seems to imply, claim that only the highest possible levels of such skill count as rational—levels that are simply out of reach for any and all of us, including Socrates himself. Instead, Plato provides us with a Socrates who bids each one of us, as he says in the *Euthydemus*, "to prepare himself by every means to become as wise as possible" (282a). When he says this, Plato's Socrates clearly recognizes that there can be degrees of this skill, and our actions will thus qualify as rational as possible under this model to the extent that we act as wisely as possible.

Moreover, I do not think that a particularly bleak picture of our capacity for rationality is borne out by our texts. Recall again what I noted earlier about the way in which Socrates characterizes his due from the Athenians—he says he *makes* them happy. He

---

[8] Woodruff, "Socrates and the Irrational," 131.

never said that he makes them masters of the *technē* of living well. The best anyone might hope to achieve along these lines from Socrates may be that he can induce in them some degree of what he denigrates as mere "human wisdom" (*Apology* 20d) in contrast to the wisdom of the god (*Apology* 23a). He is unambiguous in saying that even this advantage is one that makes the one who has it wiser than those who do not. As Socrates says of himself, after showing that some famous politician did not have the wisdom with which he was credited, "I am wiser than this man" (*Apology* 21d). Becoming aware of the extent to which one lacks wisdom, accordingly, counts to Socrates as an improvement in wisdom. I believe a case can be made just on this basis for another astonishing claim Plato has Socrates make, in this case in the *Gorgias*, where Socrates says he is the only contemporary Athenian "to take up the true political craft and practice the true politics" (521d). He does not explain this audacious claim in terms of having become a master craftsman or achieving any very impressive degree of wisdom. Instead, he claims only that "This is because the speeches I make on each occasion do not aim at gratification but at what's best. They don't aim at what's pleasant" (521d-e). Just this is enough for Socrates to bid Callicles "listen to me and follow me to where I am, and when you've come here you'll be happy both during life and at its end" (527c).

At any rate, it seems to me it is not right to say that Plato's Socrates "raises the standards for knowledge so high that no one—not even Socrates—is found to satisfy them," as Woodruff claimed. Our highest aspirational standards for craft-knowledge may, as part of the human condition, be forever unreachable. But that does not entail that none of us can attain at least some low grade of the *technē* of living well that is enough to secure that same degree of rationality in our actions, and thus also such a degree of success and happiness in our lives.

Despite these cautions, however, Woodruff is quite right to find a Socrates who makes no secret of the fact that shaming people is an important part of what he intends and achieves in his "philosophical mission" in Athens. There can be no doubt that the ways in which Socrates shames his interlocutors is plainly agonistic, not just in tone, but in its aims. Socratic discussions are competitions involving the highest possible stakes: how we should live and what values are the ones most worth following. When an interlocutor loses a debate with Socrates, he is shown to have been living by the wrong set of values and pursuing what is actually worthless as if it is worthy. And Socrates makes no secret of what he is about. In the *Apology*, we find Socrates explicitly appealing to shame in explaining why he would never willingly abandon his philosophical mission in Athens:

> I shall not cease to practice philosophy, to exhort you and in my usual way to point out to any one of you whom I happen to meet: Good Sir, you are an Athenian, a citizen of the greatest city with the greatest reputation for both wisdom and power; are you not *ashamed* of your eagerness to possess as much wealth, reputation and honor as possible, while you do not care for nor give thought to wisdom or truth, or the best possible state of your soul? (*Apology* 29d-e,[9] my emphasis)

Socratic Intellectualism

Scholars have interpreted the evidence for what has come to be called "Socratic intellectualism" in different ways, but for my purposes here, one of Terry Penner's explanations of it is especially suitable:

> According to this theory, all desires to do something are rational desires, in that they always automatically adjust to the agent's beliefs about what is the best means to their ultimate end. If in the particular circumstances I come to believe that eating this pastry is the best means to my happiness in the circumstances, then in plugging this belief into the desire for *whatever is best in these circumstances*, my (rational) desire for whatever is best becomes the desire to eat this pastry. On the other hand,

---

[9] All translations provided herein, unless otherwise noted, are those given in J. M. Cooper, ed., *Plato: Complete Dialogues* (Indianapolis: Hackett Publishing Company, 1997).

Socrates's Agonistic Use of Shame

if I come to believe that it would be better to abstain, then once again my desire for what is best will become the desire to abstain. Rational desires adjust to the agent's beliefs. In fact, on this view the *only* way to influence my conduct is to change my opinion as to what is best.[10]

In my 2010 book on Socratic moral psychology with Tom Brickhouse, we challenged the first part of this explanation of how Socrates understands motivation. The example we used just to test his claim was of a committed dieter presented with an obviously well-made pastry:

> The object of an appetite that an agent has deliberately decided not to pursue may well continue to *appear* good to the agent—the chocolate tart will continue to look and smell good to the vigilant but struggling dieter who resists eating it in spite of that desire.[11]

In our account of Socratic intellectualism—and, indeed, in any account that recognizes Socratic moral psychology as intellectualist—it is nonetheless the case that Socrates is committed to the view that the only way to influence someone's conduct from a course they might be on to a different one would be to change that person's opinion about what course is best for them, from among the options available to that person at the time of which they are aware.

It is easy enough to see why Woodruff's observations about shame in Plato's early dialogues seem to throw so-called "Socratic intellectualism" into question. Here is Woodruff's apt description of shame:

> Shame is a painful emotion one feels at the thought of being exposed in weakness, foolishness, nakedness, or

---

[10] Italics in original. T. Penner, "Socrates and the Early Dialogues," in *The Cambridge Companion to Plato*, ed. R. Kraut (Cambridge: Cambridge University Press), 128.

[11] T. C. Brickhouse and N. D. Smith, *Socratic Moral Psychology* (Cambridge: Cambridge University Press, 2010), 87 n. 13.

perhaps even wickedness, to the view of a community whose laughter would scald. Shame is closely related to fear of exclusion from one's group, since derision generally marks the exposed person as an outsider.[12]

If one acts out of a fear of shame, understood as Woodruff describes it here, one's actions must be understood in terms of emotions and not *reasons*—in terms of one's experience of emotion about another emotion they might experience, a *fear* of experiencing *shame*. Nothing in fear or shame, as motivators, seems to tell us what the one who might suffer from such experiences might *believe* as they act on the basis of such feelings. Indeed, it seems entirely possible that someone who acts on the basis of a fear of shame might allow their fear to lead them to act in a way that is *contrary* to what they believe.

Examples of just such behaviors are putatively found by Callicles when he complains about Socrates's tactics with the other interlocutors of the *Gorgias*. Callicles claims that Gorgias ended up agreeing to something that Socrates had said because he was ashamed to admit to what he really believed, and that is how Socrates ended up catching the Sophist in a contradiction (*Gorgias* 482d). Callicles goes on to say that Socrates played the same shame game with Polus, and then generalizes his accusation by saying that "…if a person is ashamed and doesn't dare to say what he thinks, he's forced to contradict himself. This is in fact the clever trick you've thought of, with which you work mischief in your discussions" (*Gorgias* 482e-483a).

Now, I do not agree with Callicles that Socrates's uses of shaming tactics amount to a "clever trick" in his discussions.[13] But

---

[12] Woodruff, "Socrates and the Irrational," 133.

[13] I find it interesting that Callicles characterizes the use of shame in such a negative way, while also attempting to use this same "clever trick" against Socrates when he describes the sorts of things the latter does as "crowd-pleasing vulgarities" (482e) of a sort that deserve a flogging (485d), as themselves shameful (486a), and as "silly nonsense" (486c). Presumably, hypocrisy is permitted in what Callicles regards as the manly speech of a good rhetorician.

I do agree with Woodruff that our texts give us plenty of evidence that Socrates not only appeals to shame in his philosophical conversations, he also does things that seem like obvious attempts to make his interlocutors feel this "scalding" emotion.[14] And even if Socrates never completely admits to using shame in his refutations of Gorgias and Polus, it seems clear enough that it is precisely *shaming* that Socrates intends when he compares Callicles himself to a "torrent-bird" (a bird reputed to excrete as fast as it eats, which might account for its name[15]), to one who spends his life delighting in the pleasures of itching and scratching himself (494c), and finally, to a *kinaidos* (passive homosexual)—all the while repeatedly (and obviously sarcastically) reminding Callicles that *aidōs* (shame) should not affect their conversation!

Is Callicles right, however, in accusing Socrates of trying to get people to say and do things they do not really believe by shaming them? To answer this, we need to examine more closely what Socrates might have thought about the relationship (or lack of it) between emotion and cognition.

A Socratic Theory of Emotion

Woodruff complains that Socrates's uses of shame cannot be defended by the standards of rationality that Socrates presents in Plato's early dialogues.[16] But the motivation Woodruff characterizes in this way is, as I have noted in passing above, one that is emotionally complex; he says that Socrates recognizes that people can be motivated by a *fear* of *shame*. If so, then there are two emotions in play here, fear and shame. But at least in the case of fear, we have some textual evidence for supposing that Socrates is a cognitivist about this emotion. In the *Protagoras* he explicitly says

---

[14] An admirable discussion of Socrates's use of mocking and humiliation may be found in D. Sanderman, "Why Socrates Mocks His Interlocutors," *Skepsis* 15 (2000): 431-441.

[15] So see T. Irwin, *Plato's Gorgias* (Oxford: Clarendon Press, 1979), 197, note on 494b; see also E. R. Dodds, *Plato: Gorgias* (Oxford: Clarendon Press, 1959), on the same passage.

[16] Woodruff, "Socrates and the Irrational,"146.

that he takes fear to be cognitive: "I say that whether you call it fear (*phobos*) or dread (*deos*), it is an expectation (*prosdokian*) of something bad" (*Protagoras* 358d). Following this lead, we could say that the fear of shame would be an expectation of something bad, namely, whatever might make that person feel shame. But then, if we assume that what he says about fear indicates a general view about emotions,[17] we should assume that Socrates would also be a cognitivist about shame, as well: shame would thus be understood as a belief of some kind. If we put this together with what Woodruff said about shame, it might be the belief that one has been exposed or perceived by ones whose opinions of one matters to one, as deserving rejection or exclusion, where such rejection or exclusion from the group would qualify as the "bad" the fear of shame would expect. Woodruff suggests that we have a natural aversion to being rejected or excluded—at least by those whose opinions of us matter to us. So perhaps—and I admit this is speculative—we should suppose that a Socratic analysis of shame would be that it is the belief that we have been exposed or perceived as deserving rejection or exclusion from a group in which one desires the opposite response, acceptance or affirmation.

Now, I am not going to defend the cognitivist view of emotion here, but I do think that we have at least some reason for thinking that Plato's Socrates held such a theory. If so, then our assessment of what Callicles accuses Socrates of—and also of what Woodruff has to say about Socrates and shame—has already become somewhat problematized. After all, if emotions *just are* cognitions, as cognitivism holds, then one can hardly accuse Socrates, as a cognitivist about emotion, of using motivational tactics involving some emotion(s) that thereby ignore or leave behind what the agent actually *believes*.

Even if we do accept that Socrates is a cognitivist about emotion, however, we should also acknowledge that, for Socrates, not all beliefs are equally worthy of our acceptance—and thus, as

---

[17] As Brickhouse and I recently argued in "Socrates on the Emotions," *Plato Journal* 15 (2015): 9-28.

an intellectualist about motivation, it will also be true that not all beliefs are equally worthy of guiding our actions. In my 2015 paper with Brickhouse, we argued that Socrates recognizes different etiologies for the production of belief—some more veridically reliable than others. But it seemed to us that the *least* veridically reliable of these processes had their origins in the non-rational processes involving our most basic attractions and aversions. Here is how Brickhouse and I describe the relevant process in that paper:

> A passage in the *Charmides* (167e) seems to indicate that human beings experience different kinds of desire, which target different sorts of goals. These include appetite (*epithumia*), which aims at pleasure, wish (*boulēsis*), which aims at what is good, and love (*erōs*), which aims at what is beautiful. Each of these seems to have an aversive alternative, as well: we avoid pains, what is bad, and what is ugly. Our natural attractions and aversions, we contend, are the grounds for a variety of non-rational beliefs: Insofar as something seems or promises to be pleasurable, beneficial, or beautiful, the agent will be naturally inclined to believe it to be something good; and insofar as something seems to be painful, detrimental, or ugly, the agent will be naturally inclined to believe it to be something bad. Unless the natural inclination to believe in such cases is mitigated or defeated by some other (for example, rational) belief-forming process, one will form beliefs about goods and evils accordingly. The beliefs created by these natural attractions and aversions, because they derive from non-rational processes, are veridically unreliable, but are also to some degree (by their nature as non-rational) resistant to rational persuasion and other belief-forming processes.[18]

In that paper, we contend that the beliefs Socrates identifies as emotions are those that have this sort of etiology. If so, then when Socrates engages an interlocutor's fear of shame, he is engaging

---

[18] Brickhouse and Smith, "Socrates on the Emotions," 14-15.

what he would regard as a non-rational process—in spite of the fact that it is a belief-forming process and thus entirely compatible with Socrates's motivational intellectualism. But there remains one more clarification I want to make about this process.

Pain and Suffering

As I have now repeated a few times, Woodruff describes shame as "a painful emotion" that one feels in relation to others whose derision or rejection would "scald." In connection with these entirely apt observations, we might remind ourselves of what Plato has Socrates say in the closing myth at the end of the *Gorgias*. Briefly, we are told that the dead are judged in the afterlife and will have no opportunity to delude the judges with clever rhetoric there. Those whose souls are judged to have been damaged by wrongdoing will be punished, for, as Socrates puts it,

> Those who are benefited, who are made to pay their due by gods and men, are the ones whose errors are curable; even so, their benefit comes to them, both here and in Hades, by way of pain and suffering, for there is no other possible way to get rid of injustice. From among those who have committed the ultimate wrongs and who because of such crimes have become incurable come the ones who are made examples of. These persons themselves no longer derive any profit from their punishment, because they're incurable. Others, however, do profit from it when they seem them undergoing for all time the most grievous, intensely painful and frightening sufferings for their errors, simply strung up there in the prison in Hades as examples, visible warnings to unjust men who are ever arriving. (*Gorgias* 525b-d)

There are several things to notice about this sobering myth. First, Socrates warns Callicles that he should not simply dismiss this story as "an old wives' tale" and feel contempt for it (*Gorgias* 527a). Socrates repeatedly says that he is convinced that the story is true (523a, 524b, 526d, 527e). But even as something that just *might* be true, it is clear that what Socrates seeks to do here is to frighten

Callicles, and we might have thought that this, again, was to employ a process that has no place in Socrates's intellectualism about motivation.[19] For the reasons I have given above, however, even if frightening Callicles is what Socrates intends, it does not follow that he is trying to motivate Callicles in a way that does not engage the younger man *cognitively*. As I am sure Woodruff would insist—and rightly—even if he is trying to change Callicles's beliefs here, the *way* he is doing it makes use of a non-rational belief-forming etiology.

The myth also has something to say in defense of Socrates's putting precisely that sort of etiology to work, however, and it is of a piece with what Socrates had earlier said about what he is trying to do with Callicles. The younger man had extolled the benefits of living one's life in ways that maximize the satiation of appetites. But Socrates entirely rejects this view and says instead that the soul of one who is "foolish, undisciplined, unjust and impious [...] should be kept away from its appetites and not permitted to do anything other than what will make it better" (*Gorgias* 505b). When Callicles feigns incomprehension, Socrates shows his hand clearly: "This fellow won't put up with being benefited and with his undergoing the very thing the discussion's about, with being punished" (κολαζόμενος[20]; *Gorgias* 505c).

But how and why would Socrates, the famous motivational intellectualist, resort to tactics that amount to *kolasis* (punishment)?

---

[19] See, for examples, C. Rowe, "A Problem in the *Gorgias*: How is Punishment Supposed to Help with Intellectual Error?" in *Akrasia in Greek Philosophy*, eds. C. Bobonich and P. Destrée (Brill, Leiden and Boston, 2007), 19-40; and T. Penner, "Inequality, Intention, and Ignorance: Socrates on Punishment and the Human Good," in *Democracy, Justice, and Equality in Ancient Greece*, eds. G. Anagnostopoulos and G. Santas, (Cham, Switzerland: Springer, 2018), 95, who seek to discredit the myth as "un-Socratic."

[20] I have modified the translation given in Cooper, *Plato*, here, which has the word "disciplined." I think the Greek word is more often associated with corrective punishment (one of the topics being discussed by Socrates and Callicles) than with maintaining a disciplined regimen (which is also part of their discussion). I do not see Socrates as "disciplining" Callicles in the way he thinks we should maintain discipline over our appetites.

Compare the interaction between Socrates and Callicles here to what Terry Penner had to say, when he claimed Socratic intellectualism implies that *"only philosophical dialogue* can improve one's fellow citizens."[21] While it is true that what we witness between Callicles and Socrates qualifies as "philosophical dialogue," what *makes* this kind of dialogue function in the way it is intended to function—if it works, that is—is that the interlocutor is improved in the only way that Socrates says it is possible for curable, but damaged, souls to be improved. Socrates seeks to improve Callicles "by way of pain and suffering, for there is no other possible way to get rid of injustice," as he puts it in the *Gorgias* myth (*Gorgias* 525b-c).

Scholars have had a lot to say about the logical and evidentiary aspects of Socratic argumentation. But in 2000, Woodruff published a paper that called our attention to a different aspect of Socratic philosophy. That aspect, I claim, he saw clearly for what it was, and though I have quibbled herein with some of the ways in which Woodruff expressed the insights he shared in that paper, he was certainly right to say that Socrates recognized clear uses for fear and shame when he engaged others philosophically. I don't know if Woodruff would agree with my taking it so far, but I would now be willing to claim that the emotional and non-rational psychological processes that Socrates recognizes and exercises in his discussions are every bit as important to it as are the logical or evidentiary aspects.[22] Indeed, if the analysis I have given here is right, Socrates sees the non-rational and emotional processes that he engages as importantly epistemic ones, since they involve a process of belief-formation

---

[21] T. Penner, "Socrates," in Cristopher Rowe and Malcom Schofield, eds., *Cambridge History of Greek and Roman Political Thought*, Cambridge: Cambridge University Press, 2000, 164.

[22] Again, see Sanderman, "Why Socrates Mocks." I have in mind, as examples of Socrates's uses of shame elsewhere, cases in which the interlocutors' own reactions seem to indicate responses to non-logical aspects of the conversation, for example with Euthyphro in the dialogue of the same name, with Critias in the *Charmides*, and especially with Thrasymachus, in *Republic* I. I do not think that these are the only examples that can be found.

that may be the *only* recourse for improvement, for those who have already allowed themselves to fall into injustice. Once an agent may come to have the correct beliefs via this process, only then may they go on to develop better epistemic habits, relying on more veridically reliable cognitive processes. The upshot is still a version of motivational intellectualism: agents will still in every case only act in the ways they believe are best for them, from the options available to them at the time of action of which they are aware. The ways in which we come to have the beliefs that guide our actions, however, appear to be a good deal more complicated than what the scholarly literature has recognized.[23]

---

[23] I am indebted to Irina Deretić for comments on an earlier draft of this paper.

Jure Zovko[1]
Agōn as Constituent of the Socratic Elenchos

The phenomenon of *agōn* (ἀγών) was a central feature of Greek culture from Homer to Socrates and a fundamental part of their daily life. Jacob Burckhardt claimed that, "the aim of the talented Greek, since Homer, was 'always to be the first and outshine the rest,' and from the same early period the wish for fame after death was also often expressed."[2] The competition (*agōn*) manifested itself, in Burckhardt's opinion, not only in the Olympic Games, but also in cultural life, theatre, poetry, art, and from the fifth century BCE in philosophy as well.[3] The model of *kalokagathia* became the ideal of the agonal way of life thanks to philosophers, especially Socrates. All human actions, life in the polis as a whole, even life connected with the fine arts and theatre were judged and valorized from the point of view of *kalokagathia*: "It was no longer the noble free individual they had in mind, but the citizen in general, and soon mankind as a whole."[4] Nietzsche argues in *Twilight of the Idols* that Socrates:

---

[1] Jure Zovko completed his MA in 1985 and his PhD in 1989 at the University of Freiburg. Since 1990 he has been employed at the Institute of Philosophy of the University of Zagreb. He is also a full professor in the Department of Theoretical Philosophy at the University of Zadar in Croatia. His research focuses on hermeneutic philosophy, Ancient Greek philosophy and classical German philosophy. He is a member of the Institut International de Philosophie (Paris) and full member of the L' Académie Internationale de Philosophie des Sciences (Brussels). He is also a member of the FISP Steering Committee. Since 2007 he has been a vice-president of the International Hegel Society and co-editor of the Hegel Yearbook and the Hegel Yearbook Supplements. The publication of this article was made possible through funding from the Croatian Science Foundation as part of his research project "The Relevance of Hermeneutic Judgment."
[2] Jacob Burckhardt, *The Greeks and Greek Civilization*; trans. Sheila Stern; edited with an introduction by Oswyn Murray (New York: St. Martin's Press, 1998), 71.
[3] Burckhardt, *The Greeks*, 233.
[4] Burckhardt, *The Greeks*, 240.

discovered a new kind of *agōn* and was its first fencing master for the noble circles of Athens. He fascinated people by stirring up the agonal drive of the Hellenes — he introduced a variation into the wrestling match between young men and youths.[5]

A significant aspect of Socrates's understanding of *agōn* was that he developed, analogous to physical athletics, a contest in argumentation in which the partners in the conversation strive to show their spiritual supremacy.

Prominent experts on Socratic method, e.g., Gregory Vlastos, Myles Burnyeat, Terence Irwin, and Gerasimos Santas, did not consider *agōn* to be a relevant aspect or important component of the elenchos. The main reason for this was probably because they wanted to portray Socrates as a model of the humanistic ideal which abandons the Greek-agonistic model as a principle of life.[6] The contest (*agōn*) remains the basic purpose and characteristic of early Platonic dialogues, but also appears in the middle dialogues as well as in late Platonic writings. The same can be said for irony as a literary form in Platonic dialogues, which was used in a similar way by the historical Socrates, as well as by the Socrates of the late dialogues. A sharp separation between the historical Socrates and the Platonic literary figure "Socrates," as Vlastos claimed and pleaded, is a problematic endeavor. Every reconstruction of the historical Socrates is carried out against the background of the Platonic literary image.

The existence of two different literary figures of Socrates in the Platonic dialogues does not necessarily mean that the image of Socrates in the early dialogues corresponds to that of the historical

---

[5] Friedrich Nietzsche, "The Problem of Socrates," *Sämtliche Werke Kritische Studienausgabe. Der Fall Wagner, Götzen-Dämmerung, Der Antichrist/ Ecce homo, Dionysos-Dithyramben/Nietzsche contra Wagner*, eds Giorgio Colli and Mazzino Montinari (München/Berlin DTV Walter de Gruyter 1980), 71.

[6] Heinrich Maier, the outstanding German expert on Socratic Philosophy, even uses the expression "Socratic Gospel," *Sokrates: sein Werk und seine geschichtliche Stellung* (Tübingen: Mohr, 1913), 296 f.

Socrates. Wolfgang Wieland plausibly argued that the attempts to uncover as authentic a Socratic legacy as possible should not issue in a sharp and strict differentiation between Socratic and Platonic teaching, "as this Socratic legacy will to us remain recognizable as a legacy adopted by Plato and stamped by his will to give it a shape."[7] Hence, an attempt to isolate such a legacy through the method of subtraction by leaving out of consideration all the additions that the long tradition passed on a genuine Platonic teaching would fail to deliver anything worthwhile.

The fact that Socrates identified the human soul with the individual personality (*Apology* 36c; *Crito* 47e; *Gorgias* 486e) does not mean that this identification does not occur in the later dialogues. The practical question of how to achieve a good and virtuous life is not a basic characteristic of the early dialogues only. It is also controversial that Vlastos attributes a skeptical view of life to the historical Socrates: "For Socrates E [earlier dialogues] our soul is our self... The queries, 'Is the soul material or immaterial, mortal or immortal? Will it be annihilated when the body rots?' are never on his elenctic agenda... both options—total annihilation or survival in Hades—are left open."[8]

The primary intent of this chapter is to show that Socrates's elenchos is fundamentally agonal in its structure and character, an ascertainment which applies equally to the purgative, defensive, and definitional forms of elenchos, as confirmed by Michael Erler, G. Klosko, and Heather Reid.[9] Socratic elenchos comprises not only the refutation of inadequate definitions but is a contest by which judgments are formed. My thesis is that elenchos in the

---

[7] Wolfgang Wieland, "Das sokratische Erbe: Laches," in *Platon: seine Dialoge in der Sicht neuer Forschungen,* eds. Theo Kobusch and Burkhard Mojsisch (Darmstadt: Wiss. Buchgesell. 1996), 5-24, 7.

[8] Gregory Vlastos, *Socrates. Ironist and Moral Philosopher* (Ithaca: Cornell University Press 1991), 55.

[9] Cf. Michael Erler, *Der Sinn der Aporien in den Dialogen Platons: Übungsstücke zur Anleitung im philosophischen Denken* (Berlin/New York. Walter de Gruyter 1987), 122; George Klosko, "Thrasymachos' Eristikos: The Agon Logon in 'Republic' I," *Polity,* 17 (1984): 5-29; Heather L. Reid, "The Socratic Agon Turning *Philonikia* toward *Philosophia* in Plato's Dialogues," *Proceedings of the XXII World Congress of Philosophy* 2 (2008): 173-183.

early Platonic dialogues represents a form of judgment in the sense of a combination of reflective and determining judgment (*die reflektierende Urteilskraft, die bestimmende Urteilskraft*), as Kant practiced in the *Critique of Judgement* (*Kritik der Urteilskraft*). In Plato's Socratic dialogues, the concrete case is usually analyzed, examined, and clarified in the context of general ethical predicates. It is discussed, for example, whether the action of Euthyphro's father is pious or not, whether the behavior of the military generals was brave or not, or could Thrasymachus's statement that justice is based on the interest of the stronger be universalized as the general standard of living.

In contrast to Vlastos, it is necessary to point out that the elenchos is closely linked to the question of how to live a good life (*eu zēn*), which Socrates repeatedly asks in the early Platonic dialogues. In the dialogue *Gorgias* this question is discussed from the standpoint of truth (*sub ratione veritatis*), and the result of the discussion is that the life forms of radical hedonism and political imperialism are rejected.

Fifty years ago, Vlastos quite rightly characterized the elenchos as a process of searching for the truth, especially in the questions of morality and correct ethical action. He maintained "that while the elenchos was adversative, pervasively negative in form, its aim was strongly positive: to discover and defend true moral doctrine."[10] Vlastos emphasizes that the peculiarity of the elenchos is manifested externally by refuting wrong opinions and attitudes, but behind the negative form of elenchos hides the search for truth: "Commitment to the elenctic method as the final arbiter of truth in the moral domain […] is common and peculiar to ten dialogues," namely, the *Apology*, *Republic I*, and the eight so-

---

[10] Vlastos, *Socrates Ironist*, 14. For Vlastos, Socrates "never troubles to say why his way of searching is the way to discover truth or even to say what this way of searching is. He has no name for it; ἔλεγχος and the cognate verb ἐλέγχειν ('to refute', 'to examine critically', 'to censure') he uses to describe, not to baptize, what he does; only in modern times has '*elenchos*' become a proper name." Gregory Vlastos, *Socratic Studies*, ed. Myles Burnyeat (Cambridge: Cambridge University Press, 1994), 1.

called Socratic dialogues: *Charmides, Crito, Euthyphro, Gorgias, Hippias Minor, Ion, Laches,* and *Protagoras.*"[11] *Gorgias* remains Vlastos's favorite dialogue for the elaboration of his concept of elenchos because here it is claimed that "the true can never be refuted" (τὸ γὰρ ἀληθὲς οὐδέποτε ἐλέγχεται; 473b), but Vlastos's critics also take this dialogue as a starting point for their confrontation with him. They say the weakness of Vlastos's interpretation of the Socratic elenchos consists in the fact that he unfortunately focused primarily on the logical form of Socratic argumentation under the motto "method is all." Unfortunately, through such methodical universalization, the ethical form of life that Socrates represented in practice is neglected.

In the *Gorgias*, one can note an especially rough attitude toward the sophists as well as an emphatic claim that it is in their rhetorical demagogy that one should seek the source of both the evils and the disorders of Athenian democracy as well as the decay of its civic ethos. In contrast to Vlastos, Heinrich Maier holds that the *Gorgias* is the site of a particular cognitive turn in the *Opus Platonicum*: philosophy is no longer conceptualized as a Socratic moral dialectic but as a science of the knowledge of the truth. According to Maier, philosophy is a science that strives for the knowledge of truth, for real knowledge, and despises the world of opinion, of seeming (*Schein*), of deceptive persuasion.[12] The argumentative contest in the discussion in the dialogue *Gorgias* certainly has agonal traits: it should be proven that the conclusion (*logos*) "doing wrong is worse than suffering wrong" is stable and unshaken. The same applies to the substantial difference between "*dokeien*" and "*einai*" with regard to the good and other ethical predicates, so that "a man must practise, not seeming good, but being good, in private and public life" (*Gorgias* 527b).[13] Socrates is firmly convinced that this *logos* should be regarded as a universal and binding norm of the good life, i.e., that it can no longer be

---

[11] Vlastos, *Socrates Ironist*, 119.
[12] Cf. Maier, *Sokrates*, 133 f.
[13] Translation by Terence Irwin: Plato, *Gorgias. Translated with Notes by T. Irwin.* (Oxford: Clarendon Press 1979), 106.

refuted as a principle of ethical action. The goal of the agonistic dialectic is to test the *logos* with regard to the truth and not according to the opinion of the majority.

In order to be superior to one's opponent in agonal competition, Socrates believes it is necessary to be consistent, to create an inner order in one's own soul, and to strive for a good life. The human soul is well constituted when it moderates desires and affects, and as such, it can strive to fight and refute the problematic forms of life. This is the characteristic of the agonistic discussions between Socrates and Protagoras, Socrates and Callicles, and between Socrates and Thrasymachus. This is the reason why most Socratic dialogues e.g., *Protagoras*, *Gorgias*, *Hippias Major*, *Euthydemus*, were characterized as agonistic (ἀγωνιστικός) in tradition, as Diogenes Laertius confirms.[14] Laertius claims that Plato distinguished two forms of agonistic dialogues: proving (ἐνδεικτικός) and refuting (ἀνατρεπτικός).[15]

Although it is obvious from the context of the ethical dialogues that Socrates succeeded in refuting his interlocutors in the competition (*agōn*), there have always been cases in the course of history where sympathies were shown for the opposing position. The example of Thrasymachus with his controversial definition of justice as the advantage of the stronger (φημὶ γὰρ ἐγὼ εἶναι τὸ δίκαιον οὐκ ἄλλο τι ἢ τὸ τοῦ κρείττονος συμφέρον, *Republic* 338c) is an interesting case. Thrasymachus's definition of justice has gained more approval in current political discourse than Socrates's view that justice is the benefit of the weaker. The famous German political scientist Ralf Dahrendorf has demonstrated an affinity for this position.[16] Dahrendorf tried to prove that in the modern democratic society the power of authority is *conditio sine qua non* for governing. Dahrendorf therefore shows a certain sympathy with the assertion of Thrasymachus that "justice is the benefit of the stronger" because

---

[14] Cf. Diogenes Laertius: *Diogenis Laertii Vitae* philosophorum. Vol. I. Libri I-X. ed. Miroslav Marcovich. (Berlin: Walter de Gruyter 2008), (III, 49-51), 222.

[15] Diogenes Laertius 3.49.

[16] Cf. Ralf Dahrendorf, *In Praise of Thrasymachus* (Eugene: University of Oregon Press, 1966).

political power is for Dahrendorf a "central concept" of democratic society; laws are established by rulers so that they can govern over citizens. Laws, namely, allow rulers to punish criminals. Therefore, justice is defined as obedience to the laws, as Thrasymachus has claimed. Furthermore, we can claim that Socrates's concept of justice as the right of the weaker has become the basic idea of social justice or a social democratic worldview.

In contrast to Vlastos's interpretation of elenchos, it is important to emphasize that elenctic argumentation is more than just the method; it is a form of careful examination of how to live well; it is a process of reflective judgment. Elenchos is not merely a methodical procedure in which wrong views and incorrect definitions are refuted, it is also a sign of concern for one's own soul (*Apology* 29e2); it is identical with self-enquiry and concern for one's own personality (*Apology* 29d). The question about the good life, or "how to live" (πῶς βιωτέον, *Gorgias* 492d), remains in the foreground of the Socratic discussion and ultimately proves to be the moral *elenchein* that strives for "moral clarity." Already in the *Apology* it was stated that "the unexamined life is not worth living" (ὁ δὲ ἀνεξέταστος βίος οὐ βιωτὸς ἀνθρώπῳ, 38a). Elenchos is a process of permanent examination of one's own life with regard to *eudaimonia* (happiness). The fundamental motif of Socrates's philosophizing, how to become as good and honorable a person as possible (*Apology* 36c5), recurs in all the aporetic dialogues. Socrates reflected intensively on this question and fervently discussed with his partners in the dialogues the genuine values (*aretai*) of human existence, which belong to all human beings as universal characteristics (*ta proshekonta*; *Gorgias* 507a7).

Socrates is aware that practical knowledge—the conditions that guarantee a good and happy life—surpasses his epistemic ability. The key difficulty implied by the effort to achieve the good life is thus how the individual is to achieve *phronēsis*, which implies good judgment and excellence of character. *Phronēsis* is reasonable thinking, ranging from judgment of a specific situation to the key question of how to achieve a good and happy life. The examination of self and knowledge of oneself prescribed by the Delphic oracle "*Gnōthi seauton*," thus necessarily implies concern for the constitution of one's own personality, the realization of one's own true *aretē*, the good in relation to one's self. The importance of self-knowledge is pointed out on several occasions in the Socratic dialogues (*Protagoras* 343b; *Charmides* 164d; *Apology* 23b;). It is telling that Socrates, for example, in the *Crito* (47a) asserts that with respect to the question of how to achieve the good life, it is not the judgment (*doxa*) of the majority of people that is crucial, but that of those who are competent, as shown by the example of the knowledge of "*technē*," where the competence of the experts (*technikos*) is decisive (*Laches* 184e; *Gorgias* 455b). In connection to this, the *Gorgias* has it thus:

> For remember, the things we are disputing over are not at all trivial, but they are practically the things which it is finest to know, and most shameful not to know; for the sum of them is to come to know or not to know who is happy (*eudaimōn*) and who is not" (*Gorgias* 472c-d).[17]

And it is precisely the human soul which enables a man to reason correctly and make the best and most reasoned decision within a given context to achieve a given goal: a personal satisfaction and *eudaimonia*. In the concrete example of whether it is imperative to attempt to escape from prison, or to accept the sentence of death, Socrates shows that it is imperative that he himself decides on the basis of prudent and reasonable reflection: "Because not only now, but always I adhered to the arguments, *logos*, that appears best to me upon reasoning" (μοι λογιζομένῳ; *Crito* 46b). The mere fact that human beings possess *phronēsis*, is thus the necessary condition, but not the sufficient cause, for achieving a happy and satisfying life. Moreover, Socrates's "*logizomai*" presupposes the faculty of judgment as a search for the best option that fulfills our meaningful life and achieves the best conditions possible for a human being (*eudaimonia*). The faculty of judgment can be either a reflective activity in which we seek general norms for concrete actions or determinative judgment in which we apply already known norms to concrete cases.

---

[17] Translation by Terence Irwin (Plato, *Gorgias*, 42).

Agōn as Constituent of the Socratic Elenchos

In the early Platonic dialogues, we distinguish three forms of elenchos:
1. purgative or cathartic refutation in which the consistency of the definition is checked;
2. defensive elenchos in which the definition or opinion is justified or defended.
3. definition-testing elenchos which answers the question "What is X?"[18]

All three forms of elenchos are in some way the forms of judgment (*krinein*).

The first book of the *Republic* offers us a beautiful example of the purgative refutation of the conventional morality which Polemarchus represents, namely that it is good to behave well and justly with friends, unkind and inhuman towards enemies. War was cited as a paradigmatic example of such behavior. We should help our fellow combatants in war and show solidarity with them in every respect, while we should do harm to our enemies. Socrates refutes this definition with the question of whether this way of dealing makes the enemy better, or does it make the enemy even worse? Justice should not make anyone worse. As an example of the defensive elenchos the claim is given that "it is worse to do wrong than to suffer wrong" (*Gorgias* 509a). This *logos* contains a principle of life, namely how one can live well and happily; therefore, Socrates claims that he will defend this *logos* "with iron argument" (*Gorgias* 509a); all other assertions (*logoi*) are refuted, only this one remains conclusive, unshakeable.

Definition-testing elenchos was practiced in the dialogues *Euthyphro*, *Laches*, *Charmides*, and early parts of the *Meno* and the first book of *The Republic*. In the dialogue *Laches*, for example, it becomes plausible that an example from war is not sufficient to define courage, even though we designate such cases as brave. Courage is found not only in war, but in perils at sea, in disease, poverty, and politics, and what he wishes to be told is what is the

---

[18] Cf. P. Woodruff, "The Skeptical Side of Plato's Method," *Revue Internationale de Philosophie*, 1986 (40) 22-37, 26.

same (*tauton*) in all these instances.[19] In Kant's terminology, we could say that the attempt to arrive at a definition through induction from individual cases is a skillful activity of reflective judgment (*reflektierende Urteilskraft*). On the other hand, the refutation (*elenchos*) of inadequate definitions could be characterized as the application of determinative judgment (*bestimmende Urteilskraft*).

In his closing words in the *Gorgias*, Socrates says that he calls Callicles and all other people to competition (*agōn*). It's about the search for the best form of life: "To this way of life and to this struggle (*agōn*), in which the prize, I assure you, outweighs all the prizes of this world, I challenge all others to the best of my ability" (527e). As a philosopher, at the end of the dialogue, Socrates promises a life that is in itself a competition (*agōn*) for truth. It is not an abstract search for the truth, but the question of how to live (πῶς βιωτέον, *Gorgias* 492d).

Vlastos's assertion that there is a radical difference between the Socratic and Platonic forms of elenchos is highly controversial. The difference should be analogous to the difference of ideas and forms in Socrates and Plato: Plato's elenchos is "different from that of Socrates as is the Platonic Form from the Socratic form."[20] Vlastos has unfortunately not explained what the real difference between Platonic and Socratic elenchos is. The common feature of the two forms of elenchos is that truth is the essential criterion for the application of the elenctic method. In the seventh book of *The Republic*, Plato sees in the discussion of the idea of the good a connection between victory in argumentation and knowledge of the truth:

> The man who cannot by reason distinguish the Form of the Good from all others, who does not, as in a battle, survive all refutations, (ὥσπερ ἐν μάχῃ διὰ πάντων ἐλέγχων διεξιών) eager to argue according to reality and

---

[19] Cf. R.E. Allen, "Plato's Earlier Theory of Forms," in Gregory Vlastos, ed., *The Philosophy of Socrates. A Collection of Critical Essays* (Notre Dame: University of Notre Dame Press, 1971), 319-334, 322.

[20] Vlastos, *Socratic Studies*, 2 n. 6.

not according to opinion, and who does not come through all the tests without faltering in reasoned discourse such a man you will say does not know the Good itself, nor any kind of good. (*Republic* 534c, trans. Grube)

The Idea of the Good as the highest philosophical principle also has, among other tasks and functions, the assignment of "regulating the activity of judgement."[21] As the principle of judgment, the idea of the good remains both the source and the principle of all reasonable private and political action: "that anyone who is to act wisely (ἐμφρόνως) in private or public must have caught sight of this" (*Republic* 517c). As in the *Gorgias*, Plato also tried in *The Republic* to link the philosophical judgment to the concept of competition (*agōn*) because the greatest agonistic challenge is to determine "whether a man prove good or bad, so that not the lure of honor or wealth or any office, no, nor of poetry either, should incite us to be careless of righteousness and all excellence" (608b).[22]

Similar to the *Republic*, Plato continues in the *Sophist* the Socratic tradition of agonal elenctic by proving that the art of testing the truth is closely tied to the art of refutation (*hē elenktikē technē*), which is itself a form of the art of contest (*agōnistikē technē*; *Sophist* 230a f.). As Socrates states in *Gorgias* (526e), the life of reasoning, "this life and this contest…is worth all other contests on this earth."

The agonal determination of elenchos in Plato's late dialogues is proof that despite certain doctrinal differences in early and late periods, his work demonstrates definite continuity in its argumentation. In the late dialogue *Philebus*, we have proof of how the agonistic dialectic is applied to the question of how to live a good life. In *Philebus*, Socrates is again given the leading role in the discussion, but in the discussion about the forms of the good life the instruments of the agonal dialectic of connection and division

---

[21] Cf. Wolfgang Wieland, *Plato und die Formen des Wissen* (Göttingen: Vandenhoeck & Ruprecht, 1982), 164.

[22] Translation by Paul Shorey, Plato, *The Republic* (Cambridge: Harvard University Press, 1987).

of concepts are used. *Philebus* should be interpreted according to the premise that a shared language is a precondition for the dialectical exchange of claims as well as of the reaching of an agreement concerning the fundamental question of which roads lead to both a good life and spiritual contentment. Plato recognized that the dialectical method relates to the whole of language and that it is only within the context of the whole language that one can make sense of true and false claims, and to debate and discuss both acceptable and unacceptable views.

In his late dialogues, he focuses on the issue of the truth and the falsity of *logos* based on the possibility of conceptual blending. Plato views *logos* as an explication of reality, while the dialectical method of conceptual collection and division helps him to uncover both the existing and the possible states of affairs articulated through our propositions. The potential interconnectivity of concepts is proposed as a logical contest, which opens the room to a multitude of both true and false propositions corresponding to a multitude of factual or non-factual states of affairs.

The return to Socratic questions in the *Philebus* is a result of Plato's profound insight that we cannot solve problems in practical life with the so-called "divine method" of dialectics, but that we also need reasonable judgment. Namely, it is easy to describe the relationship between the genera, kinds, species, and sub-species, or to explain through them the cases involved in them; however, the question of the degree to which we can live with pleasure (*hedonē*) without being swayed by it is a complex dialectical issue in which an application of the "divine method" poses a demanding and perplexing challenge. The dialectical method can supply reliable definitions of moral terms, or virtues, and create a network of their associations and interrelations, but it nevertheless must leave the question of their application to specific cases to the cultivated ability of reasonable judging. This remains the task of *phronēsis*.

Lidia Palumbo & Heather L. Reid[1]
Wrestling with the Eleatics in Plato's *Parmenides*

In his *Lives,* Diogenes Laertius classifies Platonic dialogues into several types, including *gymnastikos* and *agōnistikos* forms of inquiry; the latter are aimed at victory, the former at training the mind.[2] Although he classifies the *Parmenides* as neither of these but rather as one for instruction in metaphysics,[3] we believe that the dialogue illustrates Plato's adaptation of athletic techniques to philosophical inquiry on several levels. To demonstrate this, we will examine the *Parmenides*'s setting, its method, and its theory. On all three levels, we find an important connection between

---

[1] Lidia Palumbo is professor of ancient philosophy at the Università degli Studi di Napoli Federico II. She is co-editor of the series *Philosophike Skepsis,* and author of *Il non essere e l'apparenza. Sul* Sofista *di Platone* (Napoli 1996), Mimesis: *Rappresentazione, teatro e mondo nei dialoghi di Platone e nella* Poetica *di Aristotle* (Napoli 2008), Verba manent, *su Platone e il linguaggio* (Napoli 2014), and many articles on Plato and Aristotle's *Poetics*. She is currently working on the theatrical and protreptic dimensions of Platonic texts. Heather L. Reid was introduced in the first essay of the volume. This collaborative essay was completed during her Fulbright residence in Napoli, which was co-sponsored by the Foundation *Con il Sud*.

[2] Diogenes Laertius 3.49: "Of the Platonic dialogues there are two most general types, the one adapted for instruction and the other for inquiry…The dialogue of inquiry also has two main divisions, the one of which aims at training the mind and the other at victory in controversy. Again, the part which aims at training the mind has two subdivisions, the one akin to the midwife's art, the other merely tentative. And that suited to controversy is also subdivided into one part which raises critical objections, and another which is subversive of the main position. Τοῦ δὴ <δια>λόγου τοῦ Πλατωνικοῦ δύ᾽ εἰσὶν ἀνωτάτω χαρακτῆρες, ὅ τε ὑφηγητικὸς καὶ ὁ ζητητικός… τοῦ δὲ ζητητικοῦ καὶ αὐτοῦ δύο εἰσὶν οἱ πρῶτοι χαρακτῆρες, ὅ τε γυμναστικὸς καὶ ἀγωνιστικός. καὶ τοῦ μὲν γυμναστικοῦ μαιευτικός τε καὶ πειραστικός, τοῦ δὲ ἀγωνιστικοῦ ἐνδεικτικὸς καὶ ἀνατρεπτικός." For an analysis, see F. Ferrari, "La nascita del platonismo," in *Princeps Philosophorum. Platone nell'Occidente tardo-antico, medievale e umanistico,* eds. M. Borriello and A.M.Vitale (Roma: Città Nuova, 2016), 13-29.

[3] Diogenes Laertius 3.50. The fact that the *Parmenides* does not appear in the category of zetetic or gymnastic dialogues in this classification (presumably derived from Middle Platonism) demonstrates only that it was interpreted differently than the others.

philosophy and *agōn*, a specifically gymnastic or training *agōn* that is aimed not at victory or defeat of one's opponent, but constructively toward the achievement of a philosophical "vision," which is achieved by overcoming the theoretical challenges that philosophers encounter on their path.

This essay interprets the *Parmenides* agonistically as a constructive contest between Plato's Socrates and the Eleatics of Western Greece. Not only is the dialogue set in the agonistic context of the Panathenaic Games, it features agonistic language, employs an agonistic method, and may even present an agonistic model for participation in the forms. The inspiration for this agonistic motif may be that Parmenides and his student Zeno represent Western Greece, which was a key rival for the mainland at the Olympics and other Panhellenic festivals. This athletic rivalry was complemented by a philosophical rivalry, which is dramatized in the dialogue by pitting a very young (flyweight) Socrates against the Eleatic (heavyweight) Parmenides. Through dialectic, an agonistic form of philosophy attributed to the Eleatics, Plato subjects his theory of forms to a variety of conceptual challenges. This process is described as *gymnasia* (training) at 135d, and the power of dialectic and philosophy itself are said to depend on it.

The goal of the *gymnasia* (136c) is to achieve a full view (*kyriōs diopsesthai*) of the truth. This philosophical "vision" corresponds to the physical fitness achieved through athletic training, and it distinguishes philosophers (lovers of wisdom) from *philotheamones* (lovers of images) as explained at *Republic* 475d-476c. Just as trained athletes are able to participate in the contest while spectators merely watch it, philosophers are able to discern intelligible forms through the particulars that participate in them. In the words of the *Seventh Letter* 341c, it takes prolonged communion (*synousia*) with a subject to ignite the philosophical light in one's soul. The *Parmenides*'s *gymnasia* provides an agonistic model for this process, inviting its readers to participate in philosophical training and develop a vison that transcends the material in a way these Eleatic spectators were unable to do.

Wrestling with the Eleatics in Plato's Parmenides

Setting and Characters

The *Parmenides* has an athletic setting and its philosophical characters are compared to athletes. We learn at 127a, that Parmenides and his protégé, Zeno, have come to Athens εἰς Παναθήναια τὰ μεγάλα, for the Greater Panathenaic Games.[4] The Panathenaia was a local religious festival honoring Athena that took place annually. Every fourth year, athletic contests were added and athletes came from all over the Hellenic world to compete for the sacred olive oil contained in Panathenaic prize vases, which can be seen today in museums all over the world. Although these games, like all the "money" games that awarded valuable prizes, were less prestigious than the "crown" games at Olympia, Delphi, Nemea and Isthmia, they grew to become an important Panhellenic event. And just as the Olympic Games provided an opportunity for intellectuals to gather and exchange ideas, the Greater Panathenaia would be a likely occasion — perhaps the only likely occasion — upon which Socrates would meet the Eleatic philosophers. Socrates rarely wandered far from Athens, unlike Plato who travelled to Olympia and Western Greece.

The dialogue's narrator, Cephalus (whose name suggests the beginning of something)[5] says that he has traveled to Athens from Clazomenae in Asia Minor — home of the pre-Socratic philosopher Anaxagoras.[6] It is not clear whether the Clazomenians were also in

---

[4] See S. Campese and S. Gastaldi, "Bendidie e Panatenee," in Platone, *La Repubblica*, vol. I, bk. I, trans. M. Vegetti (Napoli: Bibliopolis, 1998), 109-131.

[5] In this case, the beginning of the Platonic dialogues, since Socrates is younger here than in any other dialogue. On the possibility of ordering Plato's dialogues according to the dramatic context of Socrates's age, see C. H. Zuckert, "Plato's Parmenides: A dramatic Reading," *The Review of Metaphysics*, 51.4 (1998): 875-906, and C. H. Zuckert, *Plato's Philosophers. The Coherence of the Dialogues* (Chicago: The University of Chicago Press, 2009). See also M.L. Declos, "Instituer la philosophie: le temps de la succession dans le Parménide de Platon," in C. Darbo-Peschanski (ed.), *Constructions du temps dans le monde grec ancien*, (Paris: CNRS Éditions, 2000), 223-52.

[6] On the reference to Clazomenae, see F. Forcignanò, *Forme, linguaggio, sostanze. Il dibattito sulle idee nell'Academia antica*, (Milano-Udine: Mimesis: 2017), 55.

town for (a later edition) of the Festival, but it is well-attested by the distribution of Panathenaic amphorae in tombs that delegations from Asia Minor as well as Western Greece attended the Games. In fact, athletes from Sicily and Southern Italy, particularly the city of Croton, were so dominant that a proverb claimed, "The last of the Crotonites is the first of the rest of the Greeks."[7] Croton, of course, is also the adopted home of Pythagoras,[8] who very likely had a hand in its athletes' success, and certainly had a major influence on Western Greek thinkers including Empedocles, Parmenides, and Zeno. That Plato was aware of the athletic side of Pythagoreanism is suggested by his decision to set up a school in the Academy gymnasium[9] upon returning from a voyage to Syracuse and Taranto, where he met the Pythagorean Archytas[10] who, by one account, rescued the Athenian from slavery after a later voyage.

The point is that the athletic rivalry between Mainland and Western Greeks was accompanied in Plato's mind by a philosophical rivalry. Furthermore, as a former wrestler,[11] Plato would have understood this rivalry as a constructive one in which good competition serves to improve the competitors. By pitting a very young Socrates against the venerable Eleatic Parmenides in dialectic (a form of inquiry attributed to Zeno),[12] Plato subjects his theory of forms to a variety of conceptual challenges in the effort to make it stronger. The dialogue's participants are also described in athletic terms. Parmenides compliments Socrates for his *hormē*

---

[7] Strabo, *Geographia* 6.1.12.

[8] For a discussion of Pythagoras's influence on athletics see Heather L. Reid, "Plato the Gymnasiarch," in *ΦΙΛΕΛΛΗΝ: Essays for Stephen G. Miller*, eds. D. Katsonopoulou & E. Partida, Athens: The Helike Society, 171-186, p 173.

[9] Diogenes Laertius, 3.7.

[10] Diogenes Laertius 3.21-22.

[11] Diogenes Laertius, 3.1.4.

[12] According to Diogenes Laertius 8.2.57, Aristotle in his *Sophist* calls Empedocles the inventor of rhetoric and Zeno of dialectic. "φησὶ δ᾽ Ἀριστοτέλης εὑρετὴν [Ζήνων] γενέσθαι διαλεκτικῆς, ὥσπερ Ἐμπεδοκλέα ῥητορικῆς."

Wrestling with the Eleatics in Plato's Parmenides

toward argument[13]—an athletic word that suggests the eagerness of a runner or racehorse bursting from the starting gate. Zeno, meanwhile, confesses to writing his book out of "competitive spirit" (*philonikia*), a vice that Plato takes to be characteristic of athletes and sophists.[14] It is worth noting, as well, that Plato himself is engaged in the parallel act of writing a book to competitively defend his theory of forms.

Finally, Parmenides himself is compared with the aging racehorse in a song from the Western Greek poet, Ibycus:

> I am obliged to go along with you. And yet I feel like the horse in the poem of Ibycus. Ibycus compares himself to a horse—a champion but no longer young, on the point of drawing a chariot in a race and trembling at what experience tells him is about to happen—and says that he himself, old man that he is, is being forced against his will to compete in Love's game. I too, when I think back, feel a good deal of anxiety as to how at my age I am to make my way across such a vast and formidable sea of words.
>
> ἀνάγκη, φάναι, πείθεσθαι. καίτοι δοκῶ μοι τὸ τοῦ Ἰβυκείου ἵππου πεπονθέναι, ᾧ ἐκεῖνος ἀθλητῇ ὄντι καὶ πρεσβυτέρῳ, ὑφ᾽ ἅρματι μέλλοντι ἀγωνιεῖσθαι καὶ δι᾽ ἐμπειρίαν τρέμοντι τὸ μέλλον, ἑαυτὸν ἀπεικάζων ἄκων ἔφη καὶ αὐτὸς οὕτω πρεσβύτης ὢν εἰς τὸν ἔρωτα

---

[13] 130b: Παρμενίδην: ὦ Σώκρατες, φάναι, ὡς ἄξιος εἶ ἄγασθαι τῆς ὁρμῆς τῆς ἐπὶ τοὺς λόγους ("what an admirable talent for argument you have!"). Also, 135d: καλὴ μὲν οὖν καὶ θεία, εὖ ἴσθι, ἡ ὁρμὴ ἣν ὁρμᾷς ἐπὶ τοὺς λόγους (Your impulse towards dialectic is noble and divine).

[14] 128de: διὰ τοιαύτην δὴ φιλονικίαν ὑπὸ νέου ὄντος ἐμοῦ ἐγράφη, καί τις αὐτὸ ἔκλεψε γραφέν... ταύτῃ οὖν σε λανθάνει, ὦ Σώκρατες, ὅτι οὐχ ὑπὸ νέου φιλονικίας οἴει αὐτὸ γεγράφθαι, ἀλλ᾽ ὑπὸ πρεσβυτέρου φιλοτιμίας. "In that competitive spirit, I wrote the book when I was a young man. [...] So in this respect, I think you missed the point, Socrates, you think it was written not out of a young man's competitiveness but out of a mature man's vainglory." Both *philonikia* and *philotimia* are considered by Plato to be vices characteristic of athletes and sophists. See M. Tabak, *Plato's* Parmenides *Reconsidered*, (New York: Palgrave Macmillan, 2015), 31-2.

ἀναγκάζεσθαι ἰέναι: κἀγώ μοι δοκῶ μεμνημένος μάλα φοβεῖσθαι πῶς χρὴ τηλικόνδε ὄντα διανεῦσαι τοιοῦτόν τε καὶ τοσοῦτον πέλαγος λόγων. (136e-137a[15])

By 137b, however, Parmenides has agreed "to play the strenuous game" (πραγματειώδη παιδιὰν παίζειν) he has been recommending to Socrates.[16] After all, he observes, they are by themselves—no one is watching.

Method: the "*Gymnasia*"

At 135c, the "game" in question is actually called "*gymnasia*" (training) and Parmenides tells Socrates that nothing less than the power of dialectic and the future of philosophy depend on it.[17] Dialectic, as we said, was a form of inquiry attributed by Aristotle to Zeno of Elea.[18] The method demonstrated by Parmenides in the dialogue is certainly an example of Eleatic dialectic.[19] But why, apart from its affinity with athletic contest, is this dialectic called *gymnasia*? The first hint comes from the aforementioned comments about it taking place in private.[20] At 136de, Zeno says it would not

---

[15] Unless otherwise stated, all English translations of Plato are taken from John Cooper, ed., *Plato: Complete Works* (Indianapolis: Hackett, 1997).

[16] It is significant that Parmenides uses the terms *paidia/paizein* here (to play a game), which suggests the sophists' abuse of philosophical tools such as dialectic. In our interpretation, the Eleatics are presented in the *Parmenides* as practitioners of a sophistical dialectic, whereas Socrates, here at the beginning of his career, and thanks to the training that he is beginning to undergo, is capable of authentically philosophical dialectic. On sophistry as a game, see Plato, *Sophist*, 234b-235a.

[17] 135c: "'In this way he [who does not allow for forms] will destroy the power of dialectic entirely. But I think you are only too well aware of that./ 'What you say is true,' Socrates said./ 'What then will you do about philosophy? Where will you turn, while these difficulties remain unresolved?'...καὶ οὕτως τὴν τοῦ διαλέγεσθαι δύναμιν παντάπασι διαφθερεῖ. τοῦ τοιούτου μὲν οὖν μοι δοκεῖς καὶ μᾶλλον ᾐσθῆσθαι. ἀληθῆ , φάναι. τί οὖν ποιήσεις φιλοσοφίας πέρι; πῇ τρέψῃ ἀγνοουμένων τούτων;"

[18] See n. 12 above.

[19] On the Eleatic method in Plato's *Parmenides*, see Samuel Scolnicov, *Plato's Parmenides* (Berkeley: University of California Press, 2003).

[20] The lack of spectators transforms the dialectic from a public *agōn* (the prefix *ag-* indicates a public gathering) into a private *gymnasia* (training exercise).

be appropriate to ask Parmenides to perform the *gymnasia* in public:

> ...it's not fitting, especially for a man his age, to engage in such a discussion in front of a crowd. Ordinary people don't know that without this comprehensive and circuitous treatment we cannot hit upon the truth and gain insight.

> εἰ μὲν οὖν πλείους ἦμεν, οὐκ ἂν ἄξιον ἦν δεῖσθαι: ἀπρεπῆ γὰρ τὰ τοιαῦτα πολλῶν ἐναντίον λέγειν ἄλλως τε καὶ τηλικούτῳ: ἀγνοοῦσιν γὰρ οἱ πολλοὶ ὅτι ἄνευ ταύτης τῆς διὰ πάντων διεξόδου τε καὶ πλάνης ἀδύνατον ἐντυχόντα τῷ ἀληθεῖ νοῦν σχεῖν.

Just as athletes train privately in the gymnasium and compete publically in the games, philosophers need to train in private before they perform in public.[21] And once a champion like Parmenides is past his prime, his experience is of special value in training younger competitors, such as Socrates.[22] By Plato's time,

---

[21] A similar point about training in private before performing in public is made at *Gorgias* 514e: "by Heaven, Callicles, would it not in truth be ridiculous that men should descend to such folly that, before having plenty of private practice, sometimes with indifferent results, sometimes with success, and so getting adequate training in the art, they should, as the saying is, try to learn pottery by starting on a wine-jar, and start public practice themselves and invite others of their like to do so? Do you not think it would be mere folly to act thus? πρὸς Διός, ὦ Καλλίκλεις, οὐ καταγέλαστον ἂν ἦν τῇ ἀληθείᾳ, εἰς τοσοῦτον ἀνοίας ἐλθεῖν ἀνθρώπους, ὥστε, πρὶν ἰδιωτεύοντας πολλὰ μὲν ὅπως ἐτύχομεν ποιῆσαι, πολλὰ δὲ κατορθῶσαι καὶ γυμνάσασθαι ἱκανῶς τὴν τέχνην, τὸ λεγόμενον δὴ τοῦτο ἐν τῷ πίθῳ τὴν κεραμείαν ἐπιχειρεῖν μανθάνειν, καὶ αὐτούς τε δημοσιεύειν ἐπιχειρεῖν καὶ ἄλλους τοιούτους παρακαλεῖν; οὐκ ἀνόητόν σοι δοκεῖ ἂν εἶναι οὕτω πράττειν;"

[22] Parmenides, in this dialogue, plays not only the role of a critic, but also a defender of the Theory of Forms. The two roles are unified in the figure of the objector (ὁ ἀμφισβητῶν, 133b8, cfr. 135a), in which he poses questions to train Socrates, who has to respond and defend the Theory of Forms. On the role of the respondent, see M.L. Kakkuri-Knuuttila, "The Role of the Respondent in Plato and Aristotle," in *The Development of Dialectic from Plato*

the training of both athletes and philosophers actually took place in the gymnasium and only the former competed in the Games. Parmenides, however, may well have performed his philosophical poem competitively during his prime. Indeed, the rhetorical contests that Plato derides may have descended from competition among serious philosophers like Parmenides and Empedocles.[23]

In any case, the *gymnasia* demonstrated in the *Parmenides* has the flavor of a master sparring privately with his students, as we see the mature Socrates doing in such dialogues as *Charmides, Lysis,* and *Theaetetus*—all of which are set in *palaistrai* or gymnasia.[24] Indeed, the *Theaetetus* echoes several of the *Parmenides*'s gymnastic themes. For example, Theodorus is reluctant to enter the "contest" (*helkein pros to gymnàsion*) and asks Socrates to (*labe*) "get a hold on" Theaetetus in the argument (162ab); also, Theaetetus agrees to wrestle only upon the agreement that Socrates and Theodorus will "put him upright" (*epanorthō*) if he falls (146c). Helping your opponent to his feet is a common feature of combat sports training. This atmosphere of friendly competition is compounded in *Parmenides* by Zeno's and Parmenides's obvious delight in Socrates's challenge to their ideas at 130a; if the atmosphere were one of *philonikia,* such criticism might draw contempt. Although some scholars see the defeat either of Socrates or Parmenides in the dialectic,[25] the very fact that

---

to Aristotle, ed. Jakob L. Fink (Cambridge: Cambridge University Press, 2012), 62-90.

[23] See N. Benzi, *Philosophy in Verse: Competition and Early Greek Philosophical Thought,* thesis, Durham University. 2016 http://etheses.dur.ac.uk/11568/, 181-186.

[24] L. Coventry, "The Role of the Interlocutor in Plato's Dialogues, Theory and Practice," in *Characterization and Individuality in Greek Literature,* ed. Ch. Pelling (Oxford: Clarendon Press, 1990), 174-196.

[25] We do not believe that the *Parmenides* depicts a dialectical defeat of Socrates, but rather shows how Parmenides's objections to his theory are ultimately inconsistent. For another interpretation of the text from this perspective, see F. Ferrari, *Platone, Parmenide* (Milano: Bur, 2004); A. Graeser, "Parmenides in Plato's *Parmenides,*" in *Issues in the Philosophy of Language. Past and Present* (Bern: Peter Lang Publishing, 1999), 43-56; M. Tabak, *Plato's Parmenides*

Wrestling with the Eleatics in Plato's Parmenides

it is unclear who "wins" illustrates that this *gymnasia* is a form of mutually-beneficial training rather than a winner-take-all contest.[26]

The *Parmenides*'s dialectic is called *gymnasia*, above all, because it is a form of preparation. Let's go back to where Parmenides asks Socrates what he will do about philosophy if his questions about the forms remain unresolved. "I don't think I have anything clearly in view," replies the young Socrates, "at least not at present" (135c). Parmenides responds:

> Socrates, that's because you are trying to mark off something beautiful, and just, and good, and each one of the forms, too soon...[*prin gymnasthēnai*] before you have been properly trained. I noticed that the other day too, as I listened to you conversing with Aristotle here. The impulse [*hormē*] you bring to argument is noble and divine, make no mistake about it. But while you are still young put your back into it and get more training [*gymnasai*] through something people think useless— what the crowd call idle talk. Otherwise the truth will escape you.
>
> πρῷ γάρ, εἰπεῖν, πρὶν γυμνασθῆναι, ὦ Σώκρατες, ὁρίζεσθαι ἐπιχειρεῖς καλόν τέ τι καὶ δίκαιον καὶ ἀγαθὸν καὶ ἓν ἕκαστον τῶν εἰδῶν. ἐνενόησα γὰρ καὶ

Reconsidered (New York: Palgrave, 2015), 29: "Part I is clearly a satirical display of various objections to the theory of Forms, which are invalid, *non sequitur* reactions to the theory of Forms that smack of sophistry."

[26] The *gymnasia* benefits Socrates (or the critical reader of Socrates) by subjecting the theory of forms to the Eleatics' critical examination, so he can overcome some important theoretical challenges (attributable partly to his young age). But it also benefits Parmenides (or the critical reader of *Parmenides*), by revealing certain materialistic biases in the Eleatic criticism of Socrates. On this last point, see F. Ferrari, "Equiparazionismo ontologico e deduttivismo: l'eredità di Parmenide nella *gymnasia* del *Parmenide*," in *Il quinto secolo. Studi di filosofia antica in onore di Livio Rossetti*, eds. S. Giombini and F. Marcacci (Aguaplano: Officina del libro, Passignano, 2010), 357-368. On the text's instruction of the reader, see A.K. Cotton, *Platonic Dialogue and the Education of the Reader* (Oxford/New York: Oxford University Press, 2014).

πρώην σου ἀκούων διαλεγομένου ἐνθάδε Ἀριστοτέλει τῷδε. καλὴ μὲν οὖν καὶ θεία, εὖ ἴσθι, ἡ ὁρμὴ ἣν ὁρμᾷς ἐπὶ τοὺς λόγους: ἕλκυσον δὲ σαυτὸν καὶ γύμνασαι μᾶλλον διὰ τῆς δοκούσης ἀχρήστου εἶναι καὶ καλουμένης ὑπὸ τῶν πολλῶν ἀδολεσχίας, ἕως ἔτι νέος εἶ: εἰ δὲ μή, σὲ διαφεύξεται ἡ ἀλήθεια. (135d)

The image of truth "escaping" the hold of a wrestler is unavoidable here. Young Socrates wants to learn the old champion's technique. "What matter of training is that? (τίς οὖν ὁ τρόπος...τῆς γυμνασίας;)," he asks (135d).

The method that Parmenides describes is a special type of dialectic—a kind of round-robin *reductio*. *Reductio ad absurdum* works by hypothesizing the opposite of what you want to prove and then showing that the consequences are absurd. Standard dialectic envisions an objector who challenges each hypothesis—not unlike a wrestling match. What Parmenides proposes is a comprehensive system that subjects a hypothesis and its opposite to a series of *reductio* challenges, then analyzes the consequences.[27] Ancient wrestling tournaments were single elimination, with wrestlers drawing lots to determine matches and the winners advancing until a victor was determined.[28] Parmenides's method looks more like a round-robin tournament, in which each competitor faces every other competitor—as in the group play phase of the FIFA World Cup.[29] The round-robin method is less efficient at picking winners, but it has the advantage of revealing each contestant's individual strengths and weaknesses. It makes sense, furthermore, to prepare for a competition, in which one never knows exactly who one will be wrestling, by testing oneself against everyone else in the gymnasium who can provide an

---

[27] For a summary of the structure of the *gymnasia*, see F. Fronterotta, *Guida alla lettura del Parmenide di Platone* (Roma-Bari, Laterza, 1998).

[28] Michael B. Poliakoff, *Combat Sports in the Ancient World* (Yale University Press, 1987), 22.

[29] In the *gymnasia*, not only does the one confront the many, and the many—each alone and all together—confront the one, but it also happens that Socrates confronts Parmenides and Zeno, and then each of them separately.

appropriate challenge. This is the kind of "comprehensive and circuitous treatment" (διὰ πάντων διεξόδου τε καὶ πλάνης) Zeno describes at 136e. So Parmenides's *gymnasia* is private, cooperative, comprehensive preparation, akin to that undertaken in traditional gymnasia by athletes preparing for the Games. But what, exactly, is the philosopher training for?

Theory: Philosophical Vision

The theory and method of the *Parmenides* come together in the idea of a philosophical vision. The dialogue's theoretical background holds that material particulars participate in intelligible forms without being identical to them or completely separate. At 136c, Parmenides says to Socrates that he must complete the *gymnasia* in order to "achieve a full view (*kyriōs diopsesthai*) of truth." The goal of the philosopher's *gymnasia*, then, is to develop the "vision" by which sensible objects can be distinguished from intelligible forms, and the latter discerned through the former's participation in them. In other words, the gymnastic method cultivates a capacity to see things philosophically just as athletic exercises cultivate the capacity to wrestle competitively. Specifically, the philosopher is able to look beyond particulars as they show up superficially in our sense-data and see through to the ideals in which they participate. This is because the round-robin *reductio*, discussed above, forces us to imagine and consider all of the different consequences of each hypothesis. The challenge provided by opposing hypotheses, which is the basic method of dialectic, pushes us to transcend the limitations of material reality (135e) and to consider what exists only in the intelligible realm. In addition, by forcing us to consider what *would be* if things were opposite, it renders the invisible visible, considers the possibility of the apparently impossible, and in short evokes that sense of wonder characteristic of philosophers (not to mention the sense of possibility characteristic of sport).[30]

Such a concept of philosophical vision is illustrated in *Republic* V, appropriately enough with a contrast between spectators

---

[30] See L. Palumbo, "La meravigliosa struttura dell' 'altrimenti'. Una lettura del *Parmenide* di Platone," *Archivio di Storia della Cultura – Anno XXXIII-2020.*

(*philotheamones*) who love to watch festivals, and philosophers who "love the sight of truth." At 476b, spectators are described as those able to see the many beautiful things but not the beautiful itself.[31] A philosopher, by contrast,

> believes in the beautiful itself, can see both it and the things that participate in it and doesn't believe that the participants are it or that it itself is the participants.
>
> ἡγούμενός τέ τι αὐτὸ καλὸν καὶ δυνάμενος καθορᾶν καὶ αὐτὸ καὶ τὰ ἐκείνου μετέχοντα, καὶ οὔτε τὰ μετέχοντα αὐτὸ οὔτε αὐτὸ τὰ μετέχοντα ἡγούμενος. (476cd)

What is interesting, maybe even ironic,[32] is that the heavyweight philosopher Parmenides himself seems to lack such vision because the mistake he makes in the dialogue is precisely to fail to distinguish between forms and particulars,[33] immaterial and material.[34] For example, when Socrates tries to explain the relation

---

[31] *Republic* 476b: "The lovers of sights and sounds like beautiful sounds, colors, shapes, and everything fashioned out of them, but their thought is unable to see and embrace the nature of the beautiful itself. φιλήκοοι καὶ φιλοθεάμονες τάς τε καλὰς φωνὰς ἀσπάζονται καὶ χρόας καὶ σχήματα καὶ πάντα τὰ ἐκ τῶν τοιούτων δημιουργούμενα, αὐτοῦ δὲ τοῦ καλοῦ ἀδύνατος αὐτῶν ἡ διάνοια τὴν φύσιν ἰδεῖν τε καὶ ἀσπάσασθαι." On this passage, see F. Ferrari, "Teoria delle idee e ontologia," in *Platone, Repubblica* vol. iv, bk. 5, ed. M. Vegetti, (Napoli: Bibliopolis, 2000), 365-91.

[32] G. A. Press, *Plato: A Guide for the Perplexed* (London-New York: Continuum, 2007), 70 writes: "If they [Plato's dialogues] are attempts to communicate theories, concepts and doctrines that are Plato's own, they do not do so directly, but only indirectly through the mediation of [...] literary and dramatic machinery."

[33] The *gymnasia*, the lengthy discourse proposed by Parmenides in the last part of the dialogue, is the Platonic way of demonstrating the absurd, self-contradictory, and therefore ridiculous conclusions arrived at by a sophistical Eleatism, which dialectically questions the ontological difference between forms and particulars.

[34] This materialistic aspect of the Eleatic argument is crucial. It is evident in the entire Eleatic perspective, which conceives the relationship between the forms and particulars, or between the one and the many, in terms of a

between form and particular using the metaphor of the light of day, Parmenides counters with the materialistic example of a sail (131bc).[35] The Eleatic is presented as hopelessly attached to the material world.

Like several Platonic dialogues, the *Parmenides* not only discusses dialectic, it attempts to engage the reader in practicing it. On Plato's view, philosophy requires active participation. Just as the wrestler improves through engagement with other wrestlers, the philosopher improves through engagement with other philosophers, and it is through this dialectical wrestling with each other that they both move closer to the ideal.[36] Socrates's refusal to write at all and Plato's insistence on writing only dialogues are evidence for this belief. The *Seventh Letter*, meanwhile, states it specifically:

> Unlike other sciences, [philosophy] can in no way be communicated by means of words. On the contrary, it is only through a prolonged communion (*synousia*) with the subject, by living with it, that, like a light that is kindled by a flickering flame, it begins to suddenly nourish itself within one's soul.
>
> ῥητὸν γὰρ οὐδαμῶς ἐστὶν ὡς ἄλλα μαθήματα, ἀλλ' ἐκ πολλῆς συνουσίας γιγνομένης περὶ τὸ πρᾶγμα αὐτὸ καὶ τοῦ συζῆν ἐξαίφνης, οἷον ἀπὸ πυρὸς πηδήσαντος ἐξαφθὲν φῶς, ἐν τῇ ψυχῇ γενόμενον αὐτὸ ἑαυτὸ ἤδη τρέφει. (*Seventh Letter* 341cd)[37]

We believe that Plato primarily imagined this communion with the subject as the kind of private dialectic modeled on athletic training

---

combination of two elements in space, or in terms of a temporal conjunction of two material entities.

[35] See Ferrari, *Platone, Parmenide*, 212, n. 45.

[36] This model can be observed in *Lysis*, see H. Reid, "The Art of Teaching Philosophy in Plato's *Lysis*," *Skepsis* XVI i-ii (2005): 278-287.

[37] Translation by Jonah Radding from H. Reid and M. Ralkowski, eds. *Plato at Syracuse: Essays on Plato in Western Greece with a New Translation of the Seventh Letter by Jonah Radding* (Parnassos Press, 2019). Even if Plato is not the author of the letter, it is widely believed to express the philosopher's views.

that is called *gymnasia* in the *Parmenides*. And we argue that the dialogue itself is set up to engage readers in that *gymnasia*, in particular to get them to think beyond materialism, here represented by Parmenides. A full analysis of the philosophical problems presented by the dialectic must be left for another time, however.

Conclusion

It has been our purpose to show that Plato's *Parmenides* can be interpreted agonistically as a constructive contest between Eleatic and Athenian philosophers. By setting the dialogue at the Panathenaic Games and using athletic language to describe its participants, Plato uses the athletic rivalry between Mainland and Western Greeks to highlight a parallel philosophical rivalry. As a former wrestler, Plato would envision this rivalry as constructive, and imagine the dialectical method, here called *gymnasia*, as a kind of philosophical training. It is a private, comprehensive, and challenging preparation designed to reveal the weaknesses in hypotheses, but also to develop the kind of "vision" described in *Republic* V, which distinguishes the philosopher from the mere spectator. This philosophical *gymnasia* resembles a round-robin training exercise in which the reader is called to participate. In *Republic* III, Socrates states that *gymnastikē* primarily benefits the soul (*psychē*, 410c), while the *Parmenides* offers a philosophical gymnasium in which all souls are invited to train.

Daniel A. Dombrowski [1]
Four-Term Analogies and the *Gorgias*:
Gymnastics, *Agōn*, and the Athletic Life in Plato

One very fruitful way to read Plato's *Gorgias* is to interpret 464-465 as the key passage that illuminates the rest of this very long dialogue.[2] Here Plato introduces two four-term analogies, one of which deals with the body and the other with the soul. It will be the purpose of the present chapter to explicate these four-term analogies so as to shed needed light on the Platonic view of *gymnastikē* and *agōn* in particular, and more importantly, on the best life for human beings in general, in which bodily and intellectual/moral excellence are fused.

The dialogue takes place among the character Socrates and several other figures: the aged Gorgias, a famous teacher of rhetoric; a pupil named Polus; and Callicles, who defends both hedonism and the might-makes-right thesis, positions that are resisted by Socrates. Consider the following lines in the dialogue delivered by Plato's presumed spokesperson, the character Socrates:

> To the pair, body and soul, there correspond two arts— that concerned with the soul I call the political art; to the single art that relates to the body I cannot give a name offhand. But this single art that cares for the body comprises two parts, gymnastics and medicine, and in the political art what corresponds to gymnastics is legislation, while the counterpart of medicine is justice [...]. There are then these four arts which always minister to what is best, one pair to the body, the other for the soul. But flattery, perceiving this [...] divided herself also into

---

[1] Daniel Dombrowski is in the Philosophy Department of Seattle University. ddombrow@seattleu.edu.
[2] See the W.D. Woodhead translation in Plato, *The Collected Dialogues of Plato*, ed. Edith Hamilton and Huntington Cairns (Princeton: Princeton University Press, 1999); and the Greek text in *Platonis Opera*, 5 vols., ed. John Burnet (Oxford: Clarendon Press, 1977).

four branches, and [...] pretends to be that which she impersonates [...]. [S]he regularly uses pleasure as a bait [...]. [C]ookery has impersonated medicine [...]. [T]his kind of thing is bad [...] not an art but a routine [...]. [A]nd in the same way gymnastics is [im]personated by beautification, a mischievous, deceitful, mean, and ignoble activity, which cheats us by shapes and colors, by smoothing and draping, thereby causing people to take on an alien charm to the neglect of the natural beauty produced by exercise [...]. [And] sophistic is to legislation what beautification is to gymnastics, and rhetoric to justice what cookery is to medicine (464b-465b).

In brief, the four-term analogy that deals with the body goes as follows:

beautification (*kommotikē*) : gymnastics (*gymnastikē*) ::
cookery (*opsopoiikē*) : medicine (*iatrikē*)

The true arts are gymnastics and medicine in that the former, which can best be seen in terms of its contribution to the athletic life (to be described momentarily), is the best way to try to bring about bodily health, whereas medicine is the best way to cure the body when it becomes unhealthy, as it inevitably will. Beautification feigns the sort of bodily health fostered by gymnastics, in particular, or more generally by the athletic life; and cookery consists in a sort of pseudo-medicine that pretends to cure disease without actually doing so.

Likewise, in brief, the four-term analogy that deals with the soul goes as follows;

sophistic (*sophistikē*) : legislation (*nomothetikē*) ::
rhetoric (*rhetorikē*) : justice (*dikaiosynē*)

The best way to develop a healthy soul, whether in an individual or in the collective soul of the state, is to properly legislate regarding which pleasures are appropriate and in what degrees. Whereas, when the soul fails in the effort at legislation, as it inevitably does, justice (including punishment) is needed so as to correct the course of a wayward soul.

Four-Term Analogies and the Gorgias

It will be noted that, as a result of these two four-term analogies, there are four bona fide arts required in the best life, two of which concern the body (gymnastics and medicine) and two of which concern the soul (legislation and justice). Unfortunately, there are also four other arts that flourish parasitically as types of flattery (*kolakeutikē*), two of which deal with the body (beautification and cookery) and two of which deal with the soul (sophistic and rhetoric).[3]

The prominent place for the beautification-gymnastics complex in this dialogue should be of interest to contemporary scholars who are interested in the concepts of gymnastics, *agōn*, and the athletic/intellectual life in Plato. Plato's view here (presumably articulated in the dialogue through the character Socrates) is challenged forcefully by the most important of Socrates's interlocutors, Callicles, who argues that the sort of self-control required in gymnastics (or the athletic life) and legislation is actually a type of weakness and cowardice (483a-e). That is, the topics treated in the present chapter should be of interest to those contemporary thinkers interested in understanding the psychology and philosophy of tyranny (an understanding that is unfortunately just as needed in our world as it was in ancient Greece), as articulated in the dialogue by Callicles's defense of the might-makes-right hypothesis (484a-c), which is reminiscent of the defense of the same thesis in Book One of the *Republic* by the character Thrasymachus.

Gorgias, one of Socrates's interlocutors, is quite explicit that he is an expert in rhetoric (449a), which, according to the character Socrates, infringes not only on justice, but also on medicine, reflecting the conceptual tie between cookery and rhetoric (449d). All of the arts in question concern the use or misuse of words,

---

[3] Of course one can re-shuffle the Platonic deck and imagine two other four-term analogies, one of which groups together the true arts/sciences: gymnastics : legislation :: medicine : justice. The other groups together the flattering routines: beautification : sophistic :: cookery : rhetoric. Although these regroupings do not add much conceptually to Plato's ideas in the *Gorgias*, they may visually facilitate understanding of these concepts.

including gymnastics due to the need for proper discourse regarding the body's condition (450a), and regarding other games that do not involve bodily excellence, like draughts (450d). In short, on Gorgias's view there is something encyclopedic about rhetoric that seems to crowd out the other arts (456a).[4] Another art in which the rhetorician claims expertise is that of the athletic trainer; this is because the rhetorician knows the words used by the trainer to make bodies strong and beautiful (452a-b). The persuasion aimed at by rhetoricians is found by Gorgias to be useful far beyond the courts and assemblies for which it was originally intended. By rhetoric Gorgias intends "the power to convince by your words the judges in court...the people in the Assembly" and the ability to "persuade multitudes" by any means (452e).

The main difference between Gorgias's expansive view of rhetoric and the character Socrates's (Platonic) view is that the latter sees quite a difference between persuasion that produces belief without knowledge and persuasion that produces belief with it (454e). Gorgias quite frankly views rhetoric as a competitive art like boxing or mixed fighting such that to engage in rhetoric is very much to be involved in an *agōn*. It is "like every other competitive art," he says (456c). Rhetoric is often victorious in battles with other disciplines, on this view (456c-d). Granted, rhetoric might at times be misused, but we should no more chastise the teacher of rhetoric for this fact, thinks Gorgias, than we would blame a boxing teacher if one of his pupils acted aggressively outside of legitimate competition (456-457). One should make proper use of athletic gifts (457a-b, 460d). On the Platonic view, rhetoric and the other flattery "arts" (including beautification and cookery) are examples of a routine (*empeiria*) rather than of a genuine art or science (*technē*) in that they aim not so much at the truth as at gratification and pleasure (462c-e). These "arts" are the occupations of enterprising spirits who trade in semblances of reality, rather than with reality itself.

---

[4] See Eric Havelock, *Preface to Plato* (Cambridge: Harvard University Press, 1963).

Four-Term Analogies and the Gorgias

It is unfortunate that there is no single word that refers to the art that cares for the body, but the two parts—gymnastics and medicine—remind one of the distinction made today between preventive medicine and curative medicine. Likewise, there is no single contemporary word that refers to the art that cares for the soul, but the two parts—legislation and justice—cover the territory in comprehensive fashion. These four arts always minister to what is best (464b-c). By contrast, the flattery routines are irrational (*alogōn*).

The four flattery "arts" masquerade as the true ones. They are routines rather than true arts/sciences because they can produce no rationally defensible principles behind what they offer, nor can they explain the nature of their subject matter, nor can they show causal connection, only temporal succession (464d-465e). Beautification, in particular, is described most negatively: it is mischievous, deceitful, mean, and ignoble! By beautification Plato means the effort to feign the athletic life by use of shapes (here one can let one's imagination run wild) and colors (one thinks of the fetish white people have for tans), by smoothing and draping the body with clothes that admittedly produce an alien charm, but they neglect the natural beauty produced by exercise (465b). Here one thinks about the contemporary multi-billion dollar industry in athletic clothing as well as the nearly ubiquitous presence of mirrors in weight training facilities. One pays a stiff price, Plato seems to be saying, by being more concerned with looking fit than with actually being so, both in terms of bodily health and health of soul. To cite an example from wood-working, there is quite a difference between a cheap veneer and quarter-sawn oak.

Everything that we do, on the Platonic account, should be directed toward the good, including running and training for an athletic event (468a-b). The four legitimate arts, including gymnastics, reinforce a familiar Platonic theme: that to do wrong, rather than to receive it, is the greatest of evils (469b, etc.). By contrast, the hedonist like Callicles, to whom the four flattery routines are pandering, thinks that the greatest evil is to be harmed. Further, the men *and women* (showing the egalitarian character of the thesis being defended) who are noble and good are happier than those who succumb to the four flattery routines, according to the character Socrates (470e, 493d). The unjust person, who initially might seem successful, is like a sprinter trying to run a long-distance race (see *Republic* 613b-c).

If one has done wrong, it is worse to escape punishment than to suffer it (474b, 509b), thus showing the importance of justice if legislation has in some way failed. Analogously, if one is unhealthy, it is worse to stay home rather than go to the doctor if gymnastics has in some way failed or if the body is unhealthy due to chance factors beyond one's control (477e-478a). Although an unhealthy soul is worse than an unhealthy body for Plato (479b), gymnastics and medicine are nonetheless necessary arts in the very best life, which should exhibit healthiness of soul *and* body. Those who give in to the four flattery routines—even beautification that deals with the body—are likely to develop ulcerous souls (480b), due to the integral connection between body and soul, to be described momentarily.

Rhetoric and the other flattery arts are not of much use to someone who does not intend to do wrong (481b). Of course, Socrates's primary interlocutor, Callicles, sees things quite differently, claiming, for example, that to suffer wrong is not fit for a real man, only for a slave, and slaves are to be simply used. Today we would say that someone with Callicles's view is pasting hair on his chest in an exaggerated display of machismo. He thinks that, although by convention (*nomos*) it is wrong to take advantage of weaker parties, by nature (*physis*) it is quite legitimate to do so. That is, our conventions are unnatural, he thinks (483c-484a, 488b, 489c).

Callicles has a much more bellicose understanding of *agōn* than Plato's, as evidenced by the controlled competitiveness of the dialogue itself. We are reminded here of the etymology of the Latin word *competitio*: to ask *with* (not against) one's partner in a dialectical *agōn*, whose view is better? (484c). In this context occurs one of the most famous (or infamous) of Callicles's criticisms of Socrates, that his philosophy (indeed philosophy, in general) is fitting for an adolescent, but not for real men. The character Socrates is like a child with a lisp, he thinks (485a-d).

Rather than master others in an exercise of sheer power, Plato would have us master ourselves in a temperate life (491d). Pleasure itself is not the problem, but pursuit of pleasure that knows nothing of the better or worse. Cookery, in particular, sees pleasure as an end-in-itself, hence it is a mere routine rather than a true art/science. (It seems that routines, for Plato, are necessarily inferior to true arts/sciences in that only the latter involve rational justification; hence the denigration of mere routines throughout the *Gorgias*.) It would be a mistake to assume that because the character Socrates does not subscribe to Callicles's aggressive sort of *agōn* that he is merely playing frivolously (*paizontos*) in the dialogue. Once again, between these two extremes—aggression and frivolous play—there is a sort of competitive play or controlled battle of ideas at work in the dialogue (500a-c). That is, Plato exhibits a sort of moderation in dialogical *agōn* that is compatible with several contemporary versions of the *homo ludens* hypothesis.[5] In this regard Platonic moderation is a philosophic expression of something similar in Homer.[6]

Medicine differs from cookery in its serious investigation of the subject, its search for causes rather than mere temporal successions, and its analysis of pleasure rather than the mere having of it. Further, medicine, in contrast to cookery, exhibits forethought regarding what will be best in the future for the body and soul of the patient (501ab). It is also concerned with the common good, in contrast to Callicles's egocentrism (502e).

The recent explosion of interest in bodily training might initially seem to be compatible with Plato's obvious interest in

---

[5] See Johan Huizinga, *Homo Ludens: A Study of the Play Element in Culture*, trans. R.F.C. Hull (Boston: Beacon Press, 1955); Randolph Feezell, *Sport, Play, and Ethical Reflection* (Champaign: University of Illinois Press, 2004); Daniel Dombrowski, *Contemporary Athletics and Ancient Greek Ideals* (Chicago: University of Chicago Press, 2009).

[6] See Daniel Dombrowski, "Homer, Competition, and Sport," *Journal of the Philosophy of Sport* 39 (2012): 33-51. Also see "Plato and Athletics," *Journal of the Philosophy of Sport* 6 (1979): 29-38; "Asceticism as Athletic Training in Plotinus," *Aufstieg und Niedergang der Römischen Welt* 36.1 (1987): 701-712; and "Weiss, Sport, and the Greek Ideal," in *The Philosophy of Paul Weiss*, ed. Lewis Hahn (LaSalle, IL: Open Court, 1995).

Daniel A. Dombrowski

bodily discipline, but the bodily *askēsis* Plato has in mind is integrally connected with the hylomorphic task of concomitantly fostering health and strength of soul. "Hylomorphism" is a view usually associated with Aristotle, which suggests that a human being is a composite of material stuff, on the one hand, and mind or soul stuff, on the other, such that the two interpenetrate and mutually reinforce each other. The word itself is a composite of *hyle* or matter and *morphē* or structure that is given to biological life by mind or soul. Rather than the common characterization of Plato as a dualist (wherein soul or mind is seen as radically different from, and separable from, body), the evidence here in the *Gorgias*, along with some evidence from the system of education in the *Republic*, is that Plato, too, along with Aristotle, is a hylomorphist. Instead of seeing human beings as souls or minds inside of (or imprisoned in) bodies, it would be more accurate to refer to human beings as "soulbodies" or "mindbodies" so as to highlight the fusion of mind/soul and body. That is, the athletic life and the intellectual/moral life are not as different from each other as they might initially seem.

Gymnastics and medicine are integrally connected to legislation and justice (504a-505b). In all of these true arts/sciences the pleasant is for the sake of the good, not the other way around (506c, 513c-d). This becomes quite evident when one particular sort of bodily discipline, swimming, is responsible for actually saving lives, in contrast to rhetoric, which is hardly useful at all (511c-d). Likewise, charioteers train their horses for useful service, in contrast to the work of (even famous) rhetoricians, who frequently make their students worse than they were before they came under the sway of rhetoric, say by inculcating into them the sense that persuasion matters more than truth or, even worse, that truth does not matter at all (516d-e).

Gymnastics and medicine should have sway over any subsidiary bodily arts/sciences because only they really know what is good for the body and indirectly for the soul due to the soul-body composite character of human existence. We should be especially skittish regarding those who practice the routine of cookery by urging us to consume food dainties or wines that are

Four-Term Analogies and the Gorgias

pleasing in a detrimental way to true health. Analogously, we should be skittish regarding rhetorical dainties that flatter, but do not really help, the soul (517e-518e).

In a peculiar way, sophistic is better than rhetoric. What Plato has in mind here (520a-c) can be understood when the analogy with bodily discipline is considered. That is, gymnastics is in a way more important than medicine in that it is better to do the best one can to lead a healthy life and then bring in medicine only when it is needed. It would seem that a healthcare system that ignored or deemphasized preventive medicine would be a defective one in that medicines and surgeries should be taken only reluctantly. However, we should not deny physicians their due in their legitimate efforts to help their patients. It is in this limited analogous sense that sophistic (as a preventive routine) is superior to rhetoric (as a reactionary measure). Likewise, a society with a bloated criminal justice system would seem to indicate a society that had not legislated properly.

It is true that laws deal in generalities and can only accommodate particular details with difficulty. This is exemplified by running coaches who deal with the general rules of running and not with each individual step of the runners (also see *Statesman* 294d). Plato's four-term analogies in the *Gorgias* that are the foci of the present chapter anticipate the discovery by Plato of relative nonbeing in the *Sophist*, or the unlimited factor in the *Philebus*, or the nonrational character of the receptacle in the *Timaeus*. Medicine and justice, in large part, owe their existence metaphysically to these unintelligible factors built into the world we live in, just as irrational numbers are built into the structure of rational mathematics. Plato is not quite the overly ambitious rationalist that many make him out to be. But then again, medicine and justice are also often propagated because of the failure of people to take preventative measures seriously by not getting their bodies and souls in the best shape possible through gymnastics and philosophic legislation.

Although in some of the dialogues (*Republic* 620b; *Phaedrus* 248) it seems that the athletic life is intermediate between the best and worst sorts of life, the above evidence from the *Gorgias* seems to indicate a more cooperative effort between the bodily arts and those that deal with the soul in pursuit of the best life. This would appear to be due, in part, to the fact that the more the appetitive part of the soul is trained well, the more the rational part can go about its proper business. Of course, the results here from the *Gorgias* may very well be compatible with evidence from other dialogues, depending on which passages are emphasized. Readers will be reminded of some well-known parts of the *Republic* (410b-c, 535d) where the proper preliminary studies in the education of youth are music (which develops the soul) and gymnastics (which develops the body and hence ultimately the soul due to the close hylomorphic connection between body and soul). Although a *purely* gymnastic education leads to a state close to savagery, in conjunction with music one can come to learn about the world in general: both the world of becoming (through gymnastics) and the world of being (through music/mathematics). The athletic life plays a necessary, if not sufficient, role in the development of a well-rounded individual.

The character Socrates reinforces the Platonic contempt for the flattery "arts" by suggesting that his upcoming trial (presumably in the *Apology*) will be like a scientific physician being prosecuted by a cook before a jury of children (521e)! He predicts that he will take his own upcoming death with equanimity (522d). At death, it seems, the soul will be separated from the body, *but not before* (524b, 527c-d). This is what prompted my aforementioned use of the concept of hylomorphism to describe Plato's view, despite the fact that this position is more usually associated with Aristotle. Avoiding the flattery disciplines is crucial for both health of body and health of soul individually *and* for the health of the hylomorphic body-soul composite found in this life.

The purpose of the above explication of the two four-term analogies at *Gorgias* (464-465) is to facilitate nothing less than the best way of life (*aristos tou biou* 527e). Plato's concern for the role of the athletics in the best possible life spans his dialogues from *Apology* to *Laws*. In this regard it should be remembered that the denigration of the body in the *Phaedo*, at a time when the body was

Four-Term Analogies and the Gorgias

of little concern to the character Socrates, certainly does not characterize all of Plato's thought.

I would like to close by gathering together the insights that might be gained by a consideration of these two four-term analogies in the *Gorgias* and by briefly commenting on the import of these analogies for an influential facet of contemporary philosophy. These analogies, which I see as the key to understanding the dialogue, are also crucial in the effort to understand nothing less than the good life, not only for Plato, but for us as well. On the evidence of these four-term analogies, we can say that a necessary condition for the good life consists in health of body, and health of body is fostered by two arts/sciences: gymnastics and medicine. The former is primary in that it is concerned with foods and exercises conducive to overall well-being, whereas the latter is needed when (not if) bodily health deteriorates. Another necessary condition for the good life is health of soul, which is also fostered by two arts/sciences: legislation and justice. The former is primary because it is concerned with the development of rationally defensible principles to live by, whereas the latter is needed when mistakes in legislation occur, at which point punishment (or at least regret regarding such mistakes) might be required. Further, these two types of health are not mutually exclusive in that each sort of health is conducive to the other on the hylomorphist view of Plato that I have emphasized. That is, health of body and health of soul are by no means contradictories but are rather mutually reinforcing correlatives. I admit that there are many passages in Plato's dialogues that might lead one to conclude that he was a dualist, but the important hylomorphist passages in Plato should not escape our notice. In this regard I would like to emphasize that the locutions "the athletic life" and "the intellectual/moral life" are not as opposed as they might initially seem, but might actually be seen as shorthand designations for each other.

Here at the end of the chapter I would like to push forward and bring these Platonic insights to bear on our contemporary situation. From the time of Friedrich Nietzsche to the present we have become familiar with the cliché that there are no facts, only interpretations. If this view were correct it would be difficult, if not impossible, to distinguish the four legitimate arts/sciences from the four types of flattery that impersonate them. This is because in the effort to balance the understandable claims of both perspectivalism and realism, there is a tendency in some philosophical circles to abandon the latter and to glorify the former. This abandonment leads to disastrous consequences on the Platonic view that I am defending, in that it prevents us from defending, say, the superiority of medicine to cookery. To take one outrageous contemporary example, Giorgio Agamben has recently criticized government leaders for taking seriously the advice of epidemiologists in the face of the covid-19 crisis that citizens should be sequestered from each other and that schools and sporting events, should be suspended until the coronavirus is contained. [7] In addition to exhibiting a sort of paranoia regarding legitimate government activity to promote the common good, Agamben's view constitutes a sort of postmodern cookery.

There are obviously important questions that still need to be asked about how exactly to differentiate between the legitimate arts/sciences and the flattery disciplines like cookery and how to get at the truth in a conflicting sea of mere opinion. It is no secret that Plato's monumental contribution to adequate responses to these questions lies in the dialectical method that he discovered and that he enshrined in his dialogues, a method that I have described above in terms of a moderate *agōn* that lies between Callicles' more aggressive contests and frivolous play. Such moderation is analogous to fair athletic competition in search of victory, with the infinitive *athleuein* meaning to compete for a prize. In dialectic the prize consists in having a certain hypothesis remain standing after several attempts at refutation by intelligent interlocutors. There *are* facts as well as interpretations.

---

[7] See Anastasia Berg, "Giorgio Agamban's Coronavirus Cluelessness," *The Chronicle of Higher Education* (March 23, 2020), which analyzes an article by Agamban, "The Coronavirus and the State of Exception," originally in *Il Manifesto,* but translated online into English in *Autonomies* (March 3, 2020).

Lee M. J. Coulson[1]
The *Agōnes* of Platonic Philosophy:
Seeking Victory Without Triumph

Jacob Burckhardt suggests that an "Agonal Age" of Greek history extended from the end of the Dorian migration to the conclusion of the sixth century BCE. He held that

> *agōn* was a motive power known to no other people – the general leavening element that, given the essential condition of freedom, proved capable of working upon the will and the potentialities of every individual.[2]

In the context of Ancient Greece, Burckhardt saw this age of *agōn* consisting "in men staking everything to win the favor of the crowd."[3] The dynamics of this motivational power to visibly win favor is not confined to the ancients, as it profoundly affects human behavior in any era. Like Plato, we also live in a agonistic age of endemic political struggle, physical competition, legal proceedings, public rhetoric and enactments of human conflict, each of which usually concludes by "crowning" winners.

For the Greeks, athletic competitions emulated and educated military skills. Rhetoric reflected those tournament values, thus oratory education implicated combat and triumph. Platonic philosophy advanced public debate on issues of morality and truth. It was a disruptive movement that sought change by encouraging a reassessment of putative canons, a personal yearning for reality and awareness of one's own beliefs – which often required the courage to concede that they were mistaken. Plato's dialogues combined social critiques and rational dialectic to induce *metanoia*, a change of heart and mind that better

---

[1] Lee M. J. Coulson, DipLangStud, BA (Hons.), PhD, is an Honorary Associate of the Department of Classics and Ancient History at the University of Sydney. His current research focuses on Plato's method and its pertinence to 21st century meta ethics and political anthropology.

[2] Jacob Burckhardt, *The Greeks and Greek Civilization*, ed. Oswyn Murray, trans. Sheila Stern (New York: St. Martin's Press, 1998), 162.

[3] Burckhardt, *The Greeks*, 164.

discerned the reality of authentic courage, temperance, justice and wisdom. Combative debate was among the mores that Plato sought to amend with a distinct engagement in and valuation of agonistic struggle. That raises two questions: why and how did Plato oppose conventional Athenian *agōn* (ἀγών)? This essay addresses those questions by considering the purpose and transmission of Platonic philosophy in the context of ancient Athens' agonal ethos. Plato's philosophy *per se* was both extrinsically and intrinsically agonistic. It publicly competed with the eristic of sophists and others, yet taught a private way to usefully struggle for a good life of inner harmony. I conclude that Plato necessarily differentiated the pride of a noble victory from the arrogance of eristic triumph, since the latter precluded the former.

The nature of Athens' rhetoric trade helps answer both the why and the how of Plato's extrinsic, or public, *agōn*. Competing philosophical arguments were evident and influential when Athenians gathered at the law courts, political assemblies and theatres. Sophists taught budding *agōnistes* the fashionable "art of disputing" (*Sophist* 232b),[4] which was doubtless highly prized by those able to afford an education in the cunning of verbal *agōn*. Plato, however, decidedly opposed the agonistic techniques taught by those he "found to be paid hunter[s] after the young and wealthy" (*Sophist* 231d), who prospered from the demand to guilefully dominate and defeat opponents in verbal contests.

The method and purpose of Platonic *agōn* is markedly differentiated from the sophists' eristic "art" in the *Gorgias*, even though the sophistic status of the character Gorgias is a matter of conjecture.[5] Nonetheless, in this dialogue Plato has him declare that:

> The greatest good [is] the ability to persuade with speeches either judges in the law courts or statesmen in

---

[4] Harold N. Fowler, trans., Plato, *Plato in Twelve Volumes*, vol. 12, (London: William Heinemann Ltd., 1921).

[5] Coleen P. Zoller, "To 'Graze Freely in the Pastures of Philosophy': The Political Motives and Pedagogical Methods of Socrates and the Sophists," *Polis* 27:1, (2010) 80-110.

the council-chamber or the commons in the Assembly or an audience at any other meeting that may be held on public affairs [for] by virtue of this power you will have the doctor as your slave, and the trainer as your slave [if] you are able to speak and persuade the multitude. (*Gorgias* 452de)[6]

Gorgias's claim that the greatest good is "the ability to persuade [and enslave] with speeches" elucidates Plato's extrinsic struggle to oppose eristic. For him, valid philosophical debate has an obligation to

> define […] and distinguish and abstract from all other things the aspect or idea of the good [for he who] does not really know the good itself or any particular good [is] dreaming and dozing through his present life, before he awakens here he will arrive at the house of Hades and fall asleep forever (τελέως ἐπικαταδαρθάνειν). (*Republic* 534b-d)[7]

Plato evidently supposed that sophists were up to no good, and, not knowing "the good itself or any particular good," were doomed to eternally sleep in Hades.[8]

Gorgias, Plato, and others vied to win the hearts and minds of those who had access to elite education. The Academy was not in the business of hawking the wily skills of disputation, still it had reason to publicly engage in an extrinsic *agōn* with those who did. Platonic philosophy thus conducted an external struggle against ill-informed and harmful schooling. Still, Plato did not want to alienate and exclude students of eristic, or their teachers, who might yet benefit from the intrinsic *agōn* induced by dialectic.

---

[6] W.R.M Lamb trans., Plato, *Plato in Twelve Volumes*, vol. 3 (London: William Heinemann Ltd, 1967).

[7] Paul Shorey trans., Plato, *Plato in Twelve Volumes*, vols. 5 & 6. (London: William Heinemann Ltd., 1969).

[8] According to Shorey (note to *Republic* 534d), "For Platonic intellectualism the life of the ordinary man is something between sleep and waking. Cf. *Apology* 31a. Note the touch of humor in τελέως ἐπικαταδαρθάνειν."

Hence, his defense of truth and justice aimed to expose casuistry and protect its misguided patrons from

> acting like professional debaters (ἀντιλογικός) [who base] agreements on the mere similarity of words [...] are satisfied to have got the better of the argument [and] claim to be, not contestants for a prize (ἀγωνισταὶ), but lovers of wisdom (φιλόσοφοι). (*Theaetetus.* 164cd)[9]

Juxtaposing ἀγωνίζομαι (sophistic ingenuity that contends for a prize), with φιλόσοφοι (true lovers of wisdoms), Plato hints at the outset of this passage, claiming to love wisdom (φιλοσοφία) while contesting for a prize (ἀγωνίζομαι) is ἀντιλογικός (*antilogikos*), against language. Sophists contradict wisdom since they do not consider other arguments and fail to discriminate (cf. *Phaedrus.* 261de).

Perhaps, Plato's extrinsic rivalry with eristic differed little from a sophistic *agonistēs*'s struggle to vanquish an opponent. My response evokes the critical difference in *agonistic* intent implied in the *Theaetetus* and other dialogues. Platonic dialectic pursued the love of wisdom, and that good entailed encounters of cooperative investigation and rational discovery. Dialectic indented to eradicate ignorance as a veridical activity, since "of all the goods, for gods and men alike, truth stands first" (*Laws* 730bc).[10] Eristic's hostile mien feigned truth to exploit ignorance and triumphantly gratify egoism. Consider Socrates's apology in the *Phaedo* that his fear of impending death made him "contentious, like quite uncultured persons ... [who] do not care what the truth is in the matters they are discussing, but are eager only to make their own views seem true" (91b).[11] Platonic philosophy's aspiration for truth is an agonistic response to uncultured *agonistes* who ignore reality to "make their own views seem true."

---

[9] Harold N. Fowler trans., Plato. *Plato in Twelve Volumes*, vol. 12 (London: William Heinemann Ltd, 1921).

[10] R.G. Bury trans., Plato. *Plato in Twelve Volumes*, vols. 10 & 11 (London: William Heinemann Ltd, 1967 & 1968).

[11] Harold N. Fowler trans., Plato, *Plato in Twelve Volumes*, vol. 1 (London: William Heinemann Ltd, 1966).

The Agōnes of Platonic Philosophy

The *Republic* begins with Socrates explaining the method and intent of Platonic *agōn* to Thrasymachus:

> if our quest were for gold we would never willingly truckle to one another and make concessions in the search and so spoil our chances of finding it [we quest] for justice, a thing more precious than much fine gold, we should [...] give way to one another and [...] do our serious best to have it discovered. (336e)

Socrates proposes a cooperative inquiry into the nature of justice to "learn from the one who does know" (337d). Thrasymachus responds with a jibe at Socrates's naïveté, and seemingly ignores the valuation of justice over gold: "but in addition to 'learning' you must pay a fine of money" (337d). He does accept Socrates's request that "we come to terms with one another as to what we admit in the inquiry [and] shall be ourselves both judges and pleaders" (348b). Thrasymachean *agōn* struggles to satisfy the appetites of ego and purse, whereas Socrates wants their encounter to jointly seek and agree an outcome. Granted, Socrates also competes for personal, arguably selfish, rewards from coming "to terms with one another" to learn about justice and himself.[12] However, his self-interest wisely shuns

> the power of the art of contradiction [unlike those who] suppose that they are not wrangling but arguing owing to their inability to apply the proper divisions and distinctions [and who] pursue purely verbal oppositions, practicing eristic, not dialectic. (*Republic* 454a)[13]

Hence, dialectic pursues truth by applying "the proper divisions and distinctions" (454a).

---

[12] For Plato, dispelling ignorance in the quest for self-knowledge was in one's authentic self-interest.

[13] Parenthetically, Paul Shorey notes that Isocrates maliciously confounded eristic with dialectic. P. Shore, trans., Plato. *Plato in Twelve Volumes*, vols. 5 & 6. (London: William Heinemann Ltd, 1966), footnote on ἀντιλογικῆς at *Republic* 454a.

The *Euthydemus*'s description of sophists' fearsome power reiterates Plato's reasons to struggle against eristic's perverse animosity. Socrates remarks to Crito, "nobody dares stand up to [the Chian brothers] for a moment; such a faculty they have acquired for wielding words as their weapons and confuting any argument as readily if it be true as if it be false" (272ab).[14] Dionysodorus then whispers to Socrates that "whichever way the lad [Cleinias] answers, he will be confuted" (275e). Socrates cannot warn Cleinias about these unfair snares, still, as the dialogue progresses he demonstrates the right conduct of dialectic by courteously involving the lad.

The comparative fairness of dialectic and eristic is also noted in the *Theaetetus*:

> It is very inconsistent for a man who asserts that he cares for virtue to be constantly unfair in discussion; and it is unfair in discussion when a man makes no distinction between merely trying to make points and carrying on a real argument. (167e)

Here Plato characterizes eristic as inconsistent, lacking in virtue, "constantly unfair" and contradicting the purpose of authentic debate. This implies that dialectic *agōn* is coherent, esteems virtue and the integrity of "real argument." Whereas, eristic wields words as weapons in a battle for triumph (cf. 272a).

Plato's extrinsic *agōn* with sophistic eristic is particularly pointed in the *Sophist*, where he divides ἀγωνιστικός (*agōnistikos*) into two parts, "the competitive and [...] the pugnacious" (225a). The Stranger describes sophists as, "nothing else, apparently, than the money-making class of the disputatious, argumentative, controversial, pugnacious, combative, acquisitive art" (226a). A sophist is "a kind of merchant in articles of knowledge for the soul [...] a seller of his own productions of knowledge [an] athlete in contests of words, who had taken for his own the art of disputation"

---

[14] W.R.M. Lamb trans., Plato, *Plato in Twelve Volumes*, vol. 3 (London: William Heinemann Ltd, 1967).

(231de). Plato was doubtless aware that the public *agōnes* of athletic competition patterned the typical demeanor and idiom of verbal *agōn*.[15] His efforts in the *Sophist* to promote objective and cooperative *agōn* acknowledge the usefulness of human competition while isolating it from the "disputatious, argumentative, controversial, pugnacious, combative, acquisitive" characteristics of combative agonistic encounters. Plato probably wanted to avoid the often antagonistic reactions to Socratic elenchos. Indeed, a number of scholars explore the contention that Socrates practiced sophistic eristic. However, even where voiced by the character Socrates, Platonic dialectic employed a more temperate and persuasive technique to better attract and grip an athlete in the contests of words, until "by the orders of reason [...] he is caught [...] in this methodical way" (235bc).

Would-be philosophers may have learnt important lessons from Platonic philosophy's extrinsic *agōn* with eristic. Plato directly advised his students in the intrinsic conduct of dialectic: "When they first get a taste of disputation, [they must not] misuse it as a form of sport, always employing it contentiously [...] delight[ing] like spies in pulling about and tearing with words all who approach them" (*Republic* 539b), as that can discredit the purpose of philosophy. Earnest initiates need to "examine truth dialectically [and not] make a jest and a sport of mere contradiction [to] be more reasonable and moderate, and bring credit rather than discredit upon his pursuit [requires] orderly and stable natures" (*Republic* 539c-d). A *Meno* passage further instructs budding dialecticians by contrasting the intent of dialectic and eristic practise. Socrates counsels, if I were addressing

> a professor of the eristic and contentious sort, I should say to him: I have made my statement; if it is wrong, your business is to examine and refute it. But if ... we were friends and chose to have a discussion together, I should

---

[15] See Heather L. Reid, *Athletics and Philosophy in the Ancient World* (London: Routledge, 2011), and *Introduction to the Philosophy of Sport* (Lanham: Rowman & Littlefield, 2012).

have to reply in some milder tone more suited to [the] dialectical way [...] not merely to answer what is true, but also to make use of those points which the questioned person acknowledges he knows. (*Meno* 75d)[16]

Plato's demarcation of temperate dialectic from contentious eristic intended to aid Platonic *agonistes'* struggle to attain wisdom by schooling them in the just motives and moderating method of collaborative *agōn*.

There are diverse opinions about Plato's soul theory and eschatology, yet it is generally accepted that his philosophy aims to achieve psychological harmony through the beautiful order of self-mastery within (cf. *Republic* 443d). Platonic philosophy's definitive *agōn* was the struggle to realize that victory. As Heather Reid points out, "*agōn* is a struggle not just against the competition; it is symbolic of the more general struggle against the human imperfection that pervades life itself."[17] For Plato, our mutual battle against human imperfection meant reconciling the rivalries of one's inner opponents, in that "great [...] struggle [...] a far greater contest than we think it, that determines whether a man prove good or bad" (*Republic* 608b). The tenacity to sustain that effort necessarily employed the psychological courage and laudable aspirations of *thumos*.

My assumption that Plato's analysis of society informed his world view is supported by Karl Popper's observation that "Plato's greatness as a sociologist [...] lies rather in the wealth and detail of his observations, and in the amazing acuteness of his sociological intuition."[18] I hold that Plato's keen scrutiny of human behavior is reflected in his depiction of dialectic and eristic *agōn*. That he especially noted their different indications of thematic spirit, which he depicts as the source of anger, aggression,

---

[16] W.R.M. Lamb trans., Plato. *Plato in Twelve Volumes*, vol. 3 (London, William Heinemann Ltd, 1967).

[17] Heather L. Reid, "Athletic Competition as Socratic Philosophy," *Acta Universitatis Palackianae Olomucensis: Gymnica*, 36:2, (2006): 75.

[18] Karl R. Popper, *The Open Society And Its Enemies: Volume I, The Spell Of Plato* (London: Routledge, 1966,) 38.

The Agōnes of Platonic Philosophy

ambition, shame, desire for honor, competitiveness and pride. Plato described eristic as contentious, uncultured, aggressive, combative and pugnacious, expressing what I term the negative manifestation of *thumos*. Nonetheless, wisely used, *thumos* provided the lover of wisdom with the "pleasures of necessity" (*Republic* 581e) that enabled *agonistes* to heroically temper thumotic anger and aggression. And, where justice "is reviled [to not] be faint-hearted ... [and] defend her so long as one has breath and can utter his voice" (*Republic* 368c).

I submit that Plato's pejorative description of eristic implies that its *agonistes* aspired to and vaunted insolent triumph. Moreover, that he considered such sentiments at odds with his dialectical aim to tell truth and cultivate wisdom. Platonic ἀγῶνες rationally modulated *thumos*'s valor and determination to embolden excellence, for "let every one of us be ambitious to gain excellence, but without jealousy" (*Laws* 731b). Plato decried Homeric "false stories" (*Republic* 377d) as imitating "images of excellence [and] not lay[ing] hold on truth" (*Republic* 600e). Like Homeric heroes, Platonic dialecticians needed real courage to uphold their intrinsic struggle for the excellence of good disposition. Plato thus eschewed impediments to attaining that victory by insulating and elevating dialectic's noble *aretē* from the imaginary excellence and deceit of eristic triumph. Consequently, he responded to the negativity of quarrelsome *thumos* by teaching the cooperative conduct of *agōn*. In my view, the "victory-loving and honor-loving" (*Republic* 581b) qualities of *thumos* significantly informed this differentiation of dialectic and eristic *agōn*. Achieving the victories and honors of philosophical struggle was an aspiration that Plato deemed worthy of love. Such seeking may teach *agonistes* how to rightly proceed and honorably satisfy their "ambition for what is noble" (*Symposium* 178d).

The hypothesis that thumotic manifestations differentiate dialectic from eristic is arguably buoyed by recent research. A 2012 study that examined nonverbal signals of victory found that actions theoretically associated with pride and triumph evidently differ.[19] Granted, applying a 21st c. study to the intent of fourth c. BCE dialectic and eristic is problematic. Yet, I am reluctant to concede that spontaneous human expressions of pride and triumph have changed to such an extent that it refutes any comparison. Research subjects purportedly expressing pride smiled happily, tilted their heads back, expanded chests, held arms away from the body or akimbo, had opened hands and did not speak. Subjects identified as triumphant grimaced aggressively, thrust heads forward, held a direct gaze, expanded chests, raised arms above the shoulders and/or punched the air. They made a fist when giving a thumbs up or clapping and uttered sounds, including shouts. According to the study these triumphant gestures and noises were often accompanied by a countenance more indicative of antagonism and anger than of happiness. Conceivably, Plato witnessed and possibly experienced similar reactions at the conclusion of *agōnes*, specifically competitive debates.

The researchers' account of emotions and gestures attendant to victory suggests that pride is a happy experience of worthy achievement, whereas triumphant subjects assert hostility and enjoy domination. These findings may confirm the variable manifestations of Platonic *thumos* in dialectic and eristic. Pride articulates *thumos*'s love of honorable victory and aspires to authentic *aretē*: triumph conveys belligerence and egoistic contempt for defeated opponents. Plato might conclude that this differentiation of inner pride and palpable triumph discloses rational dialectic's aspiration for inner excellence, whereas eristic's epidictic hunts the acclaim of hubristic triumph.

Despite dialectic pride and eristic triumph having distinctive verbal and nonverbal expressions of *thumos*, that does not infer their mutual exclusivity. A victor can concurrently experience noble pride and scornful triumph in the flux of emotive response. I contend that Platonic schooling refined *thumos* to bravely moderate unrestrained triumph by advancing the love of honorable victory.

---

[19] David Matsumoto and Hyi Sung Hwang, "Evidence for a nonverbal expression of triumph," *Evolution and Human Behavior* 33:1 (2012): 520–529.

The Agōnes of Platonic Philosophy

However, "while education brings also victory, victory sometimes brings lack of education, for men have often grown more insolent (ὕβριστος) because of victory" (*Laws* 641c). A later *Laws* passage aids our understanding of why victory can bring a lack of education that makes people grow more hubristic. The Athenian explains that "a nobler victory—that which is the noblest of all victories [is] victory over pleasures" (840bc). I have argued that that victory obliges prudently employing the thumotic "pleasures of necessity since [we] would have no use for them if there was no necessity" (*Republic* 581e). Good Platonic education sought the pleasures from self-mastery. Forgetting such poise might stimulate the enjoyment and authority of hubristic triumph. Those schooled by sophists lacked good education. As captives of *thumos*'s excesses they were trained to grow "more insolent because of victory" (*Laws* 641c), and craved the triumph that was arguably Athens' undoing.

In sum, I offer that intent and conduct differentiates the purpose and practice of Platonic dialectic and sophistic eristic. Dialectic *agōn* aspires to an honorable victory of inner excellence, whereas eristic pugnaciously battles for hubristic triumph. Each *agōn* enjoys the pleasures of Platonic *thumos*: dialectic to the extent of their necessity for courageous moderation, eristic to employ the excesses of hostility. I submit that my demarcation of dialectic collaboration from eristic conquest is supported by recent research into the emotions and gestures associated with pride and triumph, noting that the study's observations of triumph reflect Plato's representation of eristic and *thumos*.

Plato participated in Athens' agonistic ethos to change it. His extrinsic *agōn* challenged the sophistic eristic that repressed the love of authentic wisdom (σοφὸς). Dialectic *agōn* usefully employed *thumos* to moderate the hostility that hindered aspirations to jointly seek the victory of truth. That *agōn* educated and heartened the intrinsic *agōn* of aspiring wisdom lovers (φιλόσοφοι) to surrender false beliefs and risk escape from cave dwelling ignorance.

In the 21st c. Platonic philosophy is engaged in a third *agōn*: the battle to defend its values and worth against the sophistry of

Lee M. J. Coulson

academic managerialism and populist insipience. This is an *agōn* Plato might well expect each lover of wisdom to boldly enjoin.

Coleen P. Zoller[1]
Plato's Rejection of the Logic of Domination[2]

Plato's philosophy highlights that the struggle (*agōn*) for goodness is central to the human experience. Nevertheless, we should not interpret Plato as a champion of combative struggle. Far too many commentators miss the peace-seeking nature of Plato's dialogues. Some have gone as far as to read him as a proponent of war.[3] One aim of this paper is to disprove that. Historically, Plato's metaphysical dualism has been perceived in a way that caused several commentators[4] to see in him a firm acceptance of the power dynamic that philosopher Karen J. Warren calls "the logic of domination."[5] In addition to

---

[1] Coleen P. Zoller is Professor of Philosophy and Chair of the Department of Philosophy at Susquehanna University. She is the author of *Plato and the Body: Reconsidering Socratic Asceticism* (Albany, NY: State University of New York Press, 2018) in addition to numerous articles and book chapters on Plato, Kant, and Thomas Aquinas. She also works on fostering unity in divided times through the use of philosophical friendliness. 514 University Avenue, Selinsgrove, PA, 17870 USA, zoller@susqu.edu.

[2] I am grateful to Heather Reid for her insightful comments on this paper.

[3] For instance, Val Plumwood, *Feminism and the Mastery of Nature* (London: Routledge, 1993), 97-8, thinks that Plato denies the value of life and believes war is a part of an ideal society, and Eva Keuls, *The Reign of the Phallus: Sexual Politics in Ancient Athens* (New York: Harper & Row, 1985), 395, contends that Plato "seems never to have contemplated a world without constant armed conflicts." Meanwhile, Nancy C. M. Hartsock, *Money, Sex, and Power: Toward a Feminist Historical Materialism* (New York: Longman, 1983), 199, asserts that for Plato "no other relation than domination and submission is possible."

[4] For instance, Hartsock, *Money, Sex, and Power*, 199, and Genevieve Lloyd, *The Man of Reason: "Male" and "Female" in Western Philosophy* (Minneapolis: University of Minnesota Press, 1984), 5, 7, 18-9.

[5] Karen J. Warren, "Feminism and Ecology: Making Connections," *Environmental Ethics* 9 (1987): 6; Warren, "The Power and Promise of Ecological Feminism," *Environmental Ethics* 12 (1990); Warren, "Feminism and the Environment: An Overview of the Issues," *APA Newsletter on Feminism and Philosophy* 90 (1991). Eco-feminism, developed initially in the 1970s, involves a commitment to rejecting the logic of domination. The logic of domination involves the acceptance of and expectation of dominance and subjugation,

demonstrating that Plato was a peace-pursuer rather than a warmonger, I want to give Plato credit here for being an early initiator of the project to argue *against* the glorification of domination. Examining Plato's way of rejecting the logic of domination helps to show us his place in the philosophy of peace, despite *agōn* being at the heart of his moral psychology and his political theory. In short, Plato embraces *agōn* but rejects the impeding, winner-take-all version of it that is domination.

Several aspects of Plato's philosophy of peace have been obscured by the thematic centrality of souls' and cities' agonistic struggle for goodness. In this essay I will discuss factors that have caused some commentators to interpret Plato as an advocate of domination instead of discerning his idealism around peace. First, I will examine the Platonic characters who defend the logic of domination, serving as Socrates's foils. Second, I will demonstrate the subtlety of his conception of leadership in the city and the soul, respectively, as a hierarchy without domination.[6] This essay will reveal how Plato uses his Socrates to argue recurrently *against* the logic of domination in dialogues such as the *Republic, Gorgias,* and *Crito,* and how the Athenian does so in the *Laws*. Key passages from these dialogues demonstrate that Plato aspires to a radical transformation of society's values, policies, and relationships that would be oriented toward harmonious cooperation and peace.

In his corpus, Plato puts Socrates in dialogue with interlocutors who are either disinclined to question domination, such as Glaucon, Adeimantus, and Polus, or who go so far as to advocate vigorously for domination by the stronger, such as

---

and it comes in various forms. When paired with the typical set of value hierarchy dichotomies (male/female; white/black; rich/poor, etc.), the logic of domination is exemplified by the expectation that men should dominate women; that people with more resources should dominate those with fewer; that people considered white should dominate people of color; that cisgender people should dominate over transgender people; that nationals should dominate over foreigners; that human beings should dominate over the natural environment and the other animals; and so on.

[6] I will leave the study of Plato's attitudes toward women, the poor, slaves, and foreigners for a longer project, but I see these as factors that are relevant to my discussion of Plato's rejection of the logic of domination.

Plato's Rejection of the Logic of Domination

Thrasymachus and Callicles. Polus, Glaucon, and Adeimantus find dominance rather tempting, though to a lesser degree than Thrasymachus and Callicles. In the *Gorgias*, Polus defines power as getting to do whatever one sees fit (466b-469c, esp. 466e), which is suggestive of a logic of domination. And in the *Republic*, Glaucon does not mind that his desire for immoderation has all sorts of negative outcomes, including civic discord and the inevitability of war (372d-373e). In a similar class are the metics of Book I, Cephalus and his son, Polemarchus (whose name translates to 'warlord'), who have profited from the sales of weapons and shields. These interlocutors do not mind the logic of domination as long as they imagine that they will be among those doing the dominating, or at least profiting from it.

The dialogues' most extreme defenders of domination, Thrasymachus and Callicles, consider dominance conducive to their greedy goal of satisfying immoderate desires. For instance, Callicles thinks it is natural and just "that the superior rule the inferior and have a greater share than they" (*Gorgias* 483d), and Thrasymachus defines justice as the dominance of the strong over the weak, saying "justice is nothing other than the advantage of the stronger" (*Republic* 338c). By way of developing Thrasymachus's position, Plato has him say that the most unjust city will be especially inclined to try to enslave other cities and "hold them in subjection" (351b). At every turn, Plato's Socrates rejects the view that might makes right and that those with greater physical strength ought to subjugate those with less, whether we have cities or individuals in mind.

Essentially the disagreement between Socrates and such interlocutors as Thrasymachus and Callicles concerns the question of what real strength is. For example, they disagree about how a city should manifest its strength. In the *Republic*, Thrasymachus believes that being unjust will help a city be strong enough to overpower other cities, whereas Socrates contends that being just is the only thing that could ever truly strengthen a city (351b-c). In bringing to life characters such as Thrasymachus and Callicles, Plato paints vivid pictures of interlocutors who strongly endorse the logic of domination. Nevertheless, we should never be so confused by this that we wind up interpreting Plato as one who endorses the logic of domination. Instead, Plato uses Socrates to strive heroically *against* the views expressed by those interlocutors foolish enough to identify strength with unjust domination and immoderation (such as Thrasymachus at *Republic* 351b-c).

Plato uses his Socrates to undermine as far as possible the positions endorsed by interlocutors steeped in the logic of domination. Socrates attempts to get his interlocutors to accept that just people do not want to "outdo" other just people (*Republic* 349b-c) because they realize that we achieve more together by being just with each other rather than by being unjust (351b-d). It does not strike the reader that either Thrasymachus or Callicles takes to heart anything to which they finally agree after being refuted by Socrates, but interlocutors like Polus, Adeimantus, and even Glaucon seem like they want to be open to the wisdom Socrates has to offer, and therefore they appear to take their reasoned conclusions to heart. All these interlocutors are extremely interested in power and strength, and the wisdom toward which Socrates steers them is that authentic power does not come from dominating others but rather from achieving more together through friendliness, cooperative service (*Republic* 347a), and justice (*Republic* 351b-c), especially in the context of agonistic struggle.

In fact, Plato's Socrates defends humility, cooperation, justice, harmony, and peace so consistently that at times he is ridiculed by his interlocutors. As Brown writes, "Innuendos about Socrates's adequacy as a man are not limited to attacks upon his *vocation* as a philosopher. Indeed, the *content* of his philosophy, aimed as it is against the prevailing ethic of heroic action...is also the occasion for ridicule and charges of effeminacy."[7] Socrates is taunted for not

---

[7] Wendy Brown, "'Supposing Truth Were a Woman...': Plato's Subversion of Masculine Discourse," in *Feminist Interpretations of Plato*, ed. Nancy Tuana. (University Park, PA: The Pennsylvania State University Press, 1994), 161. See also Arlene Saxonhouse, "Eros and the Female in Greek Political Thought," *Political Theory* 12 (1984): 13, and Laurence Lampert, *How*

Plato's Rejection of the Logic of Domination

being manly by Callicles at *Gorgias* 484d-485d and by Thrasymachus when he asks Socrates if he "still [has] a wet nurse" "letting [him] run around with a snotty nose" (*Republic* 343a). In addition to having his manliness challenged, Socrates's theory of justice is portrayed as not appropriate for the manly: by Glaucon, who suggests it is not what men would willingly do (*Republic* 359b-c), by Adeimantus, who concurs (366c-d), and by Thrasymachus, who favors the "stronger" taking "advantage" (338a-344c) with threats of "harm" (341b) and "outdoing everyone else" (344a).

Prodding Socrates, Thrasymachus concludes their conversation at the end of *Republic* Book I with, "Let that be your banquet, Socrates, at the Feast of Bendis" (354a), which is a reference to the Thracian goddess to whom Socrates has been praying at the beginning of Book I. Given that Bendis is an erotic huntress, upending customary feminine roles in a way that is empowering to women, Thrasymachus's reference is meant to insult Socrates subtly by aligning him with the feminine. Socrates gets the temporary last word when he responds by pulling Thrasymachus away from his masculine self-expression by claiming that the banquet was "[g]iven by you, Thrasymachus, after you became gentle and ceased to give me rough treatment" (354a). The Greeks' vocabulary does not capture the full range of expression used today in regard to gender, but nonetheless it is clear that part of how Thrasymachus aggressively jabs at Socrates pertains to Socrates's lack of conformity to Thrasymachus's presumptions about men and their use of domination.

Plato uses drama to highlight for us how fearsome the logic of domination and its defenders are—even to a battle-hardened soldier like Socrates (*Symposium* 219e, 221b-c; *Charmides* 153b-d). At *Republic* 336b-c Plato has Thrasymachus indicate that the interlocutors have been acting "like idiots by giving way to one another," which demonstrates Thrasymachus's aversion to friendliness and good will in dialogue. Shortly after, Plato has

---

Philosophy Became Socratic: A Study of Plato's Protagoras, Charmides, and Republic (Chicago: The University of Chicago Press, 2010), 312.

Socrates admit to feeling "startled" and "afraid" and to "trembling a little" in the wake of these words from Thrasymachus (*Republic* 336d). Additionally, at 341b, Plato has Thrasymachus claim that he will never allow Socrates to "overpower" (*biasasthai*) him in the argument. And the author reminds us again of Thrasymachus's aggression at 345b when he has the sophist say, "And how am I to persuade you, if you aren't persuaded by what I said just now? What more can I do? Am I to take my argument and pour it into your very soul?" And Socrates replies, "God forbid! Don't do that!" Here Socrates feels shaken by Thrasymachus's violent threat of force-feeding him, and yet he remains determined to keep their conversation friendly enough to avoid bellicosity despite conversing with a man operating "with toil, trouble, and…a quantity of sweat that was a wonder to behold" (350d). This dramatic portrayal reminds us that Book I is a struggle between a sweaty sophist who wants to throw his weight around and a friendly philosopher who wants to spend his spare time today in Piraeus checking out a new festival for a girl-power goddess.

There is a stark difference between the presumption made by Thrasymachus and Callicles that reasoning is combative and Socrates's position that reasoning can be done cooperatively among friends. Plato depicts Socrates's firm belief that friends tell each other what they really think and try to get to the bottom of things together with the help of each other's questions and friendly refutations. We see this highlighted in the following four passages: (1) at *Protagoras* 337b where Socrates says, "Friends debate each other on good terms; *eristics* are for enemies at odds" (ἀμφισβητοῦσι μὲν γὰρ καὶ δι' εὔνοιαν οἱ φίλοι τοῖς φίλοις, ἐρίζουσιν δὲ οἱ διάφοροί τε καὶ ἐχθροὶ ἀλλήλοις), (2) in the *Gorgias* at 470c where Socrates reminds Polus that refuting someone is the "good turn" done for a friend (see also *Gorgias* 507e-508a), (3) in the *Meno* at 75c-d where Socrates advises Meno that a friend's job includes the requirement to refute and to do so "in a manner more gentle and more proper to discussion," and (4) at *Symposium* 182d one of the effects of philosophy is to build friendship. These passages lay out much of Plato's thinking about friendship, that people of good will have the capacity to investigate together whatever is on their minds. Throughout the corpus, Plato portrays the struggle between aggressive domination and harmonious cooperation as an important one and the harmonious cooperation model as an important part of a righteous life.

In opposition to the unjust values some of his interlocutors endorse, Plato has Socrates offer a theory of justice that features a hierarchical notion of leadership both within an individual soul and within a political community. This hierarchy in Plato's vision of leadership is sorted according to understanding the Form of the Good, and people genuinely fit to be atop a political hierarchy are rare. The commitment to try to understand the Good and to endeavor bravely to make the Good as manifest in the finite world as possible is inopportunely extraordinary. These rare leaders are "good maniacs."[8] Plato has Socrates assert that there will be no end to the bad things that befall our communities until power is bestowed upon these good maniacs (*Republic* 473c-d). That power is different from the power that lies with the *Republic*'s producer class (such as private property at 416c-417b and the control of food at 416d-e). Many readers have recoiled from Plato's notion of leadership because they assume that the logic of domination automatically accompanies any type of thinking about unequal relationships.[9] According to Kraut, "One of Plato's great contributions to political philosophy lies precisely here, in his recognition of the importance of this unequal relationships among human beings."[10] However, despite this unequal hierarchy of

---

[8] Donald R. Morrison, "The Utopian Character of Plato's Ideal City," in *The Cambridge Companion to Plato's Republic*, ed. G.R.F. Ferrari. (Cambridge: Cambridge University Press, 2007), 232-55, 243, and Coleen P. Zoller, *Plato and the Body: Reconsidering Socratic Asceticism* (Albany, NY: State University of New York Press, 2018), 144.

[9] For example, Lynda Lange, "The Function of Equal Education in Plato's *Republic* and *Laws*," in *The Sexism of Social and Political Theory from Plato to Nietzsche*, eds. Lorenne Clark and Lynda Lange (Toronto: University of Toronto Press, 1979), 7-8.

[10] Richard Kraut, "Ordinary Virtue from the *Phaedo* to the *Laws*," in *Plato's Laws: A Critical Guide*, ed. Christopher Bobonich. (Cambridge: Cambridge University Press, 2010), 52. See also N. D. Smith's essay in this volume.

power, Plato's theory of justice speaks *against* leaders utilizing the logic of domination. In *Republic* Book IV, Plato offers a cooperative theory of justice, while rejecting the vision of power that is tyrannical in nature.

Plato's Socrates's rejection of domination is not a stray element of his political philosophy isolated in the *Republic* and *Gorgias*. The anti-domination theme is a central feature of Plato's moral and political thinking throughout the corpus. In fact, at the heart of the moral theory that Plato has Socrates advance is the principle that one ought never to do harm. This principle is offered at *Crito* 49b where Socrates instructs Crito that one should never do harm, even in return for being harmed. Plato's Socrates unfailingly argues against domination of others in favor of the Socratic anti-harm principle. Insofar as dominating does harm to the Socratic anti-harm principle dictates that one should not aspire to domination.

One might object that domination does no harm if guided by knowledge of the Good, and one might think that the hierarchical power dynamic in Plato's moral psychology and political philosophy exemplifies the possibility of a logic of domination motivated by the Good. However, for Plato, being guided by knowledge of the Good leads Plato's philosopher-leaders to pursue harmonious cooperation rather than squashing domination (*Republic* 443c-444b). As we see in the *Republic*, Plato's commitment to a hierarchical notion of leadership goes hand in hand with his emphasis on cooperation, friendliness, and harmony among the parts of a soul or a city (443d-e).

Despite his emphasis on different natures, it is not true that Plato believes leaders to be more human, so to speak, than their constituents or that those who should follow are valueless or inessential for the manifestation of justice. Perhaps our understanding of what Plato intends would be benefitted by constructing an analogy between Plato's natural hierarchy and the hierarchy of valuations of iron in different forms. A recently circulated meme invites us to determine our own value through what we make of ourselves; it reminds us that a bar of iron is worth $5, but when transformed into horseshoes is valued at $12, when

Plato's Rejection of the Logic of Domination

made into needles becomes worth $3500, and when crafted into springs for watches is valued at $300,000. Iron is iron, but some iron is more useful for certain purposes than other iron. For Plato, all human beings are valuable, but he is intent on acknowledging that leaders, soldiers, and producers have different natures and those natures have different degrees of rarity. The philosophers' uncommonness is further distinguished by the type of education they are marked to receive, a program focused on their curiosity concerning goodness, justice, and harmony.

Nevertheless, Plato's hierarchy of natures tends to make his egalitarian readers suspicious that those fit to lead will rule by dominating others. Yet, leadership in the form of domination would be unjust according to Plato's theory of justice because the *Republic* makes clear that each aspect of the soul has important work to do, just as the work of each class in the city is essential (443d-e). The soul's aspects and the city's classes are not equal in terms of their abilities, but they are clearly depicted in the *Republic*'s moral psychology as interdependent. Plato has Socrates remark that the aspects of the soul and the parts of the city have different natures and accordingly have different functions.

Plato's Socrates contends, furthermore, that justice is "the having and doing of one's own" (*Republic* 433e-434a). So, what is good for a human being is the life constituted by each aspect of the soul doing what is natural for it to do and doing so in the proper amounts. Similarly what is good for the city is being a community where each part of the city does its own job well, which is only possible through a cooperative approach rather than a dominating approach. Plato's theory of justice holds that any *domination*—whether by reason in the soul or leaders in the city—undermines the cultivation of justice and is, consequently, deemed unjust.

The rational aspect of the soul is supposed to wonder and try to be wise (442c-d), while the philosopher-monarchs are similarly supposed to think things through and cultivate wisdom (428c-429a, 475b-c, 479e-480a, 484b-c, 486d, 503b, 521b). Next, the business of the soul's spirited aspect is to be courageous whenever one perceives that one has been wronged (440c-d), and the city's spirited class, the military (guardian-auxiliaries) is to be courageous and protect the city (373e, 412c-e, 414b). Additionally, the business of the soul's appetitive aspect is to desire what is moderate (442a-b), while the city's artisan class—the farmers and craftsmen—is to provide for the needs of the city in a moderate fashion (369d-e, 371a, 415c, 431e).

Socrates indicates that philosopher-monarchs are fit to lead the other segments of society (*Republic* 473c-e, 474b-c, 543a) and that the rational part of the soul is fit to lead the other aspects of the soul "since it is really wise and exercises foresight on behalf of the whole soul" (441e). The craft of genuine leadership uses relevant knowledge to provide what's best for the community. Socrates says,

> That's why I thought it necessary for us to agree before that every kind of rule, insofar as it rules, doesn't seek anything other than what is best for the things it rules and cares for, and this is true both of public and private kinds of rule. (*Republic* 345d)

Plato's Socrates thinks of leaders much like he thinks of doctors or shepherds. For instance, the doctor is not given purview over the patient for the sake of anything but the health of the patient, and the shepherd does not have power over the sheep simply for the sake of power but rather for the sake of the betterment of the sheep.

Furthermore, Plato's Socrates has confidence in the disposition of those who are truly knowledgeable; he believes that they "do not want to outdo other knowledgeable people" (349e-350b). Plato's commitment to hierarchy is not driven by the conventional concept of power-over-others but rather by the prospect of public service for the good of the whole. As Levin writes, Socrates makes an "attempt to redefine power by reference to the provision of genuine benefit."[11] However, understanding the Good is a more abstract and elusive knowledge than what is required to make a good military maneuver or good shoes. So, Plato's Socrates grants ultimate superiority to the practitioner of

---

[11] Susan Levin, *Plato's Rivalry with Medicine: A Struggle and Its Dissolution* (Oxford: Oxford University Press, 2014), 22.

the craft that requires knowledge of the Good itself. Nonetheless, for Plato, power issues solely from the ability to improve the whole not at all from the ability and willingness to dominate others.

Some would still object that in seeing some natures as superior by nature for leadership, Plato is relying upon the logic of domination. The fundamental question here concerns what type of leader the rational aspect is for the soul, and the philosopher-monarch is for the city. Plato's provision of hierarchal status to the aspects of the soul and the segments of society revolves around his notions of craft and nature rather than any glorification of subjugation. Plato could have made it easier for his readers to recognize his vision of the value of the whole if he had Socrates discuss some examples of the kinds of decisions his philosopher-monarchs would need to make and how, in order to make Goodness as manifest as possible in this imperfect world, they would need perspective from those whose expertise lies in areas relevant to the decision at hand. For instance, he could have featured Socrates conversing about examples such as a philosopher-monarch needing to make a policy about military action and seeking relevant information from the auxiliary soldiers or about agricultural policy and seeking relevant information from the farmers. Unfortunately the *Republic* still leaves many such details of the leaders' political work unspoken, but Plato may have imagined it would be relatively easy for these good leaders to recognize the importance of the different classes and the value of such consultations to their work. And unlike leaders in some other contexts, a philosopher-monarch is empowered to bring to fruition those knowledgeable nuggets of advice about what must be done to foster goodness.

Elsewhere I have already shown the parallel in the soul concerning the rational aspect of the soul, which is the one fit to lead, but it must allow the other parts to do their work and at times their agendas will take priority for the whole soul (*Republic* 433a-435b; 441d-e).[12] For instance, when the vital work of the appetite or the spirit must be done, the appetite's desire to quench thirst or the

---

[12] Zoller, *Plato and the Body*, 116-21.

spirit's desire to fight passionately against injustice, then these projects are sanctioned by the rational aspect, which coordinates the whole soul *in consultation with the needs of the other aspects.*

Despite being committed to a hierarchical notion of leadership, Plato's theory of justice very much relies upon the ideas of interdependence, cooperation, friendliness, and harmony among the parts of a soul or a city.[13] The fundamental principle driving the *Republic's* account of justice is that putting the composite in order is all about good leadership bringing harmony to the interrelations among the parts. When the largest and most disruptive aspect of the soul (*Republic* 442a), the appetite, does its work well, the soul achieves moderation, which Socrates describes as bringing the soul into harmonious "unanimity" wherein "the naturally worse and the naturally better […] all sing the same song together" (*Republic* 431e-432a).

Here we see Plato link his theory of justice to a vision of peace—both personal and political—through good leadership focused on cooperative harmony instead of domination. This echoes Socrates's earlier use of the notion of harmony. At *Republic* 401a, Plato has Socrates say, "Our bodily nature is full of [these qualities], as are the natures of all growing things, for in all of these there is grace and gracelessness. And gracelessness, bad rhythm, and disharmony are akin to bad words and bad character, while their opposites are akin to and are imitations of the opposite, a moderate and good character." The harmony is born from the unanimity Plato has Socrates mention, and the unanimity is born from having all the parts "supported and promoted," to use Klosko's words.[14] Plato's Socrates alludes to the importance of the

---

[13] Anne-Marie Schultz, *Plato's Socrates as Narrator: A Philosophical Muse* (Lanham, MD: Lexington Books, 2013), 150; Julia Annas, *An Introduction to Plato's Republic* (Oxford: Clarendon Press, 1981), 117; Daryl H. Rice, "Plato on Force: The Conflict between His Psychology and Political Sociology and His Definition of Temperance in the *Republic*," *History of Political Thought* 10 (1989): 568-76; and Daniel C. Russell, *Plato on Pleasure and the Good Life* (Oxford: Oxford University Press, 2005), 206-213, 218-9.

[14] George Klosko, *The Development of Plato's Political Theory* (New York: Methuen, 1986), 102.

just person "accustoming [the aspects of the soul] to each other and making them *friendly*" (*Republic* 589a; emphasis added) and claims that the just person "should take care of the many-headed beast as a farmer does his animals, feeding and domesticating the gentle heads and preventing the savage ones from growing" (*Republic* 589b).

Plato has Socrates give the impression that in the soul of a just person we should not expect any of its aspects to be quashed. If one aims for inner harmony, then ruling over the other parts of the soul should not involve suppressing their functions. In *Republic* 4 Plato has Socrates instruct us to expect all aspects of the soul, even the appetite, to be active when their work is what's best for the overall human being. No part of the virtuous soul will be squashed through domination. As Annas writes,

> As well as describing the just person as unified and harmonious, Plato makes a comparison with health (444c-445b); he wants us to think of justice as a state where the person is completely fulfilled...because no aspect of him or her is being repressed or denied its proper expression.[15]

So, according to the logic of the *Republic*'s theory of justice, reason ruling in an authoritarian way would hinder the soul's effort to survive and flourish, given that the soul functions best when each psychic aspect plays its own natural role and does so virtuously. Reason is not meant to rule like a tyrant.

For instance, Plato has Socrates say that one "who is healthy and moderate...best grasps the truth" when one "neither starves nor feasts his appetites" (*Republic* 571d-572a). Socrates reiterates this twice in Book 9 when he concludes,

> Therefore, when the entire soul follows the philosophic part, and there is no civil war in it, each part of it does its own work exclusively and is just, and in particular it enjoys its own pleasures, the best and truest pleasures possible for it. (586e-587a)

---

[15] Annas, *Introduction*, 132.

Schultz agrees that the harmony model of justice in the *Republic* requires giving "a voice" to even the appetitive part of the soul because it "provides necessary notes on the scale of internal justice."[16] In a just soul, reason must remain open to the voices of spirit and appetite.

This means that even a thinker who is ruled by the rational aspect of the soul must satisfy the appetitive aspect's "gentle" desires. Plato demonstrates Socrates's acceptance of natural pleasures, which actually reinforce psychic harmony, according to the *Republic*'s logic. In contrast, the tyrannical mode of leadership would starve even what Socrates thinks of as our more domesticated desires, such as for quenching thirst, being nourished, and sleeping, because even they disrupt the rational aspect's agenda. This domination over the appetite would make justice unfeasible because it precludes harmonious unanimity.

Despite the fact that the *Republic*'s moral psychology makes clear that each aspect of the soul must be given the opportunity to do its important work well (433a-435b; 441d-e), a popular but misguided interpretation contends that the rational aspect of the soul ought to dominate the soul's non-rational aspects in a tyrannical manner,[17] squashing the functions of the rest of the soul, especially the appetite. What I have elsewhere called the austere dualist reading of Plato has presumed that the proper order of the soul is one wherein reason quells appetitive desires for physical pleasure.[18] And what's more, the austere dualist interpretation has failed to recognize or reconcile the inconsistency between calling for reason to dominate the subjugated aspects of the soul and to harmonize all the parts of the soul.

Meanwhile, commentators like Plumwood recognize the inconsistency between the suppression of the appetite and the

---

[16] Schultz, *Plato's Socrates as Narrator*, 150.

[17] Schultz, *Plato's Socrates as Narrator*, 150, also uses the political term "tyrannical" in application to intrapsychic dynamics that suppress the appetite.

[18] In Zoller, *Plato and the Body*, I argue against this caricature of Socratic asceticism, showing that this austere vision of the just life is not supported by the text of the dialogues.

Plato's Rejection of the Logic of Domination

quest to harmonize the whole soul, but they read Plato as one who envisions reason crushing the appetite for physical pleasure in an uncooperative manner.[19] I agree with Schultz's conclusion that there are serious limitations to that austere dualist model of how virtue is cultivated, a tyranny by reason.[20] In particular, it misses what Plato has Adeimantus hint at when Socrates asks "where are justice and injustice to be found in [our city]? With which of the things we examined did they come in?" and Adeimantus replies, "I've no idea, Socrates, unless it was somewhere in some needs that these people have of one another" (372a). Plato portrays Adeimantus as intuiting our mutual interdependence and its importance for character-development. Those who cultivate justice recognize and honor that all the parts of the whole have valuable functions and need cooperation with each other to manifest virtues.

In his moral psychology, Plato could have had Socrates say that reason ought to dominate and crush emotion and appetite, but in fact he does not.[21] And he could have had Socrates say that the philosopher-monarchs ought to rule like dominating tyrants, but, again, he in fact does not. He argues *against* tyranny in the city (*Republic* 544c, 545a, 568b, 576d-e, 577c, 579b-580c) and the soul. Reason should rule the other parts of the soul, but not as a tyrant rules a city. Similarly in the *Laws* Plato suggests that good leaders work toward peace. He has the Athenian engage interlocutors, Clinias and Megillus, who possess a vision of all against all at every level—*polis*, village, household, individual, and even among the parts within oneself.[22] By contrast, the Athenian is driving at a different civic vision, one that has an eye on reconciliation and

---

[19] Plumwood, *Feminism*, 80, 90-1. In his response to Plumwood, Timothy A. Mahoney, "Platonic Ecology: A Response to Plumwood's Critique of Plato," *Ethics and the Environment* 2 (1997): 32, agrees with my claim that it is a bad interpretation of Plato to read him as advocating utter disdain for the appetitive aspect of the soul.

[20] Schultz, *Socrates as Narrator*, 146.

[21] For more, see Zoller, *Plato and the Body*, especially chapters three and four.

[22] Legislators and their citizens should always operate "with an eye on war" (*Laws* 626a) and that well-run states aim to ensure victory in war (*Laws* 626b-c).

peace (*Laws* 628a-b). The Athenian declares, "The greatest good, however, is neither war nor civil war (God forbid we should ever need to resort to either of them), but peace and goodwill among men (εἰρήνη δὲ πρὸς ἀλλήλους ἅμα καὶ φιλοφροσύνη)" (*Laws* 628c), and he adds that a statesman will "become a *genuine* lawgiver only if he designs his legislation about war as a tool for peace, rather than his legislation for peace as an instrument of war" (*Laws* 628de).

To conclude, for Plato, leadership is not about dominating others but about fostering goodness, harmony, and peace for all. This interpretation is stronger than the one held by Plumwood, Keuls, Hartsock, and others that entirely misses Plato's emphasis on cooperation and harmony. Ultimately, Plato cannot accept a logic of domination and remain committed, as I believe he always does, to his theory of justice and its accompanying pursuit of harmony and peace. His theory of justice as harmony puts him in company with 20th century philosopher Karen J. Warren about domination being the enemy of peace. And we should not miss our chance to give Plato credit for long ago encouraging us to make friendships, to make love,[23] to make "music and peace"[24] instead of war.

---

[23] Zoller, *Plato and the Body*, 86-103, 155, 158-9.
[24] Mary Lenzi, "Plato and Eco-Feminism: Platonic Psychology and Politics for Peace," in *Peacemaking: Lessons from the Past, Visions for the Future*, ed. Judith Presler and Sally J. Scholz, (Amsterdam: Rodopi, 2000), 91.

Index of Platonic Dialogues Cited

Alcibiades I, 88, 89, 90, 91, 101, 104, 105

Apology, 20, 24, 25, 51, 56, 60, 63, 64, 88, 94, 100, 101, 152, 159, 161, 162, 175, 176, 179, 180, 208, 213

Clitophon, 74

Crito, 175, 176, 180, 224, 230

Epinomis, 116

Euthydemus, 8, 9, 10, 18, 21-23, 25-28, 30, 33, 35, 36, 37, 40-49, 160, 216

Euthyphro, 33, 99, 170, 176, 181

Gorgias, v, 8, 9, 12, 22, 23, 24, 26, 28, 29, 30, 87, 88, 91-94, 101, 103, 104, 122, 161, 164, 165, 168-170, 175, 176-181, 182, 183, 191, 199-210, 212, 213, 224, 225, 227, 228, 230

Hipparchus, 31

Hippias Major, 178

Hippias Minor, 177

Ion, 128, 177

Laches, 21, 22, 24, 25, 51, 52-56, 57, 59, 60, 64, 65, 78, 177, 180, 181

Laws, 4, 27, 86, 116, 117, 119, 120, 122, 127, 128, 150, 179, 208, 214, 219, 221, 224, 229, 237, 238

Lovers, 119-121

Lysis, 10, 17, 33, 35-39, 44-46, 48, 52, 58, 61, 61-65, 113, 124, 192, 197

Parmenides, 11, 185-198

Phaedo, 116, 150, 208, 214, 229

Phaedrus, 19, 98, 101, 107, 116, 207, 214

Philebus, 89, 183, 184, 207

Protagoras, 7, 8, 10, 22, 28, 41, 67-86, 105, 107, 124, 125, 165, 166, 177, 178, 180, 228

Republic, v, 4, 5, 7, 8, 18, 19, 20, 26, 68, 86, 89, 91, 92, 94, 102, 104, 105, 107, 114-118, 122, 124, 127-141, 143, 144, 145, 148, 149, 150, 153, 170, 176, 178, 181, 182, 183, 186, 195, 196, 198, 201, 204, 206, 207, 208, 213, 215, 217-219, 221, 224-237

Seventh Letter, 4, 68, 70, 104, 186, 197

Sophist, 37, 183, 190, 207, 212, 217

Index of Platonic Dialogues Cited

Statesman, 207

Symposium, 11, 33, 47, 74, 87, 88, 91, 93, 96-102, 104, 106, 108-112, 123, 124, 143-156, 219, 227, 228

Theaetetus, 8, 10, 30, 33, 35, 36, 37, 38, 39, 40-49, 192, 214, 216

Timaeus, 68, 74, 86, 117, 130, 207

Index of Greek Terms

agōn, v, 1, 8, 10, 11, 12, 15, 18, 19, 23, 25, 30, 35, 52, 53, 58, 62, 67-70, 87, 88, 90, 103, 104, 106, 129, 141, 144, 148, 152, 153, 156, 173, 174, 178, 182, 183, 186, 190, 199, 201, 202, 204, 205, 210, 211-221, 223, 224. *See also:* contest, competition

aidōs, 58, 64, 165. *See also:* shame

aischros, 109, 151. *See also:* shame

andreia, 53, 134. *See also:* bravery, virtue

apodyterion, 21, 42-49, 55. *See also:* stripping.

aretē, 2, 4, 5, 7, 8, 9, 10, 15-30, 51, 57, 137, 148, 179, 180, 219, 220. *See also:* virtue

askēsis, 20, 30, 34, 206. *See also:* training

dromos, 40, 42, 43, 44, 49

elenchos, 11, 21, 23, 33, 36, 38, 39, 40, 47, 49, 51, 55, 60, 62, 152, 174, 175, 176, 177, 179, 181, 182, 183, 217

epithumia, 131, 134, 167

erastēs, 57, 63, 73, 123, 151. *See also:* homosexuality.

erōs, 11, 46, 47, 93, 94, 97, 98, 100, 101, 103, 104, 105, 109, 123, 124, 143-156, 167. *See also:* Eros, love.

euexia, 1, 2, 36, 121

eutaxia, 36, 120

gymnastikē, 2, 5, 6, 11, 18, 19, 107, 115-117, 119, 121, 122, 198, 199, 200. *See also:* gymnastics, training

kalokagathia, 20, 22, 30, 33, 46, 47, 52, 54, 120, 173

kolakeia, 27

mousikē, 5, 18, 19, 107, 115, 117, 121, 122, 123

paides, 36, 40, 57, 61, 63

paidia, 27, 28, 190. *See also:* play

palaistra, 2 15, 17, 31-49, 56, 113, 118, 182

philia, 36, 69, 109, 113, 150, 151. *See also:* friendship

philonikia, 8, 10, 29, 55, 77, 81, 189, 192

philoponia, 36, 114, 120

philosophia, 9, 28, 29, 84, 110, 112, 115, 120-126, 214, 221

philotimia, 58, 65, 77, 189

Index of Greek Terms

phronēsis, 26, 179, 180, 184

pleonexia, 92, 103, 131

psychē, 6, 19, 47, 48, 110, 154, 198. *See also:* mind, soul

sōma, 6, 19, 17, 114. *See also:* body

sōphrōn, 69, 84, 85

sōphrosunē, 8, 38, 46, 57, 64, 68, 83, 84, 85. *See also:* temperance

synousia, 72, 186, 197

technē, 20, 21, 22, 26, 28, 30, 73, 159, 160, 161, 180, 183, 191, 202

thumos, 218, 219, 220, 221

General Index

Academy, 1, 2, 7, 15, 16, 17, 18, 31, 34, 35, 37, 48, 51, 112, 113, 188, 213

Achilles, 16, 25, 95, 124

Aeschylus, 134, 135, 146

aggression, 74, 202, 205, 210, 218, 220, 227-229

Alcibiades, 11, 30, 71, 86, 87-106, 108, 111, 112, 144, 145, 147

Anaxagoras, 119, 187

Antaeus, 8

Antisthenes, 3, 15, 107

Apollo, 51

architecture, 10, 31-49

Archytas of Taranto, 4, 188

Aristophanes, 2, 16, 17, 23, 31, 95, 119, 145, 146, 152

Aristotle, 1, 4, 7, 15, 22, 34, 56, 63, 108, 149, 185, 188, 190, 191, 193, 206, 208

Atalanta, 20

Athena, 187

Athens, 11, 15, 31-35, 41, 49, 51, 67, 71, 76, 79, 80, 88, 90-95, 97, 102-105, 110, 112, 113, 121, 122, 124, 159, 162, 174, 187, 212, 221

athletics, 1-5, 8-10, 12, 15, 19, 20, 23, 34-36, 39-41, 52-53, 107, 110, 112, 114, 117, 119-121, 125, 174, 185-198, 200-205, 207-210, 211

beauty, 16, 20, 26, 35, 46-49, 57, 96-103, 120, 146-156. *See also: kalon*

body, 5, 6, 7, 10, 12, 18, 19, 20, 22, 23, 26, 28, 46, 47, 57, 63, 64, 65, 102, 107, 108, 114, 116, 121, 143, 147, 151, 153, 154, 155, 175, 199, 200, 201, 202, 203, 204, 205, 206, 208, 209, 220. *See also: sōma*

bravery, 51-56, 115. *See also: courage, andreia*

Burckhardt, Jakob, 1, 173, 211

care, 10, 51-67, 122, 162, 214, 235

Cimon, 41, 43, 92, 106

competition, 4, 7, 8, 10, 12, 35-36, 39-41, 43, 49, 52, 53, 54, 62, 64, 65, 74, 75, 79, 85, 120, 121, 144, 145, 149, 153, 162, 173, 178, 182, 183, 188-189, 192, 194, 202, 204-205, 210, 211, 216-220. *See also: agōn*

General Index

contest, 11, 13, 15, 19, 23, 30, 53, 57, 72, 96, 128, 129, 143-147, 152, 153, 156, 174, 175, 177, 183, 186, 190, 192, 193, 198, 210-218. *See also: agōn*

cooperation, 19, 48, 224, 226, 229, 230, 234, 237, 238

courage, 25, 82, 99, 100, 116, 134, 150, 181, 211-212, 218, 219, 221, 231-2. *See also:* bravery, *andreia*

Croton, 3, 15, 188

Delphi, 31, 42, 45, 59, 179, 187

democracy, 1, 77, 78, 88, 89, 90, 102, 103, 105, 110, 111, 122, 177

dialectic, 11, 12, 18, 21, 25, 63, 71, 99, 147, 153, 177-178, 183-184, 186-198, 210, 211-221

Diogenes Laertius, 1, 2, 3, 15, 67, 178, 185, 188

Dionysos, 143, 144, 145, 147, 156, 174

Diotima, 11, 98, 100, 102, 112, 123, 143, 146, 147, 149, 151, 153, 154, 155, 156

education, 5-7, 17-18, 22, 23, 28, 33, 36-38, 47-49, 57-59, 88, 90, 91, 102, 104, 105, 107, 114, 115, 116, 124, 125, 128, 136, 137, 147, 151, 154, 186, 206, 208, 211, 213, 220, 221, 231. *See also: paideia*

emotion, 11, 145, 163-170, 220, 221, 237

Empedocles, 188, 192

Eros (the god), 123, 147, 149, 150, 152. *See also: erōs*

flattery, 12, 28, 199-210. *See also: kolakeia*

friendship, 9, 10, 29, 36, 51, 62-64, 67, 73, 109, 113, 150, 151, 154, 156, 228, 230, 234. *See also: philia*

Galen, 108

Gyges, 131, 132, 133, 134

gymnasium, 1-4, 15-23, 110, 113, 118, 188-198.

gymnastics, 1, 5-6, 12, 17-19, 28, 29, 199-210. *See also: gymnastikē*

Heracles, 10, 16, 25

Hermes, 16, 39, 49, 61, 69, 113, 144

Herodotus, 110, 111

Hesiod, 139

Hippocrates, 7, 22, 73, 75

Homer, 6, 19, 139, 173, 205

homosexuality, 109, 110, 165. *See also: erastēs*

Ibycus, 189

Isocrates, 5, 8, 17, 20, 88, 215

justice, 12, 17, 25, 27, 28, 68, 83, 87, 90, 92, 129-139, 143, 154, 176, 179, 199-209, 212, 214, 215, 219, 223-238.

Kant, Immanuel, 143, 176, 182, 223

Kierkegaard, Soren 101

Krison of Himera, 8

Leontiskos, 9

love, 6, 8, 11, 28- 30, 46, 47, 55, 60-64, 89, 91, 93, 96, 97, 100, 101, 107-126, 144-156, 167, 189, 196, 214, 219-221, 238. *See also: erōs, philia*

Lyceum, 3, 15, 17, 21, 31, 33, 34, 35, 37, 40, 41, 45, 113

Marsyas, 97, 98

military training, 18, 19, 21, 34, 211. *See also: Laches*

Milo of Croton, 3, 4

Miltiades, 92, 106

mind, 5, 47, 107, 206-207. *See also:* soul, *psychē*

Musaeus, 137, 139

Nietzsche, Friedrich, 1, 95, 173, 174, 209, 229

nudity, 2, 23, 31, 35, 40, 46, 47, 53-4, 64, 108. *See also:* stripping

Olympic Games, 3, 4, 6, 8, 15, 16, 20, 111, 112, 173, 186-187

Orpheus, 139

peace, 12, 95, 223, 224, 226, 234, 237, 238

Peloponnesian War, 67, 71, 94, 103

Pericles, 92, 94, 103, 105, 106, 121

play, 27-28, 190, 205, 210. *See also: paidia*

Plutarch, 31, 41, 42, 95, 96, 102

poetry, 11, 58, 61, 62, 67-68, 86, 124, 127-141, 143-145, 148, 154, 173, 183

Porphyry, 3, 108

Prodicus, 3, 15, 72, 73, 75, 76, 77, 79, 80, 82, 83

Pythagoras, 3, 4, 15, 188

rhetoric, 8, 12, 17-18, 22, 25, 115, 140, 144, 168, 177, 188, 199, 200-202, 204-207, 211, 212

setting (of dialogues), 10, 16, 31-49, 52, 65, 185, 187-198

General Index

shame, 11, 22, 58, 60, 67, 83, 87, 98, 99, 108-110, 119, 148, 150, 157-170, 180, 219

Sicily, 96, 188

sophists/sophistry, 3, 7, 8, 9, 12, 15, 21, 22, 25, 37, 44, 58, 68, 72, 73, 79, 82, 83, 86, 105, 114, 158, 164, 177, 189, 190, 193, 200, 201, 207, 212-217, 221, 228

soul, 5, 6, 7, 10, 12, 18-29, 47-49, 53, 54, 57, 60, 64, 65, 88, 89, 93, 97-99, 102, 104, 106, 107, 116, 133, 134, 143, 150, 151, 153-156, 162, 168-170, 175, 178-180, 186, 197, 198, 199-209, 216, 218, 224, 228-237. *See also: psychē*

Sparta, 47, 95, 103, 108, 124

Strabo, 3, 15, 188

stripping, 7, 15, 21-25, 30, 46-48, 53, 57, 60, 118. *See also:* nudity, *apodyterion*

suffering, 145, 164, 168-170, 177, 181, 204

temperance, 17, 25, 51, 57-60, 138, 150, 152, 212, 217-218. *See also: sōphrosunē*

Themistocles, 92, 106

Thirty Tyrants, 67, 76, 80, 83

Thucydides, 87, 95, 96, 103, 105, 106, 111, 112, 121, 122

training, 4-7, 12, 16-18, 19, 20, 24, 25, 33, 34, 39-41, 52, 64, 107, 116, 117, 119, 121, 122, 125, 126, 185-186, 190-195, 197, 198, 203, 205. *See also: askēsis, ethos*

victory, 6, 8, 9, 12, 19, 20, 27, 29, 40, 55, 60, 61, 64, 72, 74, 78, 93, 95, 96, 106, 182, 185-186, 210-212, 218,-221, 224, 237. *See also: philonikia*

virtue, 2, 5, 6, 8, 16-30, 35-36, 47, 51-56, 60, 61, 64-65, 68, 73, 75, 83-85, 103, 105, 108, 116, 118, 132, 134, 137-138, 143, 147, 148, 150, 151, 154, 156, 157, 158, 184, 213, 216, 237. *See also: aretē, kalokagathia*

vision, 79, 80, 133, 144, 146, 147, 148, 155, 156, 186, 195, 196, 198, 229, 233, 234, 236, 237

Vitruvius, 34, 43, 45, 46

war, 4, 52, 53, 115, 117, 181, 225, 237, 238. *See also: Peloponnesian War,*

wisdom, 5, 9, 16, 17, 20, 24, 25-30, 37, 39, 54, 56, 61-64, 92, 96-102, 113, 124,

125, 134, 143, 144, 147, 150, 151, 153, 160, 161, 162, 186, 212, 214, 218, 219, 221, 226, 231. *See also: sophia, philosophia*

women, 4, 117-118, 151, 203, 224, 227

Xenophon, 3, 15, 31, 41, 42, 67, 69, 74, 89, 95, 97

Zeno of Elea, 186, 187, 188, 190, 192, 194, 195

Zeus, 16, 23

Printed in Poland
by Amazon Fulfillment
Poland Sp. z o.o., Wrocław

31491418R00145